Restorative Justice
Ideas, values, debates

Gerry Johnstone

W P

WILLAN
PUBLISHING

Published by

Willan Publishing
Culmcott House
Mill Street, Uffculme
Cullompton, Devon
EX15 3AT, UK
Tel: +44(0)1884 840337
Fax: +44(0)1884 840251
e-mail: info@willanpublishing.co.uk
website: www.willanpublishing.co.uk

Published simultaneously in the USA and Canada by

Willan Publishing
c/o ISBS, 5824 N.E. Hassalo St,
Portland, Oregon 97213-3644, USA
Tel: +001(0)503 287 3093
Fax: +001(0)503 280 8832
website: www.isbs.com

Reprinted 2003, 2005, 2006, 2008

First published 2002

ISBN 978-1-903240-42-7 Paperback
ISBN 978-1-903240-43-4 Hardback

British Library Cataloguing-in-Publication Data
A catalogue record for this book is available from the British Library

Printed and bound by T.J. International, Padstow, Cornwall

Contents

Preface

In recent years, a new way of thinking about how we should view and respond to crime has emerged and is beginning to make significant inroads into criminal justice policy and practice. Called restorative justice, it revolves around the ideas that crime is, in essence, a violation of a *person* by another person (rather than a violation of legal rules); that in responding to a crime our primary concerns should be to make offenders aware of the harm they have caused, to get them to understand and meet their liability to repair such harm, and to ensure that further offences are prevented; that the form and amount of reparation from the offender to the victim and the measures to be taken to prevent re-offending should be decided collectively by offenders, victims and members of their communities through constructive dialogue in an informal and consensual process; and that efforts should be made to improve the relationship between the offender and victim and to reintegrate the offender into the law-abiding community.

During the past decade, restorative justice has been promoted – often with evangelistic fervour – as the way forward for criminal justice, which is allegedly failing to prevent crime and to provide victims and communities with a satisfactory experience of justice.[1] These alleged failures are attributed, by restorative justice proponents, to the criminal justice system's adherence to a 'retributive' lens or paradigm, according to which offenders must be judicially punished and the state must take control of the process (Zehr 1990). Advocates have managed to persuade increasing numbers of scholars and practitioners working in the field of criminal justice that a move away from 'retributive justice' in the direction of restorative justice will solve the contemporary crisis in crime and punishment. Others, however, have greeted such ideas with a mixture of scepticism and distrust.

Such is the interest in restorative justice that there is now an abundance of literature – from a multitude of countries – explaining, describing, advocating or criticising it or specific aspects of it. For the uninitiated, working one's way through this complicated mass of literature is a daunting prospect, especially since – as Paul McCold (1998) demonstrates – there is a huge divergence of opinion regarding what is meant by the term 'restorative justice'. Accordingly, this book provides an introduction to the most fundamental and distinctive *ideas* of restorative justice and to the key arguments both for and against its use. My main aim is to make the phenomenon of restorative justice, and the major debates about it, comprehensible to relative newcomers, whether students of criminology, law or related disciplines or researchers or professionals with an interest in crime and justice issues. At the same time, the book seeks – especially in its latter stages – to extend the range of the debate about the meaning of restorative justice, its pros and cons, and its broader significance. Hence, it will have some interest to those already familiar with the topic.

The aims, scope and rationale of the book are described at greater length in chapter one. Chapter two then outlines the main themes of restorative justice thought and introduces some important critical debates about the prospects for restorative justice and about whether the idea of implementing it on a wide scale is feasible or even desirable.

In the first half of chapter three, I outline the important claim that restorative justice was the standard approach to what we now call 'crime' throughout most of human history and that it is found among nearly all aboriginal groups and in all pre-modern societies. Some dismiss this claim as a myth. I argue, however, that even if this claim is accepted, there are still good reasons for doubting whether it is realistic to think of *reviving* restorative justice traditions in modern cities and towns. Such doubts, and the answers to them, are examined in the second half of the chapter.

Chapters four and five look at how restorative justice aims to involve and meet the needs of victims and offenders. Chapter four describes the restorative approach to crime victims and distinguishes it both from the traditional criminal justice approach to victims and from some other ways which have been proposed and implemented for obtaining a better deal for victims in the criminal justice process. It also asks whether restorative justice as currently conceived is as victim-oriented as its rhetoric suggests. Chapter five describes and seeks to clarify what is distinctive about the restorative approach to offenders. It explores the key differences between restorative justice, on the one hand, and 'retributive justice' and 'therapeutic justice' on the other, as well as putting forward a positive account of the main features of the restorative response to offenders. The chapter concludes by addressing the highly topical question of whether restorative justice can be properly understood as a non-punitive response to wrongdoing. Chapter six develops this discussion by looking at how the idea of reintegrative shaming, proposed by John Braithwaite (1989), is shaping restorative justice practices and by raising some questions about the ethical issues involved in attempts to shame offenders and simultaneously to promote an attitude of forgiveness.

Chapter seven shifts attention more directly to the question of what is distinctive about restorative justice as a process. It examines, in particular, the rationale for involving victims, offenders and ordinary members of the community directly in the process by which it is decided how to deal with the aftermath of an offence. It shows that, while the standard justification of the restorative justice process involves pointing to its advantages over the conventional criminal process as a method of achieving restorative goals, there is often an underlying suggestion that restorative processes can promote moral development and help to build a sense of community. The chapter goes on to explore the implications of developing this theme for our understanding and assessment of restorative justice programmes.

Chapter eight concludes the book by outlining some different directions which the restorative justice movement might take, and exploring some implications of these different directions both for the movement itself and for the broader field of penal and social control. It also makes some suggestions about some directions which restorative justice research could fruitfully take.

In a short introductory text of this nature, which seeks to describe and examine the ideas and principles of restorative justice in reasonable depth, much else that is of interest and importance will not be covered. In particular, the book does not contain a detailed chronicle of the development of restorative justice, nor detailed descriptions of restorative justice programmes, nor an up-to-date overview of how crime policies are changing in response to the campaign for restorative justice. Nor will the book present in detail the findings of research which seeks to evaluate specific restorative justice programmes (see Braithwaite 1999a; Kurki 2000). And, although the book contains some critical analysis and introduces the main critical perspectives on restorative justice, it is not an attempt at a comprehensive critique; such a critique would require a book in its own right, at the very least. What would have been interesting, but is excluded on the ground that it is too complex to cover in a short introductory text, is a study of the range of applications of the ideas and principles of restorative justice beyond criminal justice, for example in family life, in schools, in the settlement of business conflicts, in international peacekeeping and in bodies such as the South African Truth and Reconciliation Commission. However, since the ideas and values of restorative justice remain much the same whatever context it is applied in, and since some of the issues raised overlap, I hope that the book will be of some value to those interested in these wider applications of restorative justice.

Acknowledgments

I would like to thank Brian Willan for suggesting that I write an introductory book about restorative justice and for his subsequent patience and encouragement. I am particularly grateful to Clive Coleman, who read drafts of every chapter, gave excellent advice and made some very helpful comments and suggestions. Thanks are also due to Louk Hulsman who provided some very useful insights, and to the following who read and made useful comments on some chapters: Stephen Brown, Gary Edles, Paul Gilbert, William Lucy, Tony Ward, Martin Wright, and Margarita Zernova. Chapter six of this book draws upon a paper published in a special issue of the *Liverpool Law Review* (vol. 21: 2–3, 1999), I am grateful to the editors for permission to use this material. The completion of this book was assisted by a semester of study leave, for which I am grateful to my colleagues at the Law School of the University of Hull. I would like to record a special thanks to Brigid Johnstone, for her unswerving support, and to our children Eleanor and Pierce.

Notes

1 See Garland (2001: ch. 3) for an account of the 'failure model' of modern criminal justice.

Chapter I

Introduction

In public discourse it is commonly taken for granted that the usual response to the commission of a crime should, when possible, be a court trial followed by judicial punishment of the perpetrator. However, reformers have long searched for better, and especially less destructive and more effective, responses to crime. The latest result of this search is *restorative justice*.[1]

Advocates of restorative justice suggest that, once the facts of a crime have been established, our priority should not be to punish the offender but (i) to meet the victim's needs, and (ii) to ensure that the offender is fully aware of the damage they have caused to people and of their liability to repair that damage. Achieving such goals, it is suggested, requires something other than a formal criminal trial and judicial punishment. Indeed, it is argued, the standard process of trial and punishment usually hinders the achievement of such aims. Instead, a face-to-face meeting between the victim and offender, in a safe setting, is required. Ideally, members of the families and communities of the victim and offender will also take part in the process. Professionals will be involved in the process not as chief decision-makers but as facilitators. Their role is to ensure that the parties feel safe and to guide them towards constructive dialogue and a mutually agreeable resolution.

At such meetings offenders are urged to account for their behaviour; victims are encouraged to describe the impact which the crime has had upon them, materially and psychologically; and all parties are encouraged to decide upon a mutually agreeable form and amount of reparation – usually including an apology. Frequently, assurances are sought from the offender that the behaviour will not be repeated. Also, members of the offender's family and community may resolve to monitor the offender and support them in their efforts to refrain from further law-breaking and anti-social behaviour. There is an emphasis on persuading offenders, without threats, voluntarily to repair the harm they have caused. There is also an interest in *reconciling* offenders with their victims and with the community.

According to its proponents, a shift from judicial punishment to community restorative justice, as the *routine* response to crime, will have a number of benefits. Restorative justice, they claim, will meet the needs of victims of crime much better than judicial punishment. Also, although many offenders will find restorative justice more demanding than undergoing judicial punishment (we are repeatedly reassured that it is not a soft option), they will benefit because restorative justice offers them the chance to regain – or in many cases gain for the first time – the respect of the community rather than its permanent scorn. Communities, it is claimed, will also benefit in a number of ways: offenders will be rendered less dangerous; the large fiscal costs of judicial punishment can be diverted to more constructive and crime-preventing projects; and restorative justice will help foster arts of citizenship and a sense of community which can be useful in other situations (Cayley 1998: 188).

Hundreds of experiments with restorative justice are now taking place throughout the developed world, especially – but by no means exclusively – in relation to young offenders (Galaway and Hudson 1996). Most of these experiments were started by criminal justice professionals, voluntary workers, and allied reformers working within the criminal justice system using powers and structures already available (Cayley 1998). For example, the origins of the contemporary restorative justice campaign are conventionally traced to Canadian experiments with victim–offender mediation in Elmira, Ontario in 1974 (Zehr 1990: ch. 9). Legend has it that probation officer Mark Yantzi (a member of the radical Christian sect, the Mennonites), frustrated with the usual process for dealing with offenders, had a 'pie-in-the-sky idea' (*ibid*: 158). He asked the judge, in a case where two young men had pleaded guilty to vandalizing 22 properties, to order the offenders to meet their victims, in the company of Yantzi and fellow Mennonite, Dave Worth. To their surprise, the judge agreed, ordering the offenders to go with Yantzi and Worth and 'meet your victims and bring me back a report on the damage they've suffered' (Cayley 1998: 216). From this spontaneous, idealistic experiment, restorative justice – in the form of Victim Offender Reconciliation Programmes (VORPs) – was born (or rather reborn since, as we shall see, an important claim about restorative justice is that it is an ancient way of dealing with crime).

In VORPS, restorative justice takes the form of a face-to-face encounter between the victim and the offender, facilitated by a trained mediator, who is preferably a community volunteer (Zehr 1990: 161). The mediator's role is not to impose his or her interpretation or solution upon the 'parties to the conflict', but to encourage them to tell their stories, express their feelings, ask questions of each other, talk about the impact and implications of the crime, and eventually come to an agreement about what the offender will do to make restitution. While welcoming this as an important break with the conventional criminal justice process, some of those currently promoting restorative justice regard VORPs as unsatisfactory because they are 'too individualized and private' (Zehr 1990: 256). According to this view, if restorative justice is really to take place, the *community* must also be involved. From this perspective the more important experiments are those with sentencing circles and family group conferences.

The first official use of a sentencing circle occurred in 1992 in the Yukon Territorial Court in Canada (Cayley 1998: 182). In response to the Crown's assertion that 'the community' wanted a native Canadian – a chronic offender convicted of assaulting a police officer – to go to jail, Judge Barry Stuart invited members of the offender's *actual* community to participate in a sentencing circle, thereby reviving the native way of dealing with troublesome individuals and situations. In a sentencing circle, *interested community people* take part in a discussion of what happened, why it happened, what should be done about it, and what should be done to prevent further such incidents. The judge then passes sentence and makes other orders and recommendations, based on what is proposed by the circle. Although called *sentencing* circles, it should be made clear that the discussion and decisions go well beyond what is conventionally covered in sentencing processes. In particular, circles address issues such as to what extent the community shares responsibility for the crime and for doing something about it.

In the original case, the offender's actual community indicated that they did *not* want the offender to go to jail and that they were willing to help rehabilitate him. Judge Stuart, acting on the community's wishes, ordered two years' probation and the offender responded by changing his life (Cayley 1998: 198–3; Stuart 1996). As the reputation of this case spread, the practice of circle sentencing proliferated throughout native communities in Canada and elsewhere and some argue that it should be applied throughout the whole of modern society (Cayley 1998: 197–8).

A form of 'aboriginal justice' which has already been embraced more widely is the Family Group Conference (FGC). FGCs were introduced

3

by statute in New Zealand in 1989 as a new forum to deal with youth crime as well as youth care and protection issues (McElrea 1994). Their introduction owed something to Maori concerns about the over-representation of Maori youth in custodial penal institutions; FGCs are purportedly informed by Maori justice practices and philosophies (*ibid*: 98–9; Pratt 1996). FGCs are similar to the VORPS described above, in that they are forums for 'feelings to be expressed, facts to be explored, and settlements to be negotiated' (*ibid*: 258). However, a wider range of people are involved in the encounter. The offender is typically accompanied by members of his or her family and sometimes by other people who have a relationship of care with them. Victims also bring along members of their family and other 'supporters'. In addition, members of criminal justice agencies such as the police take part. The agreement which is aimed at involves not only restitution but an action plan designed to address the underlying causes of offending behaviour and thereby prevent reoffending (Masters and Roberts 2000: 142).

In the early 1990s, the police in Wagga Wagga – a small city in New South Wales, Australia – started an experiment in 'conferencing' using their common law powers of cautioning (Moore and O'Connell 1994). These experiments were strongly influenced not just by the New Zealand FGCs, but also by John Braithwaite's theory of *reintegrative shaming* (Braithwaite 1989; Masters and Roberts 2000: 145). Braithwaite argued, in an enormously influential book, that family and community shaming directed at offenders – provided it was done within a context of respect for offenders and was followed by efforts to reintegrate them – was an extremely powerful form of social control, but one which most western societies had rejected to their cost. In the 'Wagga model', FGCs were conceptualised as forums in which offenders would be confronted with such reintegrative shaming.

Conferencing, and especially the Wagga model, has proliferated internationally with astonishing speed. It was introduced in the United Kingdom (UK) in the mid-1990s by the Thames Valley Police and has since been adopted by numerous other UK police forces (Pollard 2000). Indeed, although there had been some small-scale experiments with victim–offender reconciliation in the UK in the early 1980s (Smith, Blagg and Derricourt 1988), and although Martin Wright had explained the restorative ideas and principles underlying VORPS in an influential book (Wright 1996a, first edition 1991), it was only when the police started to experiment with 'restorative cautioning' that the restorative justice movement really took off in the UK (Johnstone 1999). One result of this is that, in the UK, restorative justice has come to be closely identified with Braithwaite's theory of reintegrative shaming and the

Wagga model of conferencing. The broader ideas and values of restorative justice – and the wider range of ways in which attempts have been made to put these ideas and values into practice – have tended to be overlooked. This situation is changing, however, among some restorative justice activists in the UK, who are beginning to explore the opportunities – created by the Crime and Disorder Act 1998 and the Youth Justice and Criminal Evidence Act 1999 – for introducing restorative justice in the youth justice system. In these attempts, the importance of developing, or holding on to, a broader conception of restorative justice is increasingly being stressed (Masters and Roberts 2000: 152–3).

Yet, despite the growing interest in the development of restorative justice – as well as the growing concern in some quarters about this development – the broad phenomenon is still little understood, and often positively misunderstood, by those not directly involved in restorative justice advocacy and practice. One significant mis-understanding is the tendency to see restorative justice as rehabilitation repackaged (Daly 2000a: 45). A quite different mistake, frequently made, is to see it as part of the victims' rights movement (Cayley 1998: 218). These mistakes no doubt occur because the aims of restorative justice do overlap with those of rehabilitation programmes and those of the victims' rights movement. However, such mistakes are also encouraged by certain ways of presenting the case for restorative justice. Hence, explaining what restorative justice is about is a complex task which sometimes involves criticizing as inaccurate and misleading the self-understandings and self-representations of its leading advocates and practitioners.

A more general mistake is the frequent failure to appreciate that the argument for restorative justice is as much, if not more, about the purposes and values which should guide our responses to crime as it is about the best methods of accomplishing existing goals such as preventing future offences (Morris and Young 2000). This book addresses this issue by paying particular attention to the range of goals and values embodied in the practice of restorative justice, emphasizing that for many advocates and practitioners preventing or reducing crime is by no means the only, and not even the top, priority. Hence, the book seeks to counter the pervasive tendency to think of restorative justice simply as a new technique for controlling crime.

In addition to explaining what restorative justice is about, the book also presents some critical analysis (albeit sympathetic critical analysis) of the ideas of restorative justice. It is therefore worth saying a few ls, at this stage, about what I think a critical analysis of restorative justice entails.

As we have seen, proponents of restorative justice have made a number of claims about the advantages of restorative justice over more conventional ways of dealing with crimes, especially that it outperforms judicial punishment in reducing reoffending and satisfying victims. Lots of 'scientific evaluations' of restorative justice programmes – designed to put such claims to the test by comparing their achievements with those of more conventional criminal justice interventions – have been carried out or are currently under way. Such programme-by-programme evaluations have tended to dominate the restorative justice research agenda, while other forms of assessment have tended to be neglected (Dignan 2000). In my view, this is a mistake. While 'programme evaluations' are important, it is crucial to realise that critical analysis of restorative justice should not end, and arguably not even begin, with attempts to ascertain whether restorative justice programmes actually achieve the measurable 'outputs' that most of their proponents claim they will achieve. So, what else does critical analysis involve?

First, it is crucial to realise that what proponents of restorative justice propose is not simply a new programme or a new technique but something much more ambitious: a fundamental change in our manner of viewing and responding to criminal acts and associated forms of troublesome behaviour and of relating to both those who commit such acts and those affected by them. To subject such a proposal to critical evaluation we need to ask how practicable the proposed transformation is and, considered in the round, whether it would make things better or worse (bearing in mind that the criteria of 'better or worse' are not only highly contestable, but that proponents of restorative justice are involved in the contest). To put this briefly we need to ask: to what extent is a shift from judicial punishment to restorative justice, as the normal response to crime, feasible and desirable?

Throughout the book we will encounter arguments which suggest that such a shift is highly unlikely to occur. However, while I will look at responses to those arguments, the main focus will be on questions about the desirability of such a shift. The main reason for this emphasis is that, regardless of whether it is feasible, restorative justice is of interest and importance as a 'sensitizing theory' (Zehr 1990: 227). What is meant by this is explained by Howard Zehr, an early and leading proponent of restorative justice. He is willing to concede that 'retributive justice' *may* be so deeply embedded in our institutions and minds that it may be unrealistic to expect fundamental change (*ibid*: 226–7). Yet he insists that development of the concept of restorative justice, through academic work and practical experiment, is a necessity. Such development enables us to understand that judicial punishment is a social *choice*, not a natural or inevitable response to crime, and it lays bare the nature of that choice. Developing the concept of restorative justice therefore enables us to question the rightfulness and reasonableness of that choice, and gives us the option of acting differently in areas of our lives where we might have some control, such as in our families, daily lives and perhaps in our schools (*ibid*: 227).

So, how do we approach the question of whether a move towards restorative justice would make things significantly better, or worse, than they currently are? First, it is necessary to recognise that, for all its troubling features, in its current form the institution of judicial punishment does perform certain essential functions tolerably well. It provides most of us, regardless of our means, with *some* degree of protection from predatory and harmful behaviour, without making us pay the price of oppressive conformity. Moreover, it meets some of our criteria of fairness to some extent, and gives some degree of recognition and protection to the rights of those accused of crime. It even provides some offenders with some protection from vengeful victims and angry members of the public. Further, under certain conditions, it can help disseminate efficiently progressive ideas of what is right and what is wrong. This is not to deny the charges of those who accuse judicial punishment of being cruel, unjust and ineffective and of often creating or at least exacerbating the very problems it purports to solve (Bianchi 1994). Nor is it to deny that there may be something much better than judicial punishment. Rather, it is simply to acknowledge that – for all its faults – the institution of judicial punishment does have certain merits and those who would replace it with something else – either as a general policy or in any particular case – need to be sure that they do not throw the baby out with the bathwater. We need to ask of proponents of restorative justice how careful and balanced is their critique of judicial punishment, and how will they ensure that the essential tasks which judicial punishment does perform tolerably well continue to be performed at least as well.

What this means is that – even if we accept the claims that a shift to restorative justice would in many ways improve the lot of offenders, victims and communities – we still need to be alert to the ways in which it could make things worse. We need to ask whether a shift to restorative justice would result in a whole range of deleterious consequences such as a trivialisation of evil, a loss of security, a less fair system, an undesirable extension of police power, an erosion of important procedural safeguards, unwelcome net-widening, or a weakening of already weak

parties. Are such consequences possible and, if so, what steps do proponents of restorative justice suggest to counter them and how adequate
are those steps?

The debate about such issues is under way, but needs to be much
better developed. There is, however, another set of questions about
restorative justice which tends to be almost completely overlooked.
Restorative justice is usually presented and construed as a radical
alternative to our current way of viewing and responding to crime.
However, it might strike some – with more radical ideas – as being
insufficiently different. It could be argued that restorative justice takes
for granted most of the language, assumptions and structures of
criminal justice, and that what it proposes is merely some minor
tinkering with the system.

This argument is clearly relevant to police-run restorative cautioning
schemes, which still tend to dominate perceptions of restorative justice
in the UK. But it is important to realise that it has relevance to the
campaign for restorative justice in general. For example, the penal
abolitionist Louk Hulsman, whose ideas correspond in many ways with
those of proponents of restorative justice, would nevertheless insist that
what we need to question is not simply the way we view and respond to
'crime', but the very notion that there really exists a discrete class of acts
which we call crimes (Hulsman 1986). For Hulsman, the assemblage of
events which we call crime have little in common and little to
distinguish them from other difficult or unpleasant situations. In fact, all
that 'crimes' have in common and all that distinguishes them from other
problematic events is that the criminal justice system is authorised to
take action against them. For Hulsman, crime is brought into being and
constructed by the criminal justice system. So once we define the
problem to be handled as 'crime' we are already thinking and working
within a criminal justice framework. If we want an alternative to
criminal justice, as opposed to a mere alternative form of criminal justice,
we need to jettison the concept of crime itself. Hulsman's strategy is to
imagine ways of handling 'difficult situations' as if the language of
crime and the assumptions and structures of criminal justice did not
exist. It is only if and when these imagined solutions are deemed
unsatisfactory, he suggests, that we should contemplate thinking within
the framework of criminal justice.

Again, Sullivan and Tifft (1998) are strong supporters of the idea of
restorative justice, but they insist that it requires much more than the
reform of correctional practices which most proponents have in mind.
They argue that injustices are incurred, not just as a result of
interpersonal violence, but as a result of 'social structural violence, that is

violence done to people through the exercise of power, and hierarchical social arrangements that support the maintenance of this power' (*ibid*: 43). Hence, they argue, if we want to achieve restorative justice, we cannot confine our attention to developing restorative approaches to conventionally defined acts of harm and injustice. Rather, it is necessary to address the social structural conditions which reproduce harm, inequality and violence. The campaign for restorative justice needs to extend its scope to include, for example, 'restorative economics'. Restorative justice must be reconceived to include 'transformative justice'.

Whatever one thinks of such arguments, it is clear that they represent a much more radical challenge to the institution of judicial punishment than that offered by many mainstream proponents of restorative justice. This means that proponents of restorative justice must defend their ideas, not only against those who see them as tinkering too much with the established machinery for handling 'crime', but also from those who think that any tinkering, no matter how drastic, is dangerously complacent since we need to replace the machine with an entirely different one.

Notes

1   See, for example, Zehr (1990); Van Ness (1993); Burnside and Baker (1994); Galaway and Hudson (1996); Wright (1996a and 1999); Cayley (1998); Marshall (1998); Sullivan (1998); Braithwaite (1999a); Bazemore and Walgrave (1999); Consedine (1999); McCold (1999); Graef (2000); Kurki (2000); and Strang and Braithwaite (2000). For lists of organisations promoting restorative justice see Marshall (1988: 6–8) and Graef (2000: 69–70).

Chapter 2

Central themes and critical issues

Introduction

In the last two decades, our society's attitude towards criminals has become increasingly intolerant, hostile and exclusionary. Offenders are increasingly represented in political rhetoric and popular culture as 'some kind of external threat, as people who are different from ourselves and who do not properly belong in our society and against whom we need to raise physical defences or who ought to be contained in their ghettoes or failing that in prison' (D. Faulkner, cited in Cayley 1998: 32).[1] In practice, we are sending more offenders to prison and making them stay there for longer periods and in tougher conditions. Nor is this in order to improve their character; prisons are increasingly being run on the basis that their purpose is simply to incapacitate and to deter. In addition to imprisonment, there is mounting interest in other stringent measures – such as electronic monitoring and curfews – and in reviving sanctions designed to expose offenders to public view and humiliation. And, of course, in parts of the United States, repeat offenders are receiving life sentences and being put in chain gangs and those convicted of murder are increasingly being put to death. Meanwhile, we are investing more in alarms, locks, closed circuit television (CCTV) and other security hardware in the hope that they will protect us from criminals.

The examples could go on and on.[2] Yet, far from assuaging public anxieties about crime and disorder, this strategy seems to be fuelling and arguably even helping to create such public angst, thereby generating 'an even greater demand for punitiveness' (McCold 1996: 85–6; Bauman 2000: 37).

10

For those who doubt whether we are morally justified or even prudent in adopting such a response to offenders, the future of criminal justice looks bleak. Few believe it is possible to reverse the trend of the last few decades and, in any case, many who are opposed to what Garland (2000) calls the strategy of 'punitive segregation' were also highly critical of the therapeutic approaches to crime which went before (Johnstone 1996a: ch. 1).

Yet, in the midst of this 'culture of control' (Garland 2001), a rather different response to crime, restorative justice, has emerged and is proving to have considerable appeal to policy-makers and practitioners. In contrast to advocates and supporters of the practices described above, restorative justice proponents espouse the principle that all participants in the justice process – including offenders – 'should be treated in a humane, egalitarian way that values their worth as human beings and respects their right to justice and dignity' (Heise *et al* 2000: 34). Its advocates point to experiments, that have been going on since the mid-1970s, which – although they make minimal use of coercion and punishment – are apparently proving highly successful in reducing crime, satisfying victims that justice has been done, and even revitalising communities which have been torn apart by crime and disorder. So far, restorative justice has operated on the margins of mainstream criminal justice, gaining its strongest foothold in the youth justice system. However, in many countries there is increasing interest in its application to adult offenders.

Core themes

It is important to recognise that those who advocate restorative justice do not all have precisely the same thing in mind (McCold 1998). Yet there are some common themes which epitomize restorative justice thought.

One theme is that our current manner of viewing and responding to crime, although it seems natural and inevitable, is not the only way we have envisioned justice in the West and is quite alien in other cultures (Zehr 1990: 97; Bianchi 1994). Our distant ancestors did not make the sharp distinction between crime and other conflicts that we make today. Unlike us, they did not regard 'crime' as a distinct species of wrong: a blameworthy transgression of some widely shared and virtually sacred social norm. Hence, they did not see 'crime' as requiring a special procedure and response: prosecution and punishment by the state, intended to make offenders repay their (abstract) moral debt to society. Instead, most of what we now distinguish as 'crime' was viewed and handled as an issue of conflict between members of the community. Unless it involved some direct challenge to the authorities or some form of religious heresy, the rulers did not get directly involved (Bianchi 1994). Communities handled their own conflicts, and their primary aim was to make peace between the conflicting parties. This was usually achieved by persuading the party which had caused harm to another to compensate the injured party and show repentance (Zehr 1990: ch. 7).

In the Western world, in a lengthy process starting in the twelfth century, we developed a public system of judicial punishment for 'crimes' of violence and against property. Community-based restorative justice was suppressed or simply fell into disuse. Moreover, we subsequently imposed this system of state punitive control on the indigenous peoples of colonized nations, suppressing their native restorative justice traditions (Pratt 1996). In recent decades, however, colonised peoples have begun a struggle to revive their native forms of justice. This has provoked much debate about whether and to what extent aboriginal peoples should be allowed to have their own legal systems. Proponents of restorative justice, however, seek to go much further. They see community-based restorative justice as a practice fit for all, and hence to be applied throughout the whole of modern developed society (Cayley 1998: 197). At a time when state punitive control is proving increasingly problematic as the standard response to crime, they urge us to follow the example of aboriginal peoples and recreate our own restorative justice traditions.

A second theme is that, when a crime is committed, our principal question should not be: what should be done with the offender? Rather, it should be: what should be done for the victim? Moreover, the starting point, in answering this question, is what the victim actually wants to happen. According to this view, one of the major shortcomings of contemporary criminal justice is its almost total neglect and disempowerment of the victim; neglect and disempowerment which amount to secondary victimization, i.e. an exacerbation of the wounds of crime. This situation has been slightly improved, but not remedied, by victim reforms of recent decades. Such reforms usually aim to ensure that victims are treated with more respect by the criminal justice system and that their voice is adequately represented and given greater weight within the process whereby it is decided how much punishment the offender should receive. Such reforms do not, however, alter the structural position of the victim, whose views on appropriate punishment may be taken into account but are still subordinate to those of the state, and whose views on wider matters (such as what charges if any should be brought) are still unheard or ignored. Hence, some argue, what we need is a paradigm-shift away from punitive justice towards restorative justice (Zehr 1990). In restorative justice, the need for restitution or reparation of harm to victims prevails over demands for the punishment (or treatment) of offenders. This involves a change in the structural position of victims, who become more like plaintiffs in a civil law action. They have much greater control over how the wrong against them is defined and over how it should be dealt with. Hence, it is maintained, restorative justice helps to *heal* the wounds of crime suffered by the victim.

A third theme concerns the way we relate to and deal with offenders. First, it is stressed that we have an ongoing relationship with offenders. They are 'one of us', not enemies from outside, even though they may be adopting the attitudes and behaviour of an enemy. As such we cannot simply cut them off and act in a totally hostile manner towards them. The strategy of 'punitive segregation' is morally inappropriate as a response to fellow members of the community: we owe them compassion as well as moral indignation (cf. Moberly 1968: 97–8). Crucially, the strategy of isolation is also highly imprudent. By segregating and ostracising offenders we render them more rather than less of a threat to us. We drive them into criminal subcultures where they become more and more like alien enemies of the community. We lose whatever chance we have of influencing them to behave better and to subject themselves to various forms of supervision and control. It is wiser to strengthen our relationship with offenders rather than weaken it. It makes sense to show them that we care about them and want to reintegrate them into the community.

Proponents of restorative justice insist – repeatedly – that this does not mean being soft on crime. To regain full membership of the community, offenders must be held accountable before those whom they have harmed. They must show a willingness to repair the harm they have caused and they must show that they repent. They must also agree to whatever measures the community deems reasonable to ensure that they do not further endanger its members.

According to advocates of restorative justice, in the very process of being confronted personally with their victims and hearing first-hand of the actual harm caused by their behaviour – something which does not happen in the conventional criminal justice process – offenders will begin to grasp the true effect of their behaviour. The psychological strategies they use to distance themselves from knowledge of these consequences will be penetrated. The conscience of offenders will be reached and they will experience shame about their misdeeds. As a result, they will be less likely to repeat them.

A fourth theme is that the community must be prepared to become involved in the resolution of conflicts between offenders and victims, in supporting victims and in supporting and monitoring offenders. Controlling and dealing with crime cannot be delegated entirely to the state and to professionals. Ordinary members of the community are needed to generate pressure for the settlement of a conflict. They might serve as mediators, or they might be involved in witnessing and helping to enforce agreements and action plans (Zehr 1990: 101). They might be involved in making offenders fully aware of the harmful consequences of their behaviour (Braithwaite 1989). And, crucially, members of the community must be prepared to befriend and support those offenders who are serious about reparation and repentance, helping them live safely in the community while at the same time taking responsibility for monitoring offenders to ensure that the community feels safe with them in its midst (Cayley 1998: ch. 16). Also, members of the community must 'provide support and assistance to victims as they proceed through the justice process and seek recovery' (Zehr 1990: 31).

However, proponents of restorative justice usually recognise that, in many areas of developed society, a sense of community has become increasingly fragile and in some places eradicated altogether. Indeed, for them, a great deal of the contemporary crime and disorder problem can be attributed to the very fact that our sense of community is dying. Hence, some acknowledge that restorative justice programmes will have to be introduced gradually and in tandem with community development programmes, ensuring that communities have the resources and education required for restorative justice initiatives to work (Marshall 1998: 30). At the same time, advocates of restorative justice stress that 'community is not a place' (McCold and Wachtel 1998):

> 'community' does not have to correspond to any particular physical or geographical entity. For the purpose of conferencing and so on, the circle of relatives, supporters and significant others that each party has is sufficient as a basis for involvement and intervention. Each person, in other words, has their own community centred on themselves.
>
> (Marshall 1998: 30–1)

It is also frequently suggested that restorative justice programmes – by providing opportunities for citizens to become personally involved in co-operative attempts to resolve conflicts and solve social problems – can themselves help foster a sense of community (Christie 1977).

A fifth theme is that we must recognise that our system of court-based, formal legal justice is not suitable for achieving restorative goals. In this system, conflicts are decided in favour of one party against the other, i.e. there is one winner and one loser (Roberts 1979: 17–23). Decisions are reached by a rigid application of legal rules to the facts and are imposed on the parties. This system, it is claimed, can hinder rather than enhance the resolution of conflicts, the reintegration of offenders into the community and victim–offender reconciliation.[3] What is required instead is a less formal meeting in which the offender, victim and others with a major stake in the outcome are encouraged, with the assistance of a mediator, to negotiate an agreed form and extent of reparation from the offender to the victim and to the community and to agree an action plan which might help to prevent a recurrence of the offence. In this process, the parties should be relatively free to determine the nature and extent of the problem and how it is to be resolved. They should not be constrained by the legal definition of the offence, by legal criteria of relevance, or by legal precedents. Participants should be allowed and encouraged to draw on their everyday experiences and express their ideas and feelings in the way they choose. The criminal behaviour should be looked at in the broader context of the relations between the offender, the victim and the community. The emphasis should be on getting offenders voluntarily to accept their liability to repair the damage done. Coercion should be kept to a minimum. None of the parties should come out of the process feeling they have been the losers; the solution should be satisfactory to all sides (Bush and Folger 1994: 16).

Differences which have surfaced in the move from margins to mainstream

In recent years, campaigners for restorative justice have enjoyed enormous success in their efforts to persuade governments and criminal justice agencies to take the idea seriously and to commit themselves to implementing and resourcing restorative justice programmes within the criminal justice system, especially in relation to youth offenders. For the majority of its proponents, the endorsement of restorative justice approaches by governments, and their adoption by criminal justice agencies like the police and probation service, are causes for celebration. The response of Tony Marshall, Chairman of the Restorative Justice Consortium (established in 1998), typifies the cautiously triumphant mood:

Restorative Justice, let no one doubt it, is well and truly on the map. I am both amazed and gratified that this idea, after struggling to see the light for over a decade, has finally emerged as a serious issue for all parts of the criminal justice system.

(Marshall 1999)

Others, however, are much more apprehensive (Sullivan, Tifft and Cordella 1998: 7). Some see the rapid spread of programmes purporting to dispense restorative justice as being accompanied by a dilution, distortion and 'co-option' of the concept (Morris and Gelsthorpe 2000: 27). Indeed, some go so far as to dispute whether some of the initiatives being described as restorative justice have anything at all to do with the idea. Zehr and Mika state: 'we fear retributive and punitive programs are simply being repackaged as "restorative justice" ' (Zehr and Mika 1998: 49). Many of the statutory processes currently being developed in the youth justice arena in the United Kingdom, are particularly susceptible to this charge (Morris and Gelsthorpe 2000).

This turn of events is not untypical of reforming campaigns. There have always been some important and fundamental differences of emphasis and viewpoint within the campaign for restorative justice. As long as restorative justice remained an experimental reforming movement on the margins of the criminal justice system, these differences remained submerged. The success of the campaign in bringing restorative justice from the margins into the mainstream of criminal justice theory and practice (Restorative Justice Consortium 2000) has simply brought these differences closer to the surface. It is important to look at these 'internal tensions' in order to offset the tendency to regard the campaign for restorative justice as a completely unified one. To understand and assess the campaign for restorative justice it is crucial to realise that it is characterised by diversity, difference and some disagreement. Here, I will introduce only the most important of these internal differences.

Should restorative justice be integrated with the criminal justice system?

Most proponents of restorative justice take it for granted that the aim should be to implement restorative justice approaches as widely as possible *within* the existing criminal justice system (Marshall 1998: 4). The vision is roughly as follows. The police – as the gatekeepers of the criminal justice system – will increasingly divert suitable cases away from the conventional track of prosecution, court trial and judicial punishment, towards an alternative restorative justice track, such as a family group conference. In addition, cases which are not diverted initially may be transferred at a later stage, for example somebody who is prosecuted and convicted might be diverted to a sentencing circle instead of being sentenced in the conventional punitive way. Also, it is envisaged that restorative justice programmes will be used to supplement and modify the effects of conventional judicial punishment; for example, an offender serving a prison sentence might, at some stage, take part in a victim-offender reconciliation programme. The hope is that as the feasibility and benefits of these 'alternative' tracks become increasingly apparent to criminal justice decision-makers, they will divert more and more cases to them so that, eventually, the 'alternatives' become the norm. Gradually, restorative justice will become the presumptive disposition; prosecution, trial and punishment will become the exception, reserved for cases where restorative justice has repeatedly failed (Braithwaite 1999b).

However, some campaigners for restorative justice doubt whether their goals can be realised in this way. They express a number of concerns. One is that many policy-makers and people involved in the administration of criminal justice have a very narrow perception of restorative justice and will tend to misapply and abuse the idea (Marshall 1998: 24). The main fear is that they will regard and assess restorative justice merely as a technique of preventing reoffending. Other central goals of restorative justice – such as meeting the needs of victims of crime – tend to be seen by most criminal justice professionals as bonuses rather than primary aims and are likely to receive low priority (Reynolds 2000). As McCold (1996: 89) puts it: 'any restorative scheme implemented and operated by correctional agencies will also necessarily be offender focused.'

Another concern is that it may be impossible to carry out restorative justice within a state bureaucracy such as the criminal justice system. The need to pursue the goals of the bureaucracy and to comply with its red-tape is likely to spoil the flexibility and informality that is crucial to the success of restorative justice initiatives. Similarly, it is difficult to imagine most of the state officials and professionals employed by the criminal justice system adopting the restricted role which the idea of restorative justice demands of them, allowing victims and offenders and other ordinary members of the community to become chief actors and decision-makers. What may be ultimately at stake here is a clash between the values of the state bureaucracy – uniformity, regularity and predictability – and those which many see as essential to restorative justice – flexibility and creativeness.

Those who are uneasy about the development of restorative justice policies and programmes within criminal justice tend to have rather different ideas about how it should be developed. For example, some envisage restorative justice as something completely separate from state criminal justice. They envisage two separate systems for dealing with 'conflicts' between members of the community operating side by side and entirely independent of each other (Bianchi 1994). This is combined with the hope that the state criminal justice system will become less and less used as the advantages of the restorative system become clear. Others think that restorative justice should be developed mainly as a 'sensitizing theory' (Zehr 1990: 227). According to this view, proponents of restorative justice should resist pressures for premature practicality and concentrate on conceptual work, i.e. on developing the *vision* of restorative justice.

Healing victims or reintegrating offenders?

As indicated above, part of the reason why some think it is *not* a good idea to integrate restorative justice with the criminal justice system is that criminal justice interventions will inevitably be focused on the offender. Those who see meeting the victim's needs for justice and healing as central to what restorative justice is all about tend to be highly sceptical of initiatives run by criminal justice agencies. This reflects a deeper tension within the restorative justice campaign between those who came into it mainly *via* involvement in victims' movements and those who came into it mainly *via* involvement in penal reform. Many of the former fear that implementing restorative justice programmes within criminal justice will result, not in victims being empowered and restored, but in them being used as mere props in programmes designed mainly to reintegrate offenders (Braithwaite 1999a: 21). On the other hand, many of the latter seek to distance the campaign for restorative justice from some of the earlier emphases placed by 'victim-oriented members' on financial restitution from offenders to victims. Hence, it has been argued that 'the emphasis in the early restorative justice literature on how much material reparation is actually paid [is] quite misguided' (*ibid*: 45).

In fact, some leading figures in the contemporary restorative justice campaign seem to want to distinguish restorative justice from the victim–offender mediation schemes which the term was originally used to describe. Morris and Gelsthorpe state:

> Both victim–offender mediation and restorative justice share some
> characteristics – for example, giving victims a voice and making

restitution or amends to victims. However, victim–offender mediation emerged very much from within the victims' movement and so tends to give primacy to victims' interests whereas restorative justice emphasises trying to make the current situation better for both victims and offenders.[4]

(Morris and Gelsthorpe 2000: 18 n.3)

This statement still allows that the restorative process should be focused on victims' needs as much as on the needs of offenders. But often it is by looking at what people do rather than what they say that we get access to their true beliefs. It is telling that family group conferences, with which Morris is associated, are often run without the victim's involvement, whereas it would be inconceivable to run them without the offender's involvement.

At the same time, it is important not to overstate this tension. Indeed, one of the most important contributions of the restorative justice campaign has been to make clear that justice need not be conceived as a zero-sum game, in which the interests of victims and offenders are inversely related. Restorative justice draws our attention to the common interest which victims and offenders have 'in setting what has gone wrong right again' (Cayley 1998: 219).

The scope of restorative justice

Restorative justice is usually understood and discussed as a way of *responding* to crimes which have already been committed. However, some proponents argue that restorative justice should be as much, if not more, about seeking to create non-violent social relationships and building a sense of community (Sullivan, Tifft and Cordella, 1998: 14*ff*). It may be possible, of course, to develop these two aspects of restorative justice in tandem. However, programmes which purport to offer an effective and relatively cheap way of dealing with the aftermath of criminal incidents are likely to interest governments much more than strategies which have the ambitious and costly aim of creating the social conditions – i.e. revitalised communities – in which restorative justice, in the narrower sense, might work. Hence, programmes which are restricted to reacting to crimes committed are likely to be developed more rapidly and with more resources than programmes which aim to revive 'killed neighbourhoods' (Christie 1993). For those – such as Sullivan and Tifft (1998) – who think that restorative justice should primarily be about transforming social arrangements, the conventional focus on programmes which deal only or mainly with individual crimes is risky: 'there is the danger that such programmes will increase the burden of expectation and involvement of local people and groups to a level they cannot sustain' (Marshall 1998: 30).

Can punishment play a role in restorative justice?

To many, this will seem like a strange question to pose since almost all proponents of restorative justice represent it as an *alternative* to punishment (but see Barton 1999, 2000; Daly 2000a; and chapter five of this book). However, on closer examination, the views of some proponents are less straightforward. What leading proponents such as Braithwaite envisage is not a future where punishment is abolished, but a future where punishment is marginalized (Braithwaite 1999b). Although Braithwaite insists that if a restorative justice process fails it should be tried again and again – one of his favourite slogans is 'restorative justice rewards the patient' (Braithwaite 1999a) – he does allow for punishment to be used where restorative justice repeatedly fails. Even more important is the fact that, for Braithwaite, it seems important to the success of restorative justice that it takes place in the shadow of punishment. He continuously insinuates that, although the threat of punishment should never be direct and obvious, it should always lurk in the background. Indeed, at one point, he attributes the success of FGCs partly to the fact that they 'may sharpen our perceptions of how bad the punitive consequences would be if we were caught again' (*ibid*: 63). This blurs the distinction between restorative justice and punishment considerably.

There is another way in which the question of punishment arises in restorative justice. Early proponents of restorative justice were insistent that the outcome should be restitution or reparation rather than penal measures. More recently, however, proponents have emphasised the importance of *symbolic* reparation over material reparation. This should raise the question of whether undergoing punishment can count as symbolic reparation. As we shall see in chapter three, there are much-cited examples from Australian aboriginal 'restorative justice' of wrong-doers agreeing to submit to ceremonial spearing through their thigh as part of a process of symbolic reparation (Ivison 1999). In modern developed societies could one make symbolic reparation, e.g. demonstrate how remorseful one is for one's behaviour, by volunteering to undergo a punishment such as community service or even a term of imprisonment? Again, if this is possible, how clear is the border between restorative justice and punishment?

The claims of restorative justice: a brief examination

As we saw in chapter one, proponents of restorative justice make some big claims about how it outperforms punitive (and therapeutic) interventions in achieving certain aims, such as crime control and victim satisfaction. These claims have prompted a plethora of programme evaluations in which the aim is usually to measure the programme's impact on reoffending rates, victim satisfaction and financial costs of processing a case. As I show below, however, such 'empirical' evaluations, need to be supplemented, indeed preceded, by an examination of the logic of the claims made. What follows then is a very brief account of the central claims made on behalf of restorative justice and an equally brief discussion of those claims.

Preventing reoffending

The most frequently heard claim is that offenders who go through a restorative justice process are much less likely to commit further crimes than similar offenders who go through a conventional punitive process (Pollard 2000: 17; Morris and Gelsthorpe 2000: 21*ff*). Occasionally, in the fine print, the more modest claim is made that such offenders are likely to offend less often and less seriously. However, the message that restorative justice breaks up the pattern of repeat offending is communicated loudly. The following, from a feature article in *The Times*, is not untypical:

> Young criminals who are forced to face their victims and hear the harm they cause are far less likely to reoffend, a pilot scheme has shown.
>
> After an 18-month trial, Thames Valley Police said that only 12 petty criminals had committed new crimes out of 350 who took part. Normally about 100 are likely to reoffend. Jack Straw, the Home secretary, is expected to recommend the scheme to other forces at a conference later this month. Known as restorative justice, it is based on New Zealand and Australian ideas which borrow from Maori family practices.
>
> The scheme deals with crimes such as breaking into cars and stealing them. Instead of a caution, the offenders take part in a conference with police and their families and meet the victim. Thames Valley Police found that many of the young criminals apologised and made reparation. In some cases they broke down in tears.
>
> (Tendler 1997)

It is important to clarify how proponents of restorative justice attempt to support the claim that it outperforms punishment (and treatment) as a method of preventing reoffending. Apart from presenting anecdotes which illustrate spectacular successes, the most usual way is to offer statistical evidence from experimental studies, as in the quotation above. However, as Braithwaite (1999a) acknowledges, such evidence needs to be interpreted very carefully. Evaluating the success of restorative justice programmes in preventing reoffending is a much more complicated task than many appreciate. Highly sophisticated research designs are required. The most obvious problem with arguments based on crude statistics is that, in the majority of programmes, offenders are not diverted to restorative justice on a random basis. Rather, particular offenders are selected for diversion precisely because, for a range of reasons, it is thought that they are likely to be influenced by it. But, even if these problems of 'selection bias' are overcome, there are many other problems of method and data interpretation.

The other main way of supporting such claims, exemplified by the work of Braithwaite (1999a), is to point to a whole gamut of criminological, psychological and sociological theories which arguably lead us to expect that restorative justice will work better than conventional punitive methods in preventing reoffending. I will give just one example of this strategy here. There is a theory – to which many criminologists subscribe – that in order to commit offences and live with their behaviour, criminals must construct elaborate rationalizations for their actions (Zehr 1990: 40–1). For example, they convince themselves that they are not really hurting anyone (their victims are big businesses or are insured and so can afford the losses) or that their victim 'deserved it' (*ibid*; see also Sykes and Matza 1957; Braithwaite 1999a: 47). According to proponents of restorative justice, conventional punitive justice, by keeping the offender and the victim apart, does little or nothing to penetrate these rationalizations and may even reinforce them. Restorative justice, on the other hand, by bringing offenders and victims together and promoting respectful dialogue between them, makes these rationalizations more difficult to sustain. Hence, it is concluded, such theories predict that restorative justice practices will reduce crime more than existing criminal justice practices (Braithwaite 1999a).

Such predictions need to be weighed, of course, alongside other predictions (based on other theories or on different interpretations of what theories predict) to the effect that restorative justice is unlikely to have any significant impact on reoffending rates.[5] They do not, therefore, eliminate the need for 'harder' evidence. But, as we have seen, producing 'hard' evidence is much more difficult than many suppose and it is probably not possible to produce conclusive evidence either way. This is not to suggest that we should simply dismiss the claim that restorative justice outperforms punishment as a way of preventing reoffending but that that claim is unlikely to be proved to the satisfaction of even the most reasonable sceptics. What this does suggest is that proponents of restorative justice would be wise not to rest their entire case for its use upon its claimed efficacy in preventing reoffending, even though making such claims seems the best way of ensuring support from governments who have much to gain from presiding over a drop in crime rates.

Satisfying victims

Another important claim is that restorative justice satisfies victims of crime better than conventional criminal justice and punishment (see Braithwaite 1999a: 20–6). It is usually conceded that victims derive some satisfaction from seeing punitive justice done to those who have wronged them. Proponents of restorative justice argue, however, that this satisfaction often turns quickly into anxiety and guilt (Zehr 1990: ch. 2). Moreover, they argue that punitive justice fails to meet the more important needs of victims, such as their needs for restitution, healing of emotional trauma and empowerment (*ibid*). It is claimed that restorative justice meets these needs and that, as a result, victims who go through the process tend to derive and express much more satisfaction and are more likely to feel that they have experienced *real* justice, than victims whose cases are dealt with in the conventional punitive way.

Again, advocates frequently attempt to support such claims by providing 'hard' evidence from empirical studies of victims' views. Some studies have purported to support these claims, although they also tend to show that – of all the groups involved in a restorative justice process (e.g. offenders, police officers, members of the community) – victims tend to be the least satisfied with it (Braithwaite 1999a: 20–6). Once more, however, the main problem with such 'hard' evidence is that, because of the complexity of the issue, it is nowhere near as conclusive as it is often claimed to be. Crucially, it is virtually impossible to disentangle the multitude of variables which together determine how satisfied people are with any social service. Victim satisfaction or dissatisfaction with the handling of their case is probably more affected by their perception of how helpful and efficient particular individuals and arrangements are, than it is by the model employed. More generally, as I show in chapter four, the question of whether a shift from punitive to restorative justice would benefit crime victims is a very complex one, and evidence of how satisfied victims are with restorative justice processes can play only a small role in helping us answer the question.

Benefits to criminal justice agencies

An important claim on behalf of restorative justice – although it is much less emphasised than the previous two – is that it will benefit criminal justice personnel and agencies. Partly, this is because it offers them the 'hope of being effective in resolving the harm of crime and reducing its likelihood in the future' (Restorative Justice Consortium n.d.). More concretely, it is sometimes argued that because victims have more to gain from a restorative process – i.e. a chance of obtaining restitution for or repair of the harm done to them – they are more likely to cooperate with it. Problems such as victims failing to report crimes or appear as witnesses, because they perceive they have little to gain from the conviction and punishment of the offender, will occur less often, it is predicted, in a restorative system (Barnett 1977, 1980). To my knowledge, there is little solid evidence in support of such claims and, again, because of the sheer complexity of the issue, providing conclusive evidence would be difficult if not impossible.

Monetary savings

It is frequently claimed that restorative justice is much less costly than punitive justice (Braithwaite 1999a: 71). This is sometimes combined with the claim that the savings can then be diverted to welfare and treatment programmes and community regeneration projects which can prevent crime.

One problem with such claims is that they frequently rest on false comparisons. For example, the cost of running a FGC for a fairly minor offence is compared, not with the cost of a simple police caution or routine trial and fine/probation order which an offender might other-wise receive, but with an expensive prosecution in a higher court and a costly custodial sentence. More importantly, there is no reason to suppose that any money saved on a reduction of judicial punishment would be diverted to social spending which *might* reduce crime. This points to a more fundamental problem with the claim that restorative justice is cheaper than conventional judicial punishment. If we conceive of restorative justice narrowly as a procedure (such as a FGC) for dealing with the aftermath of a crime, the claim that it is cheaper might make some sense. But, as we have seen, many proponents of restorative justice want to define it more broadly as including the revitalisation of dying communities and provision of a range of welfare services. So conceived, the transfer of any savings on judicial punishment to investment in communities is not an option, but is essential if a policy is to be described as 'restorative'. But this means that restorative justice is anything but a cheap option. The claim that it can result in fiscal savings is seriously and dangerously misleading. Although it might have less appeal to governments, the claim should surely be that restorative justice involves a more beneficial use of public resources.

Some limitations of restorative justice

While it has gathered a great deal of interest and support, there are grounds for being sceptical about the feasibility of restorative justice and for doubting its desirability. In this section I will outline some arguments to the effect that restorative justice suffers from fundamental limitations and will never be acceptable to policy makers or the public as the routine response to crime. The following sections will outline some arguments to the effect that the proliferation of restorative justice programmes is not the benign development it is often taken to be, but has a much more sinister side to it. Responses to such arguments will be considered throughout the book.

Public expectations of criminal justice

Most members of the public, including many victims and potential victims of crime, have certain expectations of the criminal justice system. In particular, they expect it to put wrongs right and to provide them with protection from criminal behaviour. They may no longer rely wholly on the 'criminal justice state' to do these jobs (Garland and Sparks 2000), but to the extent it does not do them it is generally regarded as failing to meet legitimate public expectations.

Proponents of restorative justice do regard such expectations as legitimate. A large part of their case for restorative justice rests on the argument that, despite appearances and claims to the contrary, conventional criminal justice fails to right wrongs and fails to protect the public. Restorative justice, they insist, could do these jobs much better. But, are these claims very persuasive? It is fairly easy to persuade people that restorative justice has a future on the margins of the criminal justice system, as a useful way of dealing with some young, first–time offenders and as a useful supplement to existing ways of dealing with crime. It is much more difficult to persuade people that restorative justice can be a true alternative to conventional punitive justice in the majority of criminal cases. Let us look at the nature of these doubts in a little more detail.

Putting wrongs right

It is useful to distinguish between two quite distinct frameworks for thinking about how we try to even things out when somebody does a wrong to another. The first is the *reparation/compensation* framework. In this, the basic idea is that the wrongdoer either tries to repair the harm done to the injured party or compensates the injured party where repair is not possible or not appropriate (I burn down your house, I build you another one, or pay you the value of the house, or give you my house).[6] This framework can be extended to include symbolic reparation, in which it is deemed important that the wrongdoer also – and perhaps primarily – acknowledges that the act was wrong and expresses repentance (I burn down your house, I apologise sincerely and I do everything within reason to compensate you for the loss).

In the second, *punitive* framework the idea is that the injured party, or agencies acting on the injured party's behalf, pays back the wrongdoer by inflicting on him or her a harm equivalent to that inflicted on the injured party (you burn down my house, in return the state burns down your house or, more likely, inflicts an equivalent harm on you). The house-burning example alerts us to what many, and especially proponents of restorative justice, find so objectionable about the punitive framework: it seems vengeful and destructive and it assumes that two wrongs make a right. Punishment, we are repeatedly told by proponents of restorative justice, adds harm to harm instead of repairing harm, which is hardly rational. And it is likely to perpetuate conflicts. So why do the public insist on the punishment of offenders? A stock answer is that they are irrational and vengeful.[7] There are, however, better and less slighting answers which we need to consider if we are going to make a proper assessment of the case for restorative justice.

Many argue that there are some wrongs which are so serious that compensation or reparation are insufficient to put them right (Ashworth 1986). What makes them so serious is not the amount of material harm caused; some crimes cause negligible material harm while some non-criminal wrongs cause enormous harm. Rather, the distinguishing factor is the mental attitude of the wrongdoer at the time the wrong was committed. It is common to distinguish those who do wrong deliberately or through reckless disregard for the safety of other persons and/or property, from those who do wrong accidentally or while being merely careless (as opposed to reckless). We generally place the former in a different moral category to the latter, in the belief that their mental attitude at the time of the offence makes their wrongdoing morally worse and also, perhaps, renders them more threatening to the community. We register this difference by referring to deliberate or reckless wrongdoing as crime.[8] Crucially, we regard it as important to mark this distinction by meeting crime with what we assume to be a more serious response than a demand for compensation or reparation, i.e. we insist that the criminal must suffer. From this perspective, to respond to crime in the way advocated by proponents of restorative justice, i.e. merely to insist that the criminal compensates the wrongdoer and expresses remorse, is to trivialise it. It is to suggest that it is no more serious than accidental or careless wrongdoing.

It is important to clarify the scope of this critique. A few proponents of restorative justice argue no more than that punishment is an inadequate response to crime and that it needs to be accompanied by reparation (Meier 1998). Some go slightly further and argue that we should address the issue of compensation/reparation first, and only when that is settled should we address the issue of punishment (Christie 1977). The question of how much (if any) suffering the wrongdoer must undergo would then be considered in a broader context, i.e. the focus would be not only on the wrongdoing and the mental attitude of the wrongdoer at the time of the offence, but also on the attitude and behaviour of the wrongdoer subsequent to the offence (I deliberately burn down your house but later genuinely regret it, apologise sincerely, try hard to compensate you and enrol in therapy designed to help me control my behaviour; I should perhaps not go unpunished but deserve to be punished much less severely than if I remained unrepentant and made no attempt at restitution). These moderate arguments for restorative justice can withstand the critique. However, other proponents are much more damning of punitive justice and look forward to a future where punishment is marginalised (Braithwaite 1999b) or even abolished and replaced by restorative justice. They acknowledge the need to even things out when a crime is committed, but insist that we can achieve this without resorting to destructive punishment; we can make things fair through restorative justice. Those who argue this extreme case need to respond to the charge that their proposals would trivialise crime and would therefore be unacceptable to the vast majority of the public.

Protection from criminal behaviour

There is a fairly widespread assumption that people who commit crime once are likely to do so again, and so represent a special danger to the community. Hence, there is an expectation that the criminal justice system will subject offenders – and especially those considered to be a particular nuisance or threat to society – to special forms of control over and above those to which non-offenders are subject. In practice, the criminal justice system attempts to control the future conduct of offenders in various ways: it attempts to incapacitate some for a period of time (e.g. through imprisonment, curfews or withdrawal of licenses); it presses some into undergoing therapy; it exercises supervision over some while they remain in the community; and it punishes them in order to teach them that crime does not pay.

There is also a widespread assumption that there are many in society who have not committed crimes but have the disposition and motive to do so, and that the criminal justice system should ensure that they are deterred. The criminal justice system responds to this demand by publicising the fact that it does punish those caught committing crime. More generally, it scandalises the commission of crime and so helps to sustain or even create a general sense that certain ways of behaving are wrong (Bussmann 1992).

Proponents of restorative justice argue that these methods of protecting society from criminal behaviour are not very effective and are often counterproductive (Cayley 1998; Braithwaite 2000a). What do they offer instead? One suggestion is that family and community shaming directed at offenders will, provided it is reintegrative shaming, reform offenders and prevent most people from even considering committing crime (Braithwaite 1989, 1998; Braithwaite and Mugford 1994). Another suggestion is that if we form support groups around feared offenders, groups which will also monitor offenders and intervene when their behaviour is 'getting risky', we can both control them more effectively and assuage community fear and distrust (Cayley 1998: ch. 16).

Such proposals will strike many as hopelessly optimistic. A common retort, heard more often in casual conversation than in published work, is that these methods may work with some offenders but not with the vast majority. Crucially, as we will see in chapter three, it tends to be argued that these methods may work in communities where there exists a strong sense of unity and mutual care, but such communities are rare in modern societies and especially in those areas of modern society with high crime rates. What we tend to have in modern society, it is argued, is not community but associations of diverse strangers between whom moral ties and mutual concern are minimal. In this context, attempts at shaming will be laughed off and circles of support – even if they could be effective – will be unsustainable on a large enough scale.

It might be added that, even if the restorative process did reform and control many offenders, the perception that people have committed crimes and avoided prosecution and punishment may encourage others, and especially more hardened and ruthless criminals, to offend. Also, since one of the aims of many proponents of restorative justice is to de-dramatize crime – to depict it less as a moral outrage, more a simple conflict between members of the community – there is the danger that a move to restorative justice could, for all its talk of shaming, reduce the sense of wrongness which attaches itself to crime (Bussmann 1992).

Some dangers of restorative justice

The above arguments suggest that proponents of restorative justice need to convince us that their vision of a future where punishment is marginalised and restorative justice is the norm is more than an appealing but impossible fantasy. Some, however would insist that it is in fact a *dangerous* fantasy (Cayley 1998: ch. 11; Alder and Wundersitz 1994: part 2). Pursuing this fantasy, even if all of the goals are not realised, could have all sorts of bad consequences: it could make weak parties even weaker, the rights of suspects and offenders could be eroded and human freedom more generally could suffer.

Making weak parties weaker

The proposal that the community should take the lead in deciding what should be done about a criminal incident is highly problematic. Communities, even small, tight-knit communities, are not the homogenous units which many suppose them to be. Rather, they contain hierarchical social arrangements based on considerations such as wealth, gender, race, ancestry and family connections, and acquired authority. Also, within communities it is possible to find all sorts of social prejudices and rivalries. One of the advantages of having conflicts between members of the community settled by trained outsiders – and by reference not to local customs but to laws reflecting much broader, if not universal, conceptions of justice – is that it helps ensure (but by no means always does ensure) that the outcome is not influenced by the relative status within the community of the parties or by local prejudices. There is a real danger that, as some of the sanctioning power currently held by the judiciary is transferred (back) to local communities, this advantage will be lost. For example, there is some evidence that experiments with communal restorative justice in patriarchal communities results in cases of serious sexual assault and domestic violence being handled as trivial misdemeanours (Cayley 1998: ch. 11). Some have also argued that communities will tend to be much more lenient with offenders considered to be important to the survival or prosperity of the community than they will be with those who commit identical offences but are considered to be less important (*ibid*: 208).

Concerns about the rights of suspects and offenders

Most of those involved in the administration of judicial punishment openly acknowledge that it is particularly harmful to those on whom it is imposed. Hence, considerable importance is attached to providing those suspected of crime with protection from undeserved conviction and punishment. Although the practice falls well short of the ideal, many vital procedural safeguards are nevertheless provided: people cannot be punished unless found guilty of a criminal offence;[9] a finding of guilt must take place in a court of law by an independent judge and jury or magistrate; the onus is on the prosecution to prove its case and there is a higher standard of proof than in civil cases, i.e. beyond reasonable doubt; defendants are entitled to legal counsel; they are entitled to cross-examine hostile witnesses and call defence witnesses; and some evidence can be excluded if its probative value is outweighed by its prejudicial effect.

But, 'as the punitive characteristic of criminal justice measures is diminished, so too is the perceived need for strong procedural protection' (Barnett 1977: 284–5). Hence, proponents of restorative justice, who regard it as a non-punitive response to crime, tend not only to be less insistent on procedural protection for suspects, but also often regard procedural strictness as an obstacle to the achievement of negotiated settlements and reconciliation.

One of the most significant results of such reasoning is that, in restorative justice, the whole process of establishing criminal guilt in a court of law is often bypassed. In many schemes, cases are referred to restorative justice programmes not after a finding of legal guilt in a court of law, but after an arrestee has admitted involvement in a criminal incident to the police. Such an admission may take place without a lawyer being present. Moreover, what the arrestee admits to may fall well short of what would be needed in order to convict them of a criminal offence.[10] Nevertheless, once they are diverted to a restorative justice programme, they are dealt with, as we shall see, on the assumption that they are guilty of a criminal offence.

Critics object that this amounts to criminal suspects being denied the procedural safeguards which are a fundamental human right (Warner 1994). One way of meeting such objections is to argue that the procedural safeguards relevant to punitive criminal justice are not relevant to restorative justice since it is not about the imposition of punitive sanctions but about the encouragement of reparation. If any procedural standards apply, they should be the much more relaxed standards governing civil law compensation claims, rather than those governing criminal trials and punishments.[11]

This response is unconvincing and dangerous. The wider context within which restorative justice takes place is one of crime and punishment, not one of civil compensation. The whole process is organised around the assumption that what is being dealt with is a criminal act, not a civil wrong. For example, the perpetrator of the act is routinely referred to as the 'offender' and the injured party as the 'victim'; the police are involved; and usually lurking in the background (and sometimes in the foreground) is the threat of formal prosecution should the 'offender' not cooperate with the restorative process. In short, the restorative justice process, no matter how benevolent the intentions behind it and no matter how different it is in its objectives from a punitive process, is still a *criminal justice* process. Hence, arguably those subject to it should be entitled to much the same level of procedural protection as defendants who are prosecuted and tried in the courts.

Principled sentencing

A closely related concern is about the danger which restorative justice poses to efforts, which are only now beginning to bear fruit, to develop 'principled sentencing' (von Hirsch and Ashworth 1998). Advocates of principled sentencing argue that justice demands that the allocation of punishment among convicted offenders should be determined by certain principles, especially: punitive sanctions should be *proportionate* in severity to the degree of blameworthiness of the conduct (von Hirsch 1990); and sentences in any one case should be *consistent* with those in related cases. These principles would seem to preclude much of what restorative justice would not only permit but positively encourage, especially what Braithwaite (1994) calls 'democratic creativity' in the search for 'remedies'. Braithwaite happily concedes that democratic creativity will compromise a rationally consistent system of justice and often result in 'idiosyncratic remedies' (*ibid*: 203).

Again, one obvious reply to the advocates of principled sentencing is that restorative justice measures are not intended as punishments and that the principles of sentencing do not therefore apply. The critics insist, however, that these principles should apply even when – indeed especially when – punishment is called something else, such as treatment or reparation. And the critics have no doubt that reparation from offenders to victims, when accompanied by any degree of coercion (even a vague threat of criminal prosecution should the offender not cooperate with the restorative process), is a form of punishment as it meets punishment's defining characteristics, that is deliberate imposition of measures assumed to be burdensome and unwelcome upon a person in response to a crime (Ashworth 1986: 94).

Net-widening

Another concern is net-widening (Hudson and Galaway 1996: 11–12; Morris and Gelsthorpe 2000: 26). It is now a conventional criminological wisdom that well-intentioned attempts to create alternatives to prosecution and custodial punishment often result in expansions rather than contractions of the number of people caught in the net of penal control (Cohen 1985; but *cf.* McMahon 1992). People who would previously have been prosecuted and imprisoned are infrequently diverted to these 'alternatives'. Instead, they tend to be used mainly for people who, had the alternatives not existed, would not have been prosecuted or incarcerated. Hence, the 'social control net' (Cohen 1985) expands overall, contrary to the intentions of reformers who sought to reduce the penal sphere. Restorative justice, critics contend, is particularly susceptible to the tendency towards net-widening and hence diminishes human freedom.

Debunking restorative justice

Such concerns shade into more cynical views of the rise of informal, community-based forms of conflict-handling such as restorative justice.[12] According to cynics, the authorities are attracted to restorative justice because, in a period during which the courts and penal systems are finding it hard to cope with escalating rates of crime, disorder and violence, it provides an economical alternative form of crime control. Restorative justice, in this view, is economical in a straightforward monetary sense (but see the discussion earlier in this chapter). Also, it is economical in the use of power; it allows control over troublesome people to be achieved at low ideological cost. The reparations which offenders agree to make appear to be undertaken voluntarily. Any censure or pressure which exists appears to come from their families and neighbours, rather than from the authorities. Hence, restorative justice allows the management of the growing number of troublesome individuals, especially youths, without the state revealing its heavy hand and thereby risking resistance. The state and the criminal justice system can expand while appearing to do the opposite. The underlying argument here is that restorative justice is not an alternative to conventional repressive justice, rather it is a complement to it. Punitive and restorative justice, it is argued, should be understood as a partnership, resulting in a broader, more diverse and more flexible network of social control institutions.

A related view is that a hidden purpose of restorative justice is to persuade victims of crime and members of victimised communities that their problems are for *them* to solve, i.e. they should seek reparation from offenders and exercise control over them, rather than relying upon the state to suppress crime and to provide compensation to victims when it fails in this task. Restorative justice, arguably, also gives victims of crime the impression that they are being empowered, which might appease more radical demands and forestall more radical action by victims.

Notes

1 Faulkner was arguing that we should not regard offenders in this way.
2 Among the many attempts to describe and explain this phenomenon, Cayley (1998), Garland (2001) and Laqueur (2000) are especially useful.
3 What is often less clear is the attitude of advocates of restorative justice towards the appropriateness of court-based formal legal justice as a way of reaching a verdict when guilt is denied. Most see the criminal trial as continuing to perform the role of ascertaining legal guilt in its current form (Pollard 2000: 11) and see restorative justice as applicable only where perpetration of a criminal act has been admitted (Marshall 1998). Others think that there are some issues pertaining to guilt or innocence which could be better resolved through mediation than by a criminal trial (Wright 1996b: 229). A few hint, without ever being explicit about the matter, that the investigation of the 'crime' itself is best conducted through such a community-based, informal process (e.g. Yazzie 1998). One of the leading exponents of restorative justice, John Braithwaite (1999a: 15–6), has stated that until the mid-1990s he believed strongly that the traditional Western criminal process was superior to restorative justice processes at fair fact-finding, but found this assumption challenged by stories of restorative justice conferences from Africa, Melanesia and Asia and among First Nation communities in North America. What he seems to have in mind is that many

crimes, which would previously have gone unrecognised, are uncovered during a restorative process.

4 If Morris and Gelsthorpe are implying (as I think they are) that victim–offender mediation emerged from within the American victims' rights movement they are mistaken. As Cayley more accurately states: 'The victim–offender mediation approach … has grown up in parallel with the victims' rights movement and shares some of its aims, but it differs fundamentally in its view of justice' (Cayley 1998: 218).

5 Some of these sceptical views are discussed later in this chapter; see also Braithwaite (1999a: 82–6).

6 The use of house-burning as an example is taken from Barnett (1980: 126ff). The idea of reparation is much more complex than indicated here (see chapter five).

7 Surprisingly, this answer is heard frequently from many critical criminologists and penal reformers who view themselves as belonging to the political left. For a critique, see Johnstone (2000).

8 It is important to note, however, that much of what is legally defined as crime is not intentional or reckless wrongdoing. For various reasons, we use the criminal law today to sanction and regulate acts which cause harm accidentally or through carelessness.

9 Recent legislation, such as the UK Crime and Disorder Act 1998, which enables the authorities to subject persons who harass, alarm or distress others to measures like anti-social behaviour orders, and to impose a penal sanction for failure to comply, is eroding this safeguard (see Johnstone and Bottomley 1998: 177).

10 For many criminal offences, in order to establish guilt it must be proved not only that the defendant performed a criminal act (what lawyers call the 'actus reus') but that they did so with the appropriate mental attitude, such as intention or recklessness (what lawyers call the 'mens rea' of the offence) (see Clarkson 2001 for a brief but authoritative guide to the general principles of criminal law; for a more detailed account see Simester and Sullivan 2000). But, in many restorative justice schemes, cases are put into family group conferences:

> not on the basis of an admission of criminal guilt, but on the basis of admitting responsibility for the actus reus of an assault ('I was the one who punched her'). Functionally, New Zealand law already accomplishes this result by putting cases into family group conferences not on the basis of an admission of criminal guilt, but on the basis of formally 'declining to deny' criminal allegations. Whether the mental element required for crime was present would be decided reactively, on the basis of the constructiveness and restorativeness of his reaction to the problem caused by his act.
>
> (Braithwaite 1999a: 62)

(As lawyers will quickly note, this is remarkable not only in that the court is bypassed, but also in that the presence or absence of *mens rea* and hence criminal guilt is decided, not by reference to the defendant's state of mind at the time of the alleged *actus reus*, but by reference to the defendant's subsequent behaviour. Nor is this due to a slip by somebody insufficiently aware of the huge legal significance of dropping the requirement of coincidence of *actus reus* and *mens rea*. Braithwaite, in the context of corporate crime, sets out a conscious argument for shifting the focus of criminal liability away from the actor's law-breaking act towards the efforts they made to minimise or repair the harm resulting from that act [*ibid*]).

11 As we have seen, however, many proponents of restorative justice do conceive of it as playing a role in deciding matters of criminal guilt. Also, if we accept that, where the goal is restitution rather than punishment, the case can be handled more like a civil case, this would raise other procedural concerns such as how a victim's claims about the extent of damage suffered by them are to be tested.

12 For a detailed account of these criticisms see Pavlich (1996: chs. 4 and 5).

Chapter 3

Reviving restorative justice traditions

Have we not neglected overmuch the customs of our earlier ancestors in the matter of restitution? We have seen that in primitive societies this idea of 'making up' for a wrong has wide currency. Let us once more look into the ways of earlier men, which may still hold some wisdom for us.

(Margery Fry 1951: 124)

The rebirth of an ancient practice

According to its proponents, restorative justice was the normal way of handling 'crime' in earlier times (Van Ness 1993: 252–7; Zehr 1990: ch. 7). In the Western world, they argue, it was suppressed from the twelfth century on, as the tasks of controlling crime and dispensing criminal justice became monopolised by an emerging central power in society, i.e. the state. In the hands of the state, doing criminal justice came to mean apprehending and punishing the perpetrators of crime. Older ideas of persuading offenders to make up for a wrong, through restitution to victims, became increasingly marginalised. By the nineteenth century, the story goes, Western powers were imposing their model of state punishment on colonised peoples throughout the world, suppressing their native restorative justice traditions. By the twentieth century, the worldwide shift from communal restorative justice to state punitive justice as the routine response to those wrongs officially classified as crimes, was almost complete. Restorative justice survived as the routine response to 'crime' only in the dwindling, distant 'simple societies' studied by social anthropologists (Christie 1977; Roberts 1979) and to some extent in oriental societies such as Japan (Braithwaite 1989).

In the 1960s, however, a slight reversal of this long historical process began. Colonised peoples in North America, Australia, New Zealand and elsewhere started struggles to revive their native justice traditions (Galaway and Hudson 1996: part II). Some Western legal theorists have responded to this phenomenon by suggesting that indigenous peoples should be permitted to have their own justice systems, based on native values and customs (Cayley 1998: 197–8). For proponents of restorative justice, such a response – radical as it may seem to some – is far too conservative. For them, the point is not to tolerate native justice traditions but to embrace them. They argue that we should follow the example of the New Zealand Maori and Native Americans and recreate our own older conceptions of conflict resolution.

It is worthwhile looking at this argument in more detail because it plays a crucial rhetorical role in the campaign for restorative justice and because it links that campaign with broader themes in social and legal scholarship, for example about the historical roots of Western legal institutions and about how their dominance and assumed superiority has blinded us to other, and perhaps better, ways of preventing and handling conflicts in the community. As we will then see, those who suggest that pre-modern justice was invariably restorative in character have been criticised as romanticising both the past and other cultures. I suggest, however, that the more interesting question is whether the traditions of pre-modern societies and indigenous peoples today have any relevance whatsoever to the problem of controlling crime and dispensing criminal justice in modern, Western cities and towns. I outline the reasons for being sceptical, and the responses of proponents of restorative justice to such scepticism.

Pre-modern criminal justice

Proponents of restorative justice seek to show that the 'retributive model' of justice, in which offenders must be punished and the state must take charge, is not the only way we have conceived of justice in the West (Zehr 1990: 97). Throughout most of our history, they argue, other models of justice have prevailed. Moreover, they suggest, in dealing with what we now call crime, restorative justice was usually the normal response. This argument flies in the face of many widespread and deeply rooted assumptions about the general direction of the history of

Western criminal justice. Hence, restorative justice proponents seek to dispel these (mistaken) assumptions. I start, then, with a very brief summary of the standard understanding of 'penal evolution' which proponents of restorative justice contest.

Conventional images of 'penal progress'

It is often assumed that primitive societies were lawless (Roberts 1979). According to this assumption, in the absence of a strong central power in society, most of those who perceived themselves as wronged by another had no means of redress. However, those who had the means to do so responded by taking personal revenge (Miller 1999). This was usually violent and often indiscriminate. Little distinction was drawn between intentional and non-intentional wrongdoing. And, depending on the degree of anger provoked, not just the individual wrongdoer but their entire kin and clan might be attacked.

Unregulated private vengeance became increasingly problematic as societies developed (*ibid*: 71). In particular, the 'victims' of revenge often regarded it as a wrong against them, and hence retaliated in turn. Private vengeance therefore led to the escalation of conflicts and to long-running blood-feuds. Hence, the story goes, as societies developed they tended to create alternative, less destructive, ways of dealing with wrongs. First, the practice of 'composition' or buying off vengeance became institutionalised: 'An offender could buy back the peace he had injured by a system of fines, by paying *bot* (betterment) to the offended party and *wite* to the king' (Gorringe 1996: 89). This reduced the brutality of 'private justice' and prevented the escalation of conflicts. But it also perpetuated the problem of there being one law for the rich and another for the poor. The wealthy could easily make amends for their wrongs, while the poor, unable to pay restitution for the act of one of their kin, were frequently ruined and pushed into economic dependence and slavery (Pollock and Maitland 1898: 460). This problem was aggravated by the fact that the size of the offence, and hence the amount of compensation due, was determined mainly by the social status of the victim. To the modern mind, the system of composition was almost as bad as the private vengeance it replaced:

> there is good reason to believe that for a long time past the system of *bot* and *wite* had been delusive, if not hypocritical. It outwardly reconciled the stern facts of a rough justice with a Christian reluctance to shed blood; it demanded money instead of life, but so much money that few were likely to pay it. Those who could not

pay were outlawed or sold as slaves. From the very first it was an aristocratic system; not only did it make a distinction between those who were 'dearly born' and those who were 'cheaply born', but it widened the gulf by impoverishing the poorer folk. One unlucky blow resulting in the death of a thegn may have been enough to reduce a whole family of ceorls to economic dependence or even to legal slavery. When we reckon up the causes which made the bulk of the nation into tillers of the lands of the lords, *bot* and *wite* should not be forgotten. At any rate to ask the *villanus* of Henry I's day to pay £5 as an atonement for his crime is to condemn him to outlawry.

(Pollock and Maitland 1898: 460)

As societies developed further, and in particular as a strong central power emerged, composition gave way, in turn, to state punishment (Miller 1999: 71). In the hands of 'the state', the practice of punishment remained violent. A system of fines (corresponding to composition) did develop, but was of little relevance to the majority of offenders who were too poor to pay them (Braithwaite 1993). But, while state punishment remained violent, the use of violence became more controlled and discriminating. Punishment became restricted to the individual wrongdoer. A distinction began to emerge between malicious wrongdoers who deserved to be punished and accidental wrongdoers who need only pay compensation, i.e. a distinction between criminal law and civil law emerged. And the severity of punishment came to be based on the wrongdoer's guilt, rather than on the status of the injured party or on the degree of anger provoked.

Gradually, as society became more and more civilised, state punishment became less and less violent and its use was increasingly regulated by legal principles. More generally, some perceive a long-term tendency for the social reaction to crime to become less punitive, more restitutive.[1] While, according to many, the practice of state punishment in most modern societies is still in need of significant reform (Cragg 1992: 7), there is a general sense that the history of punishment has, at least until recently, been one of gradual progress towards a more rational, humane and decent response to offenders.[2] To this sense, the idea of reviving ancient ways of dealing with crime seems highly reactionary.

A revised image of premodern justice and of the roots of state punishment

In the conventional story, our earliest response to crime was unregulated private vengeance. From there, things could only get better. The history of our responses to crime therefore unfolds as a story of unambiguous progress.

Proponents of restorative justice, however, challenge the assumption that violent retaliation was the normal response to a perceived wrong in primitive societies. From the earliest of times, they suggest, societies developed other mechanisms for dealing with conflict. Compensation was nearly always a significant option and usually the first option, even before the emergence of a relatively institutionalised system of composition. Personal revenge should be understood, therefore, as having always been 'only one of a much richer set of options' (Zehr 1990: 98; cf. Roberts 1979: 56–69). Wronged parties were usually expected to accept compensation if the appropriate amount was offered. For most offences, it was only if the offender refused to negotiate or if negotiations failed to produce a settlement that vengeance could take place with community approval. Indeed, according to proponents of restorative justice, those who offered and paid an appropriate amount of compensation were, from an early time, given some protection by the community from violent retaliation (see also Schafer 1960; Jacob 1977).

While proponents of restorative justice do acknowledge some problems with ancient systems of restitution, what they tend to emphasise are their advantages over the systems of state punishment which eventually replaced them. Most importantly, they argue, pre-modern people saw clearly what has become obscured to us: that crime 'is at its core a violation of a person by another person' and that the priority of the community should be, not to determine the guilt of the offender and to impose an appropriate punishment, but to make peace and even things out by persuading offenders to acknowledge and meet their liability to repair the harm they caused (Zehr 1990: 182). This focus on repair and reconciliation benefited injured parties, who could expect useful compensation rather than the mere short-term gratification of seeing those who had injured them suffer in return. It also benefited offenders, since the spotlight was on the harmful consequences of their behaviour and on their liability to repair damage rather than on their motives for committing the crime and their moral guilt. Hence, in the restorative justice processes of olden times, it is argued, there was little place for the expression of moral indignation which one finds at the centre of the practice of judicial punishment (Bianchi 1994).

If ancient justice practices had much to recommend them, the characterisation of the historical process, whereby they gave way to a system of state punishment, as 'progress' becomes much more problematic. So why was this system of restitutive justice abandoned for a system of state punishment?

According to advocates of restorative justice the change was not due to humanitarian concern, nor was it an inevitable response to needs for greater social stability. Rather, among the motives for the state's appropriation of the people's conflicts were greed for money and power. Or, put more politely, the creation of state punitive control, and the concomitant suppression of the restorative justice of local communities, occurred for a combination of narrow fiscal and political reasons (Braithwaite 1999b: 1730; Barnett 1980: 119). Around the twelfth century, feudal Barons, ecclesiastical powers and the king began to take control of the justice process in order to take for themselves the 'fines' paid by offenders to their victims. They regarded these fines as a useful source of revenue, a substantial supplement to unpopular taxes (Wright 1996a: 11–19). Jacob summarises this transformation as follows:

> In England, the king and his lords or barons required that the offender pay not only 'bot' or 'wer' to the victim but a sum called 'wite' to the lord or king as a commission for assistance in bringing about a reconciliation between the offender and victim and for protection against further retaliation by the victim and victim's clan or tribe. In the twelfth century as the central power in the community increased, its share increased, and the victim's share decreased greatly. The 'wite' was increased until finally the king or overlord took the entire payment. The victim's right to restitution at this time was replaced by what has become known as a fine … The state, in the person of the king, came to be defined as the offended party in matters of criminal law.
>
> (Jacob 1977: 46–7)

In roughly the same era, European princes began to think of public displays of punitive power as a useful way of symbolizing their political power (which was in reality still weak) and hence as useful for their centralizing project (Braithwaite 1999b: 1730; *cf.* Foucault 1977). As Barnett (1977: 285–6) puts it: 'The king abandoned the composition system for the system of punishment because punishment struck terror in the hearts of the people, and this served to inspire awe for the power of the king and state'. According to this view, the emergence of a theoretical distinction between crimes and private wrongs followed rather than preceded this 'state' takeover of the business of handling 'crime' and of the revenues which this business generated, and the distinction was developed in part to justify and rationalize this takeover (Christie 1977; Barnett 1980: 119–20).[3]

Most proponents of restorative justice would accept that the creation of state judicial punishment did, nonetheless, bring some gains. For example, in many ways it created greater equality before the law and helped to pacify society by suppressing crime and disorderly conduct. Restorative justice proponents, however, seek to draw attention to what was *lost* in the transition from communal restorative justice to state retributive justice:

- The state takeover of criminal justice resulted in the needs of victims being neglected. From then on, if they wanted compensation they would have to seek it through private actions in the civil courts. But pursuing redress in this way was, and still is, prohibitively expensive for most people.

- The rise of state punitive control resulted in ordinary people losing the sense that controlling crime and dispensing justice was any of their responsibility. Communities lost their confidence, their ability and eventually their desire to handle their own crime problems and to regulate themselves. They became mere consumers of criminal justice services provided by the authorities (Christie 1977; Garland 2001: 32). In the process, they ceased to become communities in quite the same sense (Cayley 1998: 168). So, although on the one hand it provided greater security, state punitive control tended, in the long term, to debilitate the community controls which, arguably, are ultimately more powerful, efficient and just as mechanisms of crime control (Braithwaite 1989).

- The decline of communal restorative justice traditions meant the withering of a constructive, educative and reintegrative response to wrongdoing – a response which both created within offenders a sense of the magnitude of the harm they had inflicted on another person and gave them an opportunity to redeem themselves by repairing that harm (Geis 1977: 147). In place of such a response, it put a punitive system which meets violence with violence and which possibly creates more criminality than it prevents, especially by making moral outcasts of people who break the law (Bianchi 1994: 18; Braithwaite 1999b: 1738–41).

- What was originally seen as a revenue generating enterprise soon became a very costly affair as demands for the judicial punishment of impoverished deviants grew (Braithwaite 1993).

Others recognise some of these problems with our system of judicial punishment. Their response is to try to *reform* the system by, for example, developing state compensation schemes, reducing sentences, ameliorating penal institutions and introducing measures designed to rehabilitate offenders. For some proponents of restorative justice, however, the system cannot be reformed. Rather, what is needed is a fundamentally new approach. We need to abandon the institution of state punishment and return to the restorative justice traditions of our distant ancestors.

The renaissance of native justice traditions

As part of broader anti-colonial struggles, indigenous peoples in many colonised countries have sought to revitalize their traditional approaches to conflict handling (Taraschi 1998; Findlay 2000). What follows are just two of the most important examples.

In New Zealand, British forms of justice and punishment were introduced in the first half of the nineteenth century. Thereafter, the Maori way of dealing with wrongdoing, which was initially regarded by colonisers as quaint but later viewed as irritating and threatening, was first restricted to intra-Maori crime and eventually almost entirely 'silenced', continuing to exist only sporadically in outlying areas (Pratt 1996). By the 1980s, however, a number of developments – accelerating rates of Maori offending and imprisonment, disenchantment with formal and impersonal legal processes, and 'a resurgence of interest in the rights and cultures of indigenous peoples' – had converged to create a revived interest in Maori forms of justice and punishment (*ibid*: 149).

In 1988, a report by Moana Jackson, commissioned by the New Zealand Department of Justice,

> advised that the Maori be allowed to deal with conflicts that affected them in a way that was culturally appropriate. This meant a return to the principles of restorative justice that were embedded in the pre-colonial method of dispute resolution.
>
> (Pratt 1996, describing Jackson 1988)

A year later, the practice of family group conferencing, which was partly informed by Maori justice practices and philosophies, was established for 'youth offenders' (Tauri 1999). Western observers have shown considerable interest in this as a model for youth justice more generally (McElrea 1994; Morris and Gelsthorpe 2000), and something like the approach has since been imported to England, among other places (Pollard 2000).[4]

A similar revival of restorative justice traditions has taken place in the Navajo Nation.[5] In the late nineteenth century, western-style courts enforcing western-style rules (albeit often interpreted, to the exasperation of outsiders, in line with native values) were established in the Navajo Nation and traditional Navajo legal institutions were driven underground (Yazzie and Zion 1996; Yazzie 1998; Zion 1998). By the early 1980s, however, a campaign for the revival of traditional Navajo justice principles, methods and institutions was under way. By the 1990s a Navajo legal system had been resurrected and was dealing with much that non-Navajos would classify as serious crime according to the principle that the aim was not:

> to punish or penalize people, but to teach them how to live a better life. It is a healing process that either restores good relationships among people or, if they do not have good relations to begin with, fosters and nourishes a healthy environment.
>
> (Yazzie and Zion 1996: 160–1)

Western responses to native justice revivals

These developments have given rise to debates about how much control aboriginal peoples should have over their own justice systems. Some seemingly radical voices call for complete legal sovereignty for in-digenous peoples within their territories. 'Conservatives', on the other hand, refuse to concede legal sovereignty and warn against the creation of 'racially segregated justice' (Cayley 1998: 197). Nevertheless, many accept that aboriginal peoples might have their own police, courts, trials and even interpretations of the law and sentences (*ibid*).

For campaigners for restorative justice, even the so-called radical voices in this debate are too conservative. They argue that, as was the case to a limited extent with New Zealand FGCs, traditional aboriginal approaches to justice should be applied throughout the whole society. Aboriginal justice alternatives should be seen as a model for a reform of *Western* justice. As the president of the American Bar Association put it, in the subtitle of an article: 'Our Navajo peers could teach us a thing or two about conflict resolution' (Cooper 1995; see also Wright 1996a: ch. 4; Roberts 1979).

Navajo peacemaking

In order to see what kind of lessons advocates of restorative justice might want to draw from native justice practices and to assess how realistic they are being, it is necessary to give some idea of the nature of these practices. To do this, I will very briefly describe one process, Navajo peacemaking. One reason for choosing this example is that, according to its practitioners, Navajo peacemaking is a virtually universal process found among nearly all aboriginal groups and in all pre-modern societies. There is an implication that Navajo peacemaking represents a natural, authentic form of justice, a form abandoned by modern western societies in favour of a more 'artificial' system of state punitive justice. James Zion states:

> In recent travels to Bolivia and South Africa and in discussions with indigenous leaders, lawyers, and academics who visit the Navajo Nation Courts, I have found that the indigenous legal process now popularly known as peacemaking is fairly universal among indigenous peoples. I suspect it is the law which preceded modern state law.
>
> (1998: 144n1)

Navajo peacemaking, according to its proponents and practitioners, can be described with caution as a form of restorative justice (Yazzie 1998: 123). Briefly, it operates as follows. When there is a dispute, the injured party will make a demand that the perpetrator puts things right, which often involves not just material compensation but a readjustment of the relationship between the wrongdoer and the injured party. However, according to Navajo concepts of freedom and individuality, one person cannot impose a decision on another – to the Navajo way of thinking coercion is witchcraft (Yazzie 1998: 130; Zion 1998: 145n8). The perpetrator must agree to make things right. In order to reach such an agreement, the victim will often seek the assistance of a *naat'aanii* or peacemaker. The *naat'aanii*-peacemaker is a respected community leader 'usually someone who thinks well, speaks well, plans well, and shows by his or her behavior that his or her conduct is grounded in spirituality' (Yazzie 1998: 125; Yazzie and Zion 1996: 164–5; on spirituality in restorative justice see Braithwaite 1999a: 25–6).

The *naat'aanii*-peacemaker calls on the interested parties – the victim and the perpetrator and their families and clan relations – to participate in a meeting in which the aim is to resolve the dispute between them. The meeting, which takes place as soon as possible, begins with a prayer, which is a summons for supernatural help. Victims then have an opportunity to state what happened and to vent their feelings about it. The accused person then has an opportunity to speak. Frequently, they will put forward excuses or justifications. One of the purposes of the process appears to be to expose the weakness or unacceptability of the excuses which people habitually use to justify unacceptable behaviour such as drunk-driving and spouse-abuse (Yazzie 1998: 125). To achieve this, the plausibility of excuses are assessed, not by lawyers through Western methods of cross-examination, but by people who know the wrongdoer intimately and who will use their intimate knowledge of the wrongdoer to expose the frailty of their excuses.

The group, led by the peacemaker, will then seek to construct a reparative plan of action. This search is guided by principles drawn, not just from legal precedents (in the Western sense), but from a rich range of traditional sources:

> Navajos have a great deal of respect for tradition and they recognize both a form of traditional case law and a corpus of legal principles. The case law can be in the form of what happened in the time of creation, e.g., what First Man and First Woman, the Hero Twins or the Holy People did to address a similar problem. The case may involve Coyote or Horned Toad, and the foolishness of what Coyote did or the wisdom of Horned Toad to resolve a similar conflict. There are principles to be derived from ceremonial practice, songs, prayers or other expressions of Navajo doctrine. The *naat'aanii* draws upon traditional teachings to propose a plan of action for the parties in order to resolve their dispute.
>
> (Yazzie and Zion 1996: 168)

The parties themselves will then decide whether to commit themselves to the plan of action. The plan of action will often involve restitution from the wrongdoer to the victim. But crucially, the main focus is not on making adequate material reparation but upon making *symbolic* reparation (*ibid*: 168; Yazzie 1998: 127; *cf*. Retzinger and Scheff 1996). Compensatory payments are important as much for what they symbolise – acceptance of responsibility for the damage caused – as for their ability to make up for material losses.

The failure to realise that reparation is symbolic often leads outsiders to misjudge Navajo peacemaking. For instance, sexual misconduct cases are sometimes settled by the perpetrator compensating the victim by giving her horses, cows or sheep (Yazzie and Zion 1996: 168). To some non-Navajos, this amounts to putting a price on rape and a fairly inadequate price at that. This interpretation, it is argued, misses the symbolic significance of this form of compensation:

The act of delivering cattle as compensation is visible in a rural community. Members of that community will most likely know about the event, and the public act of delivering cattle or horses shows the woman's innocence. It reinforces her dignity and tells the community she was wronged.[6]

(*ibid*: 168)

Yazzie and Zion claim that the peacemaking process works in the sense that parties usually agree to the proposed plans of action and carry them out and that this resolves disputes and reduces rates of recidivism (*ibid*: 170). It is important, though, to look at why they think it works, since Navajo peacemaking, it is claimed, does not employ the authority, force and coercion which Westerners usually regard as essential to the success of legal regulation, however much in the background they may sometimes be (*ibid*: 171).

Zion describes Navajo peacemaking as a 'consensual' or 'discussion' method of justice (1998: 140). It works, not by telling people what to do and using coercion when they do not do as they are told, but by persuading people to buy into or accept decisions which they help to make (Yazzie and Zion 1996: 171). To achieve this, it uses emotions of respect and *ties to the community*. These methods, it is claimed, work with Navajos because *they cannot conceive of life outside of their communities*. In Navajo thinking 'an individual is a person within a community, it is impossible to function alone' (ibid: 170). Hence, errant individuals will try to comply with the community's expectations of proper behaviour, when these expectations are made clear and the relationship between the individual and the rest of the community is strengthened, because having good relations with the rest of the community is fundamentally important to them (Yazzie 1998: 129). There are also some hints that this system works so well because of the rural economy and lifestyle of the inhabitants of the Navajo Nation (Yazzie and Zion 1996: 170–1).

Can one characterise ancient and indigenous justice as restorative?

Kathleen Daly has described the claim that restorative justice has been the dominant mode of criminal justice throughout human history as 'extraordinary' (Daly 2000b: 10). She suspects restorative justice proponents of romanticising the past, ignoring evidence of harsh physical punishment and banishment. She also suggests, following Blagg (1997), that they may be guilty of 're-colonising' indigenous justice practices by interpreting them as exemplars of restorative justice (Daly 2000b: 25). Daly argues that we should view such histories and anthropologies as 'origin myths', rather than as attempts at serious historical or anthropological understanding, which function to 'authorise' contemporary restorative justice experiments:

> If the first form of human justice was 'restorative justice', then advocates can claim a need to recover it from a history of 'takeover' by state-sponsored retributive justice. *And*, by identifying current indigenous practices as 'restorative justice', advocates can claim a need to recover these practices from a history of 'takeover' by white colonial powers who instituted retributive justice.
>
> (Daly 2000b: 12)

In my view, Daly's assessment of the historical and anthropological arguments of proponents of restorative justice is somewhat harsh. She is right to emphasise the way in which the theme, that restorative justice was the dominant form of pre-modern justice, functions as a metaphor and a myth. However, she overstates the case when she implies that such myths have virtually no relation to the 'real story'. Even allowing for the gross over-simplifications in some accounts, there is a significant historical truth, confirmed by 'professional historians', which they expose: that there was once a mode of life in which some part of the law belonged to the community and was theirs to enforce; in which justice was not wholly delegated or bureaucratised; and that there is much to lament in the decline of this mode of life (*cf.* Thompson 1992: 530; Berman 1983). Daly is quite right to take proponents of restorative justice to task for their tendency to romanticize this mode of life, representing its justice as almost purely 'restorative' and glossing over its more tyrannical aspects. But such criticisms can be made without dismissing the whole story as a mere metaphor or origin myth.

However, even if we accept the characterisation of the justice systems of pre-modern societies (and current indigenous justice revivals) as restorative and the claim that these systems were abandoned, not because they were inferior to the state retributive justice which displaced them, but because of more complex political and cultural developments, we are still left with the question of whether it is feasible and desirable to revive such restorative justice traditions in contemporary Western society. Pointing to a time when the state was weak and justice belonged to the community is one thing; suggesting that community-based restorative justice can be resurrected in modern society, as an alternative to the violence and coercion of an existing state justice, is quite another matter.

Can one *revive* restorative justice traditions?

A number of questions and criticisms inevitably spring to mind, or at least to the minds of sceptical Western lawyers and social scientists, when presented with the idea of reviving restorative justice traditions in modern developed societies. Here I will outline just some of the most obvious doubts and look at how proponents of restorative justice respond to them.

Can restorative justice work in a world of weak geographical communities?

> One day, we had a group of visitors from Africa, and their US guide listened to my presentation on peacemaking. At one point the guide jumped in and said that something like peacemaking might work with people who share the same language and culture or in a rural situation, but it won't work in modern industrial society.
> (Yazzie 1998: 128)

John Braithwaite has stated that his ideas of reviving restorative justice and reintegrative shaming are frequently dismissed as resting on 'a romantic plea for a bygone communitarian era' (Braithwaite 1993: 2). He does not name his critics, but it is easy enough to see what they mean. As we have seen, proponents of Navajo peacemaking think it is possible to bring delinquent individuals into compliance with the community's norms of proper behaviour, without coercion or threats of punishment, by using the emotional bonds between them and their community. Just as some people meet their obligations to family even though they may find them onerous, because retaining close ties with the family is very important to them, Navajos apparently will, with a little help and persuasion, meet their obligations to the community because retaining close ties to the community is for them equally important. But in modern towns and cities, and indeed in most rural areas in developed societies, individuals are not so strongly attached to their communities. This does not mean, as some contend, that we are completely individualistic or that in modern society the individual is thrown back entirely on their own reflexive devices (Giddens 1991). In our own way, we are just as interdependent as our medieval ancestors and as the Navajos. But, our relations to most of those with whom we interact tend to be less intimate, complete, and continuous than their communal relations. Our social relations are arguably too lacking in familiarity, emotional depth, moral commitment, and continuity for ancient practices of restorative justice to work.

According to sociologists, the trend away from communal relations (or *Gemeinschaft*) towards non-communal relations (or *Gesellschaft*) is coterminous with processes of industrialisation and urbanisation which date back at least to the eighteenth century.[7] However, many see this trend as having gathered speed in the twentieth century: 'it is impossible not to sense the social disintegration, the breakdown of communities, that has taken place in Europe, North America and other parts of Western civilization in the twentieth century' (Berman 1983: *vi*). And some think it has reached its zenith in recent decades, spurred on by changes in technology, social mobility, the size of institutions, and increase of central government intervention (Schluter 1994; Garland 2001: ch. 4).[8] How do proponents of restorative justice respond?

I will focus on the response of Braithwaite, since among advocates of restorative justice, he has addressed these criticisms most directly and most thoroughly. He regards such views as 'misplaced pessimism' (2000: 121). He agrees that a 'communitarian' society is most conducive to the successful practice of restorative justice (Braithwaite 1989: ch. 6). But he responds to critics with two related arguments. The first is that that modern developed societies are more communitarian than the critics assume. The second, linked argument is that restorative justice does not depend for its viability on the existence and involvement of a *geographic* community to which both offenders and victims will feel strongly attached. Rather, it can work with the *personal* communities of offenders and victims, i.e. with individuals who know and are personally involved in the lives of offenders and victims (see also McCold 1996: 92).

Braithwaite's first argument suggests that his critics adhere to a geographic conception of community, which they then find absent in modern society. What the sceptics have in mind is the sense of community which presumably existed in the pre-industrial revolution village. The homogenous village community has certainly declined, but in other ways, Braithwaite argues, communitarian relations have flourished in modern developed societies (1993: 12–3). The modern family, he suggests, while much smaller than the extended family of pre-industrialised and pre-urbanised society, is much more communitarian (*ibid*: 11). The crucial argument, however, is that the modern city-dweller is enmeshed in a wide range of communitarian relationships which are favourable to the operation of restorative justice. Braithwaite writes:

The contemporary city-dweller may have a set of colleagues at work, in her trade union, among members of his golf club, among drinking associates whom he meets at the same pub, among members of a professional association, the parents' and citizens' committee for her daughter's school, not to mention a geographically extended family, where many of these significant others can mobilize potent disapproval. There are actually more interdependencies in the nineteenth- and twentieth-century city; it is just that they are not geographically segregated within a community. ... No matter how exotic my interests are, in the city those interests can become a basis for constructing communities.

(Braithwaite 1993: 13)

It might be objected that this misses the point. Interdependencies do not on their own amount to 'community'. The relationships of the modern city-dweller with those with whom they interact are not so intimate, deep or continuous as those of the premodern village-dweller with their neighbours, or even as those of the 1950s city dweller with their neighbours. As Braithwaite himself recognises: 'we can be in relationships of interdependency with people without sharing a community with those people in any genuine sense of mutual help and trust' (Braithwaite 1989: 85). Hence, in modern cities community control is frail and easier to escape. Braithwaite suggests the issue is more complex:

Admittedly, it is easier to cut oneself off from disapproval by some of these non-geographical communities of modernity (by simply withdrawing from them) than it is to cut oneself off from the disapproval of fellow villagers. But the reverse is also sometimes true. One cannot withdraw from the disapproval of one's international professional community by moving house; to do that one must learn a new career.

(Braithwaite 1993: 14)

This links with the second argument, which is that restorative justice can work by involving the offender's and the victim's micro-communities of care in the process. All that is required, in other words, is a small handful of people who have a relationship of mutual care with the offender and a small handful who have such a relationship with the victim. The communitarianism of restorative justice:

is an individual-centred communitarianism that can work in a world of weak geographical communities. It looks for community on many and any bases that can be built around a single person.

(Braithwaite 2000: 122)

Even so, some would argue that there are individuals who are so isolated that even this more modest requirement cannot be met. Braithwaite simply refuses to believe this. Hence, in the programmes with which he is connected, when people charged with the task of organising a family group conference for an offender,

come back with the claim that the offender is alone in the world, estranged from their family, unemployed, alienated from school, homeless, that a community of care cannot possibly be organized around them, we tell them to go back and try again. However estranged they are from the nuclear family, there will usually be a grandparent or aunt or cousin whom they respect and trust, even if they have to be brought in from another city. There will usually be someone at school who has treated them decently. This is because human beings are fundamentally social organisms; some are more lonely than others, but few are devoid of anyone who cares.

(Braithwaite 2000: 121)

How persuasive is this response to the critics? We can accept Braithwaite's point that we should think of community, not as a place, but as a type of relationship and that, so conceived, community does exist in modern societies: individuals tend to be in community with various others but not necessarily with their neighbours. This is a useful corrective to the rather crude and simplistic critique which suggests that we are moving rapidly towards an era of total *Gesellschaft* in which community no longer exists, rendering restorative justice impossible. But, it does not address the harder question of whether the so-called 'individual-centred communitarianism' which we do have is sufficient to make restorative justice feasible as the routine response to crime. Braithwaite simply asserts this and, throughout his work, provides examples of particular cases in which restorative justice has worked. But these individual examples would not convince many sceptics that *most* offenders would change their ways if only their micro-communities could be mobilised to shame and support them.

Braithwaite simply makes too little of the fact that, unlike the medieval village dweller and apparently unlike contemporary Navajos, many individuals can withdraw from 'the non-geographical communities of modernity' and join other communities. This means that most of our community relationships are weak, relative to those of the medieval village dweller. To the extent that this is the case, the capacity of micro-communities to influence modern delinquent individuals will be relatively weak. It might not be as weak as some suppose, and there may be a case for saying that we should make much more use of what capacity for community control there is. But this is well short of insisting, as Braithwaite does, that the absence of strong geographic communities in modern societies poses no problems whatsoever for the idea of reviving restorative justice traditions. The response of Braithwaite and others to the critique, so far, has been no case to answer. There is a case to answer and until it is answered persuasively many will remain sceptical about the viability of the proposed revival of restorative justice.

There is a further problem: Braithwaite's refusal to believe that modern societies contain many individuals who are so socially isolated that the idea of organising something like a Navajo peacemaking circle around them and expecting it to work is unrealistic. An earlier generation of penal reformers had no problem finding, among the population of convicted offenders, a significant portion who were 'cut off from society' (Johnstone 1996a: 85). For example, in the 1960s and 1970s, surveys of habitual drunken offenders (who accounted for thousands of arrests and prison sentences per year) found that many had no contact at all with family or friends, few had employment, many were homeless, and most of them typically had few, if any, social affiliations:

> Forty per cent had not attended a cinema, dance, church, or other social function during the preceding five years. Less than ten per cent belonged to a club, union or formal organization.[9]
>
> (Gath 1969: 22)

For many of these offenders, human interaction consisted only of extremely thin, fleeting relationships with other vagrant alcoholics or with criminal justice professionals, social workers and charitable volunteers.

Braithwaite's response, as we have seen, would be stubbornly to insist that they must have someone, somewhere who cares about them and to send organisers of restorative justice processes out to find these people so that a restorative conference could be organised. In the 1960s and 1970s, those concerned to do something constructive about this significant group of offenders, as an alternative to pushing them repeatedly through the 'penal revolving door', had rather different ideas. Their method was to try to *socialise* habitual drunken offenders by placing them in hostels, organised as therapeutic communities, where they could gradually acquire social competence. This 'hostel treatment' was combined with the creation of facilities half-way between the community and 'skid row', such as sheltered employment and drop-in centres, which would provide stepping stones for those making the journey from isolation to integration. Their point was that such individuals needed sustained support, which would have to be co-ordinated by welfare professionals, in order to get them into anything remotely resembling a relationship of community with other members of society.

The ideas of this earlier generation of reformers are frequently rejected by proponents of restorative justice, who tend to be dismissive of the 'individual treatment model' (Bazemore 1996). Yet, it seems to me that such ideas would be quite consistent with a broader conception of restorative justice. If we cease thinking of restorative justice simply as a process, in which the community must take part in conferences geared towards the reintegrative shaming of offenders, and start thinking of it more as an attitude – characterised by a commitment to creating and nurturing bonds between the community and those excluded from it, where this exclusion is in some way bound up with their being involved in crime, as offenders or victims, there would be no problem in recognising the fact of widespread social isolation and dealing with socially isolated offenders (and victims) in a manner designed to alleviate their isolation.

This points to a wider problem with Braithwaite's manner of responding to critics of restorative justice, a manner which is followed by many, but not all, of his fellow advocates. Although his writings sometimes indicate otherwise, Braithwaite seems strongly attached to a particular idea of what restorative justice involves: the use of micro-communities of care to shame and reintegrate offenders. This approach can only work if offenders actually have micro-communities of care and if these communities have a strong enough bond with offenders to be able to influence their attitudes and behaviour. Hence, Braithwaite perseveres in the belief that every individual in modern society has such a micro-community, despite strong evidence to the contrary. To be blunt, he allows his commitment to a particular form of restorative justice to influence his interpretation of the facts.

It is not necessary to respond to criticism in this manner. An alternative response would be to accept that there are huge differences between the social relations of, on the one hand, premodern society and the Navajo nation and, on the other, modern cities. The former are strongly communal, the latter are not. The difference should not be exaggerated, but nor should it be denied. This makes the idea of reviving restorative justice traditions problematic, but not impossible. What we may have to do is ask what would somebody committed to the values of restorative justice do in our current situation? One answer could be that we should respond to those offenders (and victims) who are socially isolated, who lack communities of care, in a rather different way than we should respond to those who are clearly in community with others.

How are tensions between state law and community custom to be handled?

Proponents of restorative justice do not usually envisage giving communities complete legal sovereignty, i.e. the right to make their own laws. Rather, what most advocate is the devolution, from state pro-secutors and courts to community forums, of responsibility for deciding what should be done about breaches of state criminal law. In this scheme, the limits to how we can behave are still decided by the state, through its law-making process, not by the community by reference to local customs and norms. Restorative justice is by no means popular justice. This would seem to preclude the possibility of using restorative justice forums – at least where they are part of the criminal justice system – to bring pressure on individuals to comply with customary ways of behaving, where local customs are not enforced by state law.[10] But there are still certain problems to do with the occasional discord between state law and community custom. These problems would not have arisen in the ancient practice of restorative justice, before the emergence of state criminal law. However, they do arise, often quite sharply, in native justice revivals, where indigenous peoples gain control of criminal justice process, but without obtaining full legal sovereignty (Cayley 1998: ch. 11).

One problem is what happens when community support for a particular state criminal law is weak or even where community support for action to be taken against particular individuals and groups is weak? Such problems are not unknown in the conventional criminal justice process, where juries sometimes decline to convict individuals apparently on grounds of 'conscience', i.e. where it seems clear that there is very strong proof of legal guilt, but where the prosecution is unpopular. But in an approach which relies on ordinary members of the community to determine the 'sentence', such problems are amplified.

Again, it is Braithwaite who has done most to see and grapple with this quandary. However, once again, his response is to deny that it is such a serious problem. Braithwaite does not completely reject the claim that, given the existence of cultural diversity and ethical disagreement in modern society, certain criminal laws will inevitably be unpopular in certain communities. Nevertheless, he insists that the extent of such disagreement should not be exaggerated. In particular, he argues, no matter how divided they may be on contentious ethical issues, virtually all members of modern society share a strong commitment to the prohibition of behaviour whereby one person harms another through acts such as rape, violent assault, theft and destruction of property. Hence, he argues that there does tend to be 'a *powerful consensus* ... over the rightness of criminal laws which protect our persons and property' (Braithwaite 1989: 13, emphasis added). The implication is that restorative justice is feasible as a response to 'predatory crimes' (*ibid*). It is only when the state uses the criminal law to prohibit non-predatory behaviour, in line with some more contested conception of morality, that it is likely to find community censure weak.

Even if we accepted this argument, we would still be left with the problem of what to do about 'non-predatory' criminal behaviour, the prohibition of which does not always enjoy strong support in all communities. Braithwaite's response appears to be that if the community does not support the prohibition, then the prohibition should not exist, so there is no problem if the community does nothing about it.

> A nice moral feature of restorative justice ... is that restorative justice might only work with crimes that ought to be crimes. If a group of citizens cannot agree in an undominated conference that an act of obscenity is wrong, then the obscenity should not be a crime; and the conference will fail in controlling obscenity.
>
> (Braithwaite 1999a: 50)

This argument may have some appeal to those who think there are many types of behaviour currently defined as crimes which ought not to be. However, I find it seriously misguided. Some state criminal laws are designed to protect a minority of weaker members of communities from the majority of stronger members, and are unpopular within those communities for precisely that reason. One of the advantages of state punishment over informal community control is that it can be used to enforce prohibitions which are highly unpopular among the majority, or even a strong minority, but are necessary for the protection of weaker members of the community. Bans on smoking in many public places, on drink-driving, and on many other harmful but not predatory social practices are often highly unpopular when first introduced because they strike at customs widely regarded as quite acceptable. If it is not feasible to use restorative justice to enforce such prohibitions at the time of their unpopularity then that must be acknowledged as a weakness or limitation of restorative justice. It should not be represented as a strength or useful by-product.

Even more important, Braithwaite's claim that there is 'a powerful consensus' about predatory crime is highly disputable. It may well be that virtually everyone agrees that acts of rape, violent assault, and theft are wrong. But there is by no means a powerful consensus around the legal definition of these crimes or about their seriousness. This is most obvious in relation to rape and domestic assault. It is quite clear that within many communities, condemnation of acts which many women regard as abominable violations is quite weak (Cayley 1998: ch. 11). For instance, in some indigenous restorative justice experiments, men who have committed serious domestic assaults, but pleaded drunkenness and personal problems as mitigating factors, expressed remorse and agreed to do something about their problem, have been dealt with very leniently by sentencing circles in which male voices were clearly dominant (*ibid*). It is also worth returning here to the example, from Navajo justice, of a sexual assault case being settled by the assaulter compensating his victim by giving her horses, cows or sheep. As I pointed out, those who object to this tend to miss the symbolic significance of this form of compensation, i.e. the fact that the public act of delivering cattle demonstrates the woman's innocence. Yet even those who fully understand this might still object that the punishment is wholly disproportionate to the crime and sends out a message that rape is a relatively trivial offence. Such cases help explain why many aboriginal feminists are so tepid about the idea of reviving indigenous community restoration (Cayley 1998: ch. 11).

The question of how to prevent restorative processes resulting in what many, appealing to norms of justice which are not strongly recognized within the community, would regard as an over-lenient outcome is a pressing one for the campaign for restorative justice. It is not useful to respond to it by playing down its significance. It would be much better, in my view, to face up to the problem and recognise that unless restorative justice is accompanied by much deeper cultural reforms, there is a significant danger that it could result in an inferior, rather than superior, way of responding to crime.

What about forms of symbolic reparation regarded by 'outsiders' as unacceptable?

A further problem arises when some of the things which communities regard as acceptable ways of making amends for wrongdoing are regarded as unacceptable and even criminal by the standards of state criminal law (Ivison 1999). A frequently cited example is the practice of spearing among aboriginal peoples in Australia, where (allegedly) one way of making symbolic reparation is to submit voluntarily to being speared through a fleshy part of the thigh (*ibid*: 95–6). If we subscribe to the principle of allowing parties to a conflict to negotiate appropriate reparation in accordance with community norms, on what grounds do we veto such practices?

Such extreme problems might be easily solved, in practice at least, by ruling that restorative justice processes must comply with laws designed to protect fundamental human rights. Methods of symbolic reparation which would result in an infringement of what the state or international community regards as the fundamental rights of the individual could be vetoed, even if the local community and the individual involved do not object to them. However, this does not completely solve the problem.

Because of their very symbolic nature, many acts of symbolic reparation will be regarded as highly unacceptable by the ethical and indeed aesthetic standards of many 'outsiders', but not necessarily be deemed in contravention of the person's human rights. Examples include a case where, 'an offender in a domestic violence case was made to stand before his ex-wife while she spit [sic] in his face' and a case where: 'A probationer was required to live in a halfway house and comply with its rules. When the probationer was accused of "acting like a baby," he was told to wear diapers outside of his clothes' (Karp 1998: 282).[11] There is no consensus, even among those strongly committed to protecting offenders' human rights, that such punishments violate their basic rights; many argue to the contrary (Whitman 1998). It might be thought that such 'punishments' have no place in a process which is called restorative, but there is a significant emphasis in restorative justice on the need for offenders to feel and express shame (Retzinger and Scheff 1996; Johnstone 1999), and we can have no guarantees about how this emphasis will be interpreted by local communities in practice. There are reports of restorative justice processes resulting in a decision, eagerly pushed by the offender's parents and his victim, that a young offender should wear a T-shirt inscribed with 'I am a Thief' (Braithwaite 1999a: 97).

One obvious solution is to ensure that all restorative action plans are overseen by judges, who will have power to disallow those plans which do not comply with certain standards. The question is to what extent should this legal oversight of the restorative justice process take place? The more legal oversight, the less room for what Braithwaite (1994) calls 'democratic creativity' in the search for 'remedies', creativity which is essential to the idea of restorative justice and will sometimes be used in ways which liberal-minded penal reformers will find heart-warming, but sometimes in ways which they will find disquieting or even appalling.

Conclusion: did restorative justice ever die?

Having pointed to some difficult, but not insurmountable, problems with the idea of reviving restorative justice traditions, I want to conclude on a more hopeful note. The whole idea of *reviving* restorative justice traditions rests on the assumption that such traditions have died out, to be replaced by state punitive control. This would seem to be the case if we draw our understanding of trends in social responses to 'crime' from public discourse. However, an understanding drawn from the study of actual social practices could be quite different. As Louk Hulsman (1986) points out, in practice only a small proportion of 'criminalizable events' are actually criminalized, i.e. interpreted and handled as crimes. In fact this is well known, but the profound significance of the 'dark figure' of crime is not often appreciated.[12] Most of the thousands of events which occur everyday which *could*, without straying from existing legal definitions, be construed as crimes are in fact interpreted and handled quite differently, i.e. in a non-punitive framework. The *'actual criminalisation* of criminalisable events – even in the field of traditional crime – is a rare event indeed' (*ibid*: 70, italics in original). So, what happens to the rest of these events? As Hulsman makes clear, they are defined in a variety of ways – as accidents, disputes, wrongs requiring compensation, signs of illness, or even legitimate responses to the actor's situation – and handled accordingly. Most are handled by those involved and affected by the event, and by the families and friends of each. Only infrequently do they invoke the legal system. Moreover, even when the legal system is invoked, it is often the civil law system. Resort to criminal law is quite exceptional.

One implication of this is that it is highly likely that many criminalisable events are already being interpreted and handled within a restorative justice framework, i.e. they are handled without the state's involvement and with an emphasis on recompense and contrition rather than punitive suffering. It is indeed likely that, in social practice, restorative justice is more the norm, and state punitive justice the exception. Restorative justice is probably much more deeply embedded in social life than is assumed either by those who deny the viability of a revival of restorative justice traditions and by those who are seeking to bring about such a revival. The task then may well be, not to try to revive a dead tradition, but to recognise that the tradition is very much alive and to find out why we deviate from it in a tiny, but growing, minority of cases and whether such deviation is ever necessary.

Notes

1 Emile Durkheim developed a complex sociological explanation of why such a change could be expected (Durkheim 1933; Garland 1990: ch. 2; Cotterrell 1999).

2 This assumption has been dented but not destroyed by various revisionist penal histories which have appeared since the 1970s (see Garland 1990).

3 This rather simplistic 'conspirational' account is supplemented by some proponents of restorative justice with a much more complex account of how, around the eleventh and twelfth centuries, new theological doctrines, themselves influenced by legal concepts, helped give criminal law a new status and crime a new moral meaning. A brief summary of these very complex accounts is provided in the appendix to this chapter.

4 Although the argument is too complex to deal with here, it is important to note that some regard the 'appropriation' of native justice traditions by white New Zealanders and Western nations as a form of recolonisation, in which the point of reviving traditional ceremonies and practices and the nature of those practices are seriously distorted (see Blagg 1997; Tauri 1999; Findlay 2000).

5 The Navajo Nation consists of over 200,000 inhabitants and 25,000 square miles of territory in Arizona, New Mexico and Utah (Yazzie and Zion 1996: 157).

6 I will return to this example later in the discussion.

7 See Nisbet (1967: ch. 3) for a classic and still very useful account. The German words are *Tönnies* (1887/1963) and are frequently used untranslated in sociology and social theory. But *cf.* Davies (1994) who shows that there was not a rigid unilinear relationship between the rise of urbanisation and industrialisation, on the one hand, and the decline of communal relations on the other. Drawing on the work of social and cultural historians of Victorian Britain, she describes a more complex development in which the rise and decline of 'relational institutions' (such as Sunday schools, friendly societies and the recognition of moral character as pertinent to assessments of whether one would be a good worker) in *Gesellschaft* society have to be taken into account.

8 Schluter acknowledges that these changes can sometimes create community and have other positive effects, but he highlights the negative impact of changes in these spheres on communal relationships.

9 See Johnstone (1991 and 1996b: ch. 4) for more details.

10 It would not, of course, prevent the informal use of the broader ideas and principles of restorative justice in efforts to make deviants from the norms of

any community repent and change their ways; for example, there is nothing to prevent trade union activists attempting to reintegratively shame strike-breakers, provided their methods of doing so are not themselves illegal.

11 The recent revival of judicial shame sanctions is discussed in more detail in chapter 6. See also Garvey (1998); Karp (1998); Whitman (1998); Book (1999), Johnstone (1999) and chapter 7 of this book.

12 I am grateful to Hulsman for explaining this implication of the 'dark figure' of crime to me in personal communications.

Chapter 4

Healing the victim

Retribution seeks to right the balance by lowering the offender to the level to which the victim has been reduced. It tries to defeat the wrongdoer, annulling his or her claim to superiority and confirming the victim's sense of worth. Restitution, on the other hand, seeks to raise the victim to his or her previous level.

(Howard Zehr 1990: 193)

Introduction

One of the main complaints which proponents of restorative justice make about conventional punitive justice is that it ignores the needs of victims of crime (Zehr 1990). In fact, they argue, the criminal justice system, through its apparent blindness to the fact that crime is at its core a violation of a particular person as well as a wrong against society, often adds to the injury suffered by victims. As a result, it is claimed, victims rarely experience justice when their case is dealt with by traditional punitive methods (*ibid*: 33).

Such claims will sound strange to anyone familiar with the recent history of crime policy. In the same year that Zehr was bemoaning the neglect of the victim by society and the criminal justice system, Paul Rock was charting the emergence of a determined concern to help the victim (Rock 1990). Since then, government policy has, if anything, come to be dominated by concerns about victims of crime (Garland and Sparks 2000: 16). Moreover, in practice, victims have obtained, or are close to obtaining, a bundle of rights: to make victim impact statements;

to be consulted about prosecution, sentencing and parole; to be notified about the offender's post-release movements; and to receive compensation (Garland 2000; Elias 1993).

Proponents of restorative justice are, of course, aware of such developments and to some extent they welcome them. In a recent work, Martin Wright, adopting the guise of a victim assistance worker, states:

> My main concern … is about the way victims are treated by what is loosely called 'the system'. I have to say that this is not the picture of thoughtless disregard of victims' needs that I would have described to you only two or three decades ago, when victims felt treated as non-persons … We have come a long way since it could be said that the victim is ignored, kept in the dark, and treated like just another witness, rather than as the person who was on the receiving end of the crime.
>
> (Wright 1999: 91)

But, after describing various reforms, Wright continues:

> If all these improvements are being made … isn't the system at least on the way to doing almost everything necessary to treat victims with respect. The answer is 'No', and the reason lies in the nature of the system itself.
>
> (Wright 1999: 102)

Wright's view, which is shared by many other proponents of restorative justice, is that existing 'victim reforms' do not fundamentally alter the structural position of victims in the criminal justice system (Cayley 1998: 290). No matter how much the position of the victim is strengthened, within a punitive system the victim's interests will necessarily remain secondary to the wider public interest represented by the Crown. So, the argument goes, in order to meet the victim's needs it is necessary to abandon punitive justice in favour of restorative justice (Van Ness 1993).

In this chapter I will describe this argument in more detail by looking at how proponents of restorative justice tend to answer the following questions: What are the needs of victims? Why does punitive justice fail to meet these needs? Why are the various 'victim reforms' which have been proposed and implemented inadequate? How would a shift from punitive to restorative justice ensure that victims' needs are met?

As well as describing the restorative approach to victims, this chapter will also contain a brief critical examination of that approach. This will pose the following questions: If meeting the needs of victims is really the primary concern, should we not concentrate on developing some improved form of state compensation or communal clubbing together for victims, which would arguably meet those needs much more efficiently than they can be met through reparation by offenders? Does restorative justice really prioritise the meeting of victims' needs, or is it more about using victims to help reform and reintegrate offenders into society? Why should we suppose that victims need restorative justice when, on the face of it, what most seem to want is a system that is even more punitive than that which exists? Can we not accept that victims' needs should receive much more attention, without going down the more extreme and perhaps dangerous path of restorative justice, which seems to place the relatively narrow needs of the victim above the wider needs of the community of law-abiding citizens?

The experiences and needs of victims

According to proponents of restorative justice, the main reason crime is wrong and requires some response is not because it is an offence against society, but because it is 'a violation of a person by another person' (Zehr 1990: 182). It is not denied that 'the effects of crime ripple out touching many others' and that society also has a legitimate interest in how the crime is dealt with (*ibid*), but it is asserted that these 'public dimensions' should not be the starting point for consideration of what to do about a crime. Rather, our starting point should be the fact that one person has been harmed by the wrongful actions of another.

Advocates of restorative justice also insist that what is problematic about crime is not that it is a wilful attack on some *abstract* right which people possess (*cf*. Brown forthcoming). Rather, it is the concrete damage which crime causes to the victim that is the problem. This damage is partly material, i.e. property is lost or destroyed or physical injuries are incurred but mostly, it seems, the damage is psychological and relational; being a victim of crime is a deeply traumatic occurrence because it damages the victim's sense of autonomy, order and relatedness (Zehr 1990: ch. 2). What proponents of restorative justice emphasise is the need to repair this psychological and relational damage. This, they contend, should be our overriding priority when deciding what to do about a crime. Let us look, then, at the nature of this damage in more detail.

Drawing upon the sizeable literature about the victim experience which now exists, Zehr suggests that it is possible to identify a pattern of reaction which is common to most victims (1990: 20). This consists of two phases: an initial impact phase and a recoil phase. He also identifies a third phase, a recovery phase, which some victims, who are fortunate enough to have their needs met, go through. These phases are characterised in terms of changes in the victim's emotions, self-image, world-image and relations with others.

In the initial impact phase the reactions are mostly emotional: victims tend to be 'overwhelmed by feelings of confusion, helplessness, terror, vulnerability' (*ibid*). In the recoil phase, these feelings decline in intensity but powerful new emotions arise. These include anger, guilt, anxiety, wariness, shame and feelings of self-doubt (*ibid*: 20–2). Typically, victims experience wide mood swings, their feelings of being safe and in control of their life are shattered and their trust in others is damaged. During this recoil phase, victims undergo a traumatic adjustment in their self-image. For example, those who saw themselves as trusting and caring persons have to adjust to take account of their increased caginess and fantasies of vengeance. Their view of their environment also changes. What they felt to be a secure and predictable environment becomes a potentially perilous place. Relationships also become strained in this phase. At a time when the victim needs the emotional and practical help of others, others tend to distance themselves from the victim. This is not simply because others are unwilling or unable to bear the burden of providing the level of support required by the victim. In addition, Zehr suggests, those who hear victims tell their story, themselves often experience some of the painful feelings of victimisation; they seek to avoid such feelings by insisting that the victim puts the experience behind him or her and 'moves on' (*ibid*: 22–3). Zehr argues that the experience of being a victim of crime can impinge on all areas of life. It can have a detrimental affect on the victims' health, close relationships and sex life (*ibid*: 23–4).

Crucially, Zehr maintains that while the reactions he describes are most marked in victims of violent crime, they also arise, although perhaps with less intensity, in victims of what we consider to be less serious offences (*ibid*: 24). He contends that all crimes, including property crimes, are *experienced* as attacks on the *person*.

> Crime is in essence a violation: a violation of the self, a desecration of who we are, of what we believe, of our private space. Crime is devastating because it upsets two fundamental assumptions on which we base our lives: our belief that the world is an orderly, meaningful place, and our belief in personal autonomy. Both assumptions are essential for wholeness.
>
> (Zehr 1990: 24)

If the needs of the victim are met they often move on to the recovery or 'reorganization' phase. In this phase, they recover from the emotional trauma, regain their sense of autonomy and power, and resume normal relationships with others. While their experience may still affect them, it no longer dominates them (*ibid*: 25). If the victim's needs remain unmet, however, recovery can be difficult and limited. In many cases, perhaps the majority, these needs are unmet and victims remain permanently in the recoil phase. So what are these needs?

According to Zehr, chief amongst them is the need for compensation from the offender. Even if full compensation for material damage is not possible, some compensation from the offender is essential because of its *symbolic* value (*ibid*: 26; Retzinger and Scheff 1996). As Jan van Dijk puts it:

> The arrangement of compensation to be paid by the offender has ... a great symbolic significance for the victim which far exceeds its monetary value. The imposition of an obligation to pay compensation is tantamount to inviting the offender to admit to the victim that he was in the wrong. Such a gesture can help to restore the victims' shattered sense of justice and feeling of community.
>
> (van Dijk 1988: 125)

For all the importance of compensation, proponents of restorative justice insist that victims have other, equally important, needs which should be met through the justice process. In particular, victims have needs for answers to basic questions such as why the crime happened to them, why they responded in the way they did, what they should do if it happens again, and what the whole thing means to them (Zehr 1990: 26–7). Some of these questions can and must be answered by the victims themselves, but others, such as 'what happened?' and 'why did it happen to me?' require answers from others and especially from the offender.

Victims also need opportunities to communicate their emotions – such as their anger and fear – and to have these endorsed by others (*ibid*: 27). According to advocates of restorative justice, the expression of what many would regard as distasteful 'retributive emotions' can be a crucial part of the healing process for victims. A criminal justice system which positively disapproves of and inhibits such emotional expression can therefore deprive victims of the experience of justice (Johnstone 2000b; cf. Pratt 2000).

Another need of victims is for empowerment. As Zehr puts it: 'Their sense of personal autonomy has been stolen from them by an offender, and they need to have this sense of personal power returned to them' (1990: 27). Finally, victims need to recover their sense of security – they need reassurance that steps are being taken to avoid a recurrence of the crime (*ibid*: 28).

The inadequacy of punitive justice for the victim

As indicated, our criminal justice system has traditionally been guided by what it assumes to be the general public interest in punishing crime rather than by a concern to meet the more particular needs of victims. In David Cayley's words: 'Modern criminal justice has stressed the aggrandizement and edification of the state, rather than the satisfaction of victims' (1998: 217). Or, as Margery Fry once put it: 'The tendency of English criminal law in the past has been to "take it out of the offender" rather than to do justice to the offended' (1951: 125). As a result, the victim's interests, needs or wants have tended to be barely considered. Or rather, the tendency has been to assume that the victim's interests are identical with the wider public interest represented by the Crown.

Proponents of restorative justice contend that this latter assumption is quite mistaken. As Zehr insinuates, victims have particular needs which go way beyond those of other members of the public who are affected indirectly by the commission of a crime in the community. Furthermore, in some ways the needs of victims can conflict with what is conventionally taken to be the public interest. For example, a crown prosecutor might argue that a particular offender should go to prison in the public interest. If the offender's victims had a voice in the process, they might well point out that by sending the offender to prison and thereby preventing them from earning money, the court prevents them from compensating the victims, where compensation may be of more value to them than any satisfaction or sense of security which they might receive from knowing that the person who caused them pain is suffering in return.

In any event, it is argued, a system which deems the state to be the victim and which denies the direct victims of crime any special legal standing – unless 'as members of a larger population of witnesses who claim to have direct knowledge of some crime' (Rock 1994, *xi*)[1] – is hardly likely to do well at meeting victims' needs. Hence, despite the rhetoric suggesting that 'victims must be protected, their voices heard, their memory honoured, their anger expressed, their fears addressed' (Garland 2000: 351), we still, claims Zehr, do little concrete for actual victims:

We do not listen to what they have suffered and what they need. We do not seek to give them back some of what they have lost. We do not let them help to decide how the situation should be resolved. We do not help them to recover.

(Zehr 1990: 32)

Zehr contends that the way our criminal justice system responds to victims amounts to secondary victimization:

Such neglect of victims not only fails to meet their needs: it compounds the injury. Many speak of a "secondary victimization" by criminal justice personnel and processes. The question of personal power is central here. Part of the dehumanising nature of victimization by crime is the way it robs victims of power. Instead of returning power to them by allowing them to participate in the justice process, the legal system compounds the injury by again denying power, Instead of helping, the process hurts.

(Zehr 1990: 30–1)

Some might reply that one of the main reasons we punish offenders is to demonstrate to victims that the crime committed against them is taken seriously by the rest of society. It is pertinent here that we do not judicially punish all those who do harm to others through wrongful acts. Indeed, for most wrongs we insist that the victims must themselves seek non-punitive redress.[2] However, we classify certain wrongs as crimes and follow them with state punishment of the perpetrator. This is not only because the effects of such acts reach far beyond the direct victim, instilling fear and distrust in other members of society (Schluter 1994: 17). It is also because some wrongs are so serious a violation of the victims' rights that it would show a complete lack of solidarity with the victims to expect them to seek their own non-punitive redress. The state, if it is to live up to its claims of being the guarantor and ultimate provider of security, must intervene.[3] Moreover, in order to demonstrate how seriously it regards the violation of the victim's rights, the state must take punitive action against the offender. Simply to demand compensation would be to trivialise the wrong. Hence, Jean Hampton contends, 'it is natural for the victim to demand punishment because it is a way for the community to restore his moral status after it has been damaged by his assailant' (1984: 217).

It seems to me, however, that such an objection misses the point. Punishing offenders may well be a way of demonstrating to victims that society regards the wrong committed against them as a serious matter.

But, it is not plain that it shows victims that society is concerned about the damage which they have suffered. Punishment shows that the wrongdoer's behaviour is regarded as unacceptable, which may provide some comfort to victims. But, that is not the same as demonstrating that the victim's injury is a matter of deep social concern. As Brown (forthcoming) points out, 'nothing obvious is restored to the crime victim by punishing the offender'.[4] If we want to show that the victim's specific injury concerns us, we must do something to heal that injury. Punishment of the offender may help the healing process, but it is not on its own adequate to heal the injury. Moreover, as we shall now see, punishment may sometimes prevent healing.

It is plausible that in many cases, punishment of the offender, whatever the intent behind it, can actually make things worse for the victim. As we have seen, the most obvious example of this is where being punished interferes with the offender's ability to earn and hence to pay compensation to the victim. Also, a very likely outcome is that offenders will feel that they are paying their debt to society by undergoing punishment, and hence have no further obligations, such as an obligation to compensate their victims (Cayley 1998). In addition, while punishment of offenders may reassure some victims that their rights and need for security are taken seriously, it may make others more anxious. Some victims may worry that the offender or the offenders' associates will hold them responsible for the punishment and take revenge on them. Some, indeed, may feel responsible for the offender's punishment and experience guilt (van Dijk 1988: 126).

Martin Wright (1999: 102ff) introduces another consideration. He argues that because, in a punitive system, the consequences of being convicted of a crime are so severe, those who commit crime will go to enormous lengths to avoid being convicted. Those who regret their behaviour and might be inclined to 'put things right' are unlikely to own up to their crime and hence leave themselves open to punishment. Hence, the very punitive nature of our response to crimes makes reparation and reconciliation, which the victim might welcome, less likely. Also, again because the consequences of conviction are so nasty, we are obliged to provide those suspected of crime with strong safeguards to ensure that they are not wrongfully convicted and punished. Those who have committed crimes, and the lawyers who represent them, have considerable incentive to exploit these safeguards to the full. Inevitably, in any system which is serious about avoiding wrongful conviction, many actual offenders will also escape conviction and so their victims will receive no redress through the criminal justice system. Their only hope of legal redress will then be if they have the considerable resources required to bring a claim for civil damages against the offender. What is more, one of the things which suspects will do, in order to avoid the pain of punishment, is raise doubts about the reliability of prosecution witnesses, one of whom is often the victim. Hence, the legal representatives of suspects, and sometimes suspects themselves, will subject victims to gruelling cross-examination, an experience which many victims, especially but not only of sexual offences, find extremely shocking and which tends to aggravate rather than heal the emotional wounds they suffered as a result of the crime.

So, for Wright and other proponents of restorative justice, the criminal justice system will continue to fail to meet victims' needs and will continue to give victims a hard time so long as it is oriented towards the punishment of offenders. So long as people who commit crime have so much to lose, they and their lawyers will continue to do everything they can to resist conviction and, where that fails, to ensure they receive a light sentence. A large part of what they will do involves making things worse, rather than better, for the victims of crime. So long as the system is oriented towards what Nils Christie (1982) calls 'pain delivery', most enlightened legal figures and penal reformers will seek to strengthen the offender's position within the system even when this is at the expense of victims.

Victim reforms

As indicated earlier, proponents of restorative justice are not the only group seeking a better deal for crime victims. Others have somewhat different ideas about how to improve the crime victim's lot. Some, depicting the victim as a 'consumer' of the services provided by the criminal justice system, have complained bitterly about the standard of service provided. This has led to campaigns to ensure that criminal justice agencies and personnel provide victims with better facilities and treat them with more respect. One of the triumphs of such campaigns was the British government's publication of a *Victims' Charter*, requiring criminal justice agencies to meet certain standards of service in their dealings with crime victims (Home Office 1996). As a result of this and related developments, victims may now expect to receive more 'respect from the police and lawyers during questioning, accurate information about the progress of the case and any court hearing, separate waiting areas and active support at courts, and so forth' (von Hirsch and Ashworth 1998: 307).

Proponents of restorative justice usually welcome such reforms

(Wright 1999: ch. 4), although some are wary of the consumerist ideology which has helped bring them about. The main limitation of such reforms, from the perspective of restorative justice, is that they do nothing to alter the fundamental nature of the justice system. For proponents of restorative justice, the problems which victims have in obtaining justice are mostly to do with the punitive nature of the system. Attempts to solve these problems without changing the nature of the system are doomed to failure (Barnett 1977: 279).

Victim involvement in the criminal justice process

Much more contentious than attempts to secure better services for victims are efforts to secure for victims rights to have their voice heard in the criminal justice process and even to participate in the making of major decisions about the punishment of offenders. One proposal, which has been taken up in many jurisdictions, is that the victim be allowed to provide information to the court, prior to sentencing, through a victim impact statement.[5] This provides the victim with an opportunity to indicate, in writing and sometimes orally:

> what impact the offence has had, what property was lost or damaged, what other financial losses resulted, and how the event has disrupted the life of the victim. It thus provides the victim with an opportunity to inform the court of how the offence has affected him or her physically, mentally, and otherwise.
>
> (United Nations 1998)

In some places, as part of this process, victims are also allowed to express an *opinion* on the sentence to be inflicted on the offender (*ibid*). Nor do those who seek such rights confine their attention to the sentencing stage. There are strong moves in the direction of consulting victims or otherwise involving them in decisions to prosecute, to accept guilty pleas, to grant bail and to grant parole (van Dijk 1988; von Hirsch and Ashworth 1998: 307).

At first sight, the granting of such rights to victims would seem to be a way of meeting at least some of their needs and, especially, ensuring that they receive justice. Such reforms provide victims with an opportunity to explain how the crime has affected them materially and psychologically and to express their feelings in the justice process. They also empower victims. Not only are victims increasingly allowed a voice in the justice process, but in the more radical proposed reforms they can also directly influence the outcome. If, as Zehr contends, one of the main ways in which crime harms victims is by robbing them of their sense of personal power, then giving them a significant say in how the offender is punished surely helps repair the harm.

Above all, such reforms are designed to ensure that victims get the justice they need. According to the proponents of victims' rights, criminal justice decision makers are insufficiently aware of, or inadequately attentive to, 'the traumatic, devastating effects of crime on the lives of its victims and the community at large' (National Center for Victims of Crime n.d.). On the other hand, the perspective of offenders, and especially factors mitigating their guilt, are well represented. As a result, decision makers tend to hear only one side of the argument, or at least hear the offender's voice much more directly and comprehensively than they hear the victim's voice. The results of this biased procedure, it is claimed, are decisions which are too lenient and tolerant towards offenders: offenders receive lighter sentences than they should, are granted bail and parole when they should not be, and so on. As one American campaigning group states:

> results of the National Victim Center's public opinion poll also revealed that 55% of Americans feel that sentences handed down to criminals by the court are too lenient. Perhaps this is why seven out of 10 Americans believe that it is very important for the judicial system to provide victims and their families with "... an opportunity to make a statement prior to the sentencing of the offender about how the crime has affected them." In essence, for the court to impose fair and just sentences, it is critical that information be provided to the sentencing and paroling authorities on the emotional, financial and physical impact of crime – information that only victims can accurately define and provide through the use of victim impact statements.
>
> (National Center for Victims of Crime n.d.)

Despite the important overlaps between the victims' rights campaign and the restorative justice campaign, campaigners for restorative justice tend to be unenthusiastic about such rights. For example, Wright describes the introduction of victim impact statements as 'a problematic reform' (1999: 98). He regards them as positive in that they are a means by which the victim's hurt can be recognised in the criminal justice process and because they draw attention to the concrete damage resulting from the crime (*ibid*). However, he is less sure that the courtroom is the right place for the victim's voice to be heard or that it should influence the sentence (*ibid*: 98–9). Crucially, he expresses concern about such developments not only because of their implications for the rights of offenders but also because he doubts whether inviting victims to participate in a punitive process is in the interest of the victims:

> Victims might then be exposed to hostile cross-examination, to make sure they had not exaggerated. … victims might fear retaliation because the offender may see the statement … some victims are disillusioned if they expect it to influence the outcome and it doesn't.
>
> Wright (1999: 100)

In a similar vein, van Dijk suggests that allowing and encouraging victims to participate in a punitive process may add to their angst:

> By making the victim responsible for the imposition of a punishment, the victim's capacity to 'walk away from' the crime may be negatively affected. … In the long term, the satisfaction of a desire for vengeance through the passing of an excessive sentence in line with that demanded by the victims would seem to me to be a source, not of reassurance, but of anxiety to the victim.
>
> (Van Dijk 1988: 126)

In short, while proponents of restorative justice want victims to have rights to participate in the justice process, they also maintain that in order to benefit from such rights, the justice process must become restorative rather than punitive. To invite victims into an adversarial confrontation with offenders is clearly not in the interest of offenders, but nor they claim is it in the interests of victims. What victims will benefit from, it is claimed, is participation in a non-confrontational attempt to reach a restorative solution to the wrong which has been committed.

State compensation

One obvious way of deflecting the criticism that in confining itself to punishment of the offender the criminal justice system does little if anything for the victim, is to supplement punishment with state compensation to victims. Since the 1960s, state compensation schemes for victims of crimes of violence, funded by tax revenues, have been developed in most western countries (Ashworth 1986: 99ff). These schemes have, however, attracted a number of criticisms, including:

- they are usually limited to crimes of violence;

- compensation tends to be regarded as a welfare payment to those in need rather than 'an assumption by the state of legal responsibility for the criminal loss suffered by the victim' (Barnett 1977: 287);

- many victims, e.g. those with criminal records, tend to be excluded;

- schemes tend to be set up without regard to or even inquiry into the expressed needs of victims (Shapland 1984: 137).

Proponents of restorative justice tend to reject these schemes as inadequate to meet the needs of victims by citing these familiar criticisms. What this leaves open is the question of whether victims' needs could be met through a vastly improved system based on the idea of collective responsibility for the costs of crime victimisation; i.e. the costs of crime victimisation, insofar as they can be distributed, could be distributed as widely as possible so that individuals do not suffer unduly from being targeted by offenders. Compensation, in such schemes, would be represented as a sign of communal solidarity with the victim, which any victim has a right to expect, rather than as a matter of welfare or charity. This would not meet all the needs of victims identified by Zehr, but it could form a significant part of an attempt to meet the victim's needs.

Some might object to such schemes because of their cost to the taxpayer. Those looking for a more principled argument could claim that the victims of criminal injuries do not have as strong a claim to state compensation as victims of other social misfortunes, where there is not an obvious perpetrator, since they have or ought to have a legal claim against the offender. Such objections might be combined with recommendations that people might insure themselves against crime victimisation. All of these arguments could be the subject of much debate, which is beyond the scope of this work. What is pertinent here is whether, from the victim's perspective, compensation by the offender is preferable to compensation by the state (van Dijk 1985). To address this issue, we need to turn now to the argument that punishment should give way to restitution.

Restitution from the offender

As we have seen, many of those who seek a better deal for crime victims take it as self-evident that criminals should be punished by the state.

Their aims are to ensure that victims receive better service, or state compensation, or more consideration in the sentencing process and other key decisions. However, others, such as Randy Barnett, argue that once we view crime not as an offence against society, but as an offence by one person against another person, it becomes much less obvious that what is required to restore the balance is punishment of the offender (Barnett 1977: 287–8). The offender's debt is not to society, but to the victim (*ibid*: 288). As such, it might be discharged through restitution, i.e. monies or services paid by the *offender* to the victim (Barnett 1980: 118),[6] and, according to Barnett, a suitably refined system of restitution is easier to justify morally than is the forcible imposition of suffering on an offender (*ibid*: 122ff; *cf*. Brown forthcoming).[7] In addition, he claims, a restitutive system is workable as a way of dealing with crime and would have a number of advantages over a punitive system, for victims, offenders and taxpayers (Barnett 1977: 293–4).

Barnett favours a system of 'pure restitution' over a system of 'punitive restitution'. In the latter, the court orders the offender to compensate his victim as part of his punishment, i.e. restitution is added to the paradigm of punishment. Punitive restitution is already fairly widely used in the criminal justice system. What Barnett prefers is 'pure restitution', in which restitution is not intended to have any punitive effect (although, as with the payment of civil law damages, it is burdensome) (1977: 288–9). The refinements Barnett envisages are: a system of 'victim crime insurance', which would result in offenders owing restitution to insurance companies rather than the victim; direct arbitration between victim and criminal; and a system of sureties whereby a concerned group pays the restitution and then has a claim on the offender which they might not enforce if the offender complies with certain conditions (*ibid*: 290–91). From the victim's perspective, the chief advantage is that it would provide them with some tangible compensation for damage suffered, making it easier to bear (*ibid*: 293). In addition, in a restitutive system, objections to adding the voice of the victim to the deliberations would fade (*ibid*: 301).

There are, of course, a whole range of practical and moral objections to Barnett's proposal:

- restitution may fail to satisfy either the victim's or the community's sense of justice;

- it may be insufficient to deter crime;

- the idea rests upon the naïve assumption that profitable employment projects for offenders are feasible;

- a restitutive system could not deal with 'victimless crimes';

- where crimes have multiple victims, all suffering serious losses, restitution from the offender may be impossible;

- rich people will be able to commit crime with impunity (*ibid*: 295–300).

Barnett argues that such problems are either over-stated or are only problems if one continues to think within the punitive paradigm. It is instructive to look at his dismissal of the latter objection, since it illustrates the full implications of Barnett's proposed paradigm shift from punitive to restitutive justice. In response to those who might object to a restitutive system on the ground that the rich would not be hurt enough, he states that hurting people in proportion to the wrong they have committed:

> is the prime motive behind *punitive* restitution proposals. However, we reject the moral consideration outright. The paradigm of restitution calls not for the (equal) hurting of criminals, but for restitution to victims. Any appeal to 'inadequate suffering' is a reversion to the paradigm of punishment … *Equality of justice means equal treatment for victims.*
>
> (Barnett 1977: 298, emphases in original)

Beyond restitution: restoring victims

From the perspective of restorative justice, the problem with Barnett's proposal is quite different from the sorts of problems identified by other critics, and seems far easier to resolve. Barnett and other proponents of restitution simply place far too much emphasis on financial restitution and reparation of material damage (Braithwaite 1999a: 45).[8] Such emphasis is due to an inadequate understanding of the way in which crime harms people and of what the offender can do to help restore the victim to the material, psychological and relational state they were in before the crime was committed.

As we saw earlier, for Zehr (1990) what is so hurtful about crime is the damage it does to our beliefs in the orderliness of the world and to our sense of personal dominion (see also Braithwaite and Pettit 1990). Such damage outweighs the physical injuries and property loss which crime causes, although the importance of such material damage should not be under-emphasised. This being so, applying the principle that the offender should be forced or persuaded into repairing the damage caused by his or her behaviour means they should be required to do something to help restore the victim's sense of order and personal power, as well as attempt to make good the material damage caused.

By compensating victims for their losses, through money or services, the offender can in fact go some way towards repairing the psychological and relational damage caused (although, on the other hand, 'many victims feel insulted by the assumption that money can put right the whole wrong that they have suffered', Baker 1994: 73). Once again, for proponents of restorative justice, such restitution is valuable mainly for what it symbolises – the fact that the offender has wronged the victim and so owes them a debt – rather than for its material value. It is accepted that, in a great many cases, offenders will not be able to repair or make adequate compensation for all the material harm they caused. However, by putting themselves out to repair what they can, they can help heal the psychological and relational damage which they cause.

But restitution, despite its symbolic value, is not on its own sufficient to heal the wounds of crime. Offenders can and must do more. In particular, proponents of restorative justice emphasise the importance to victims of offenders showing remorse and shame and offering genuine apologies for their crimes (Retzinger and Scheff 1996; Braithwaite 2000; Johnstone 1999). Offenders must also be prepared to meet face-to-face with their victims, in a safe atmosphere, to explain their acts and to answer the victim's questions about why they were victimised and other matters. A mediation meeting with offenders can also play a role in reducing the victim's fear and sense of powerlessness, since it allows them to see the offender as an ordinary vulnerable person rather than the threatening, all-powerful figure which, in line with public stereotypes, they often imagine criminals to be. Face-to-face meetings can also be a forum where victims can 'vent feelings of bitterness and hurt directly to the one who caused them' (Baker 1994: 75). While advocates of restorative justice insist that victim-offender meetings or restorative conferences should not become forums for the simple vilification of offenders, they do see one of their chief advantages over formal legal procedures as being their ability to act as mediums for emotional expression (*ibid*; Braithwaite and Mugford 1994).

Meetings between victims and offenders, focusing on restitution and reparation, can also help victims to recover a sense of personal power. By discussing and negotiating with the offender and others about what would be a suitable form and amount of restitution, victims can take part in the justice process and gain control over the outcomes to their conflicts. Such meetings can also result in reconciliation between offenders and victims, which allows the victim to achieve closure – to reach a point where the offender and the offence no longer dominate them. Victim-offender meetings and restorative conferences frequently result in victims forgiving those who have harmed them (Braithwaite and Mugford 1994), which, quite apart from its benefits to offenders, helps victims to recover from their traumatic experience (Estrada-Hollenbeck 1996; Gehm 1992; Johnstone 1999).

In sum, face to-face meetings between victims and offenders, in an atmosphere in which both feel safe, in which the focus is on getting the offender to express remorse and shame, offer meaningful restitution, and answer the victim's questions, can go some way towards meeting the victim's needs and hence towards helping the victim to recover from the traumatic experience of being victimized. Such meetings, pro-ponents of restorative justice argue, are far more beneficial to victims than are formal criminal trials, in which victims and offenders are kept apart and positioned as adversaries, and in which the focus is solely on determining the moral guilt of offenders and determining how much suffering they should be forced to undergo in order to pay their debt to society.

Restorative justice or 'clubbing together'?

One of the most obvious limitations of restorative justice as con-ventionally conceived, from the perspective of victims, is that few victims will benefit by it. Only a small minority of criminal incidents result in the arrest of the perpetrator(s) and an even smaller minority result in either an admission of the offence or conviction (Braithwaite 1999a: 79). Restorative justice, which emphasises restitution and other forms of reparation from the offender to the victim, seems therefore to have nothing much to offer the majority of crime victims. It shares this limitation with every other criminal justice intervention. Hence, it might be argued that, if our priority when a crime is committed is really to restore the victim, we should not waste our energy trying to reform the criminal justice system. What is needed is not so much an alternative form of criminal justice, but an alternative to criminal justice.

This would not, of course, imply the abolition of criminal justice, which could continue to perform its current functions of trying suspects and processing those who admit crimes or are convicted. Nor would it preclude attempts to reform the criminal justice system in order either to improve its treatment of offenders or to ensure that it serves society better. Crucially, nor would it preclude attempts to reform the criminal justice system in order to ensure that it better serves victims whose offenders are caught. What it does mean is that, for those who are serious about prioritising the task of restoring the victim, reform of criminal justice should be a secondary consideration. The main concern should surely be to establish some system of victim restoration outside of the criminal justice system and with only the loosest of links to it.

This would seem to take us back to the idea of a more fully developed and much reformed system of collective responsibility for the costs of crime victimisation, conceptualised not as state welfare but as a 'clubbing together for mutual protection' (Fry 1959: 192). In other words, we could provide collective support for victims of crime along the same lines as those committed to a communal ethic would provide support to 'neighbours' who become victims of illness, accidents, natural disasters or any other social misfortune. What would be important, in such a system, is the establishment of a procedure for determining that a person had in fact been victimised, for determining the nature and extent of the damage – material, psychological and relational – suffered and for repairing that damage. Such a process, and the people involved in it, would have to be highly sensitive to the nature of the experience of crime victimisation and the needs it generates, as depicted by Zehr and others, otherwise it could end up doing more damage.[9] The nature of the repair required would depend, of course, on the nature of the damage suffered and on the circumstances of the victim. Some may need only financial compensation. Others may need to have established around them long-lasting circles of support, of the kind which Cayley (1998: ch. 18) advocates for certain offenders. The crucial point is that the task of restoring the victim should take place irrespective of whether the perpetrator is caught.

Such a system of 'clubbing together' is in fact quite consistent with the broad values of restorative justice. I suggest that it is the first solution which a proponent of restorative justice would come up with if they did not start by thinking within a criminal justice framework.

There is, however, a complexity in the case of crime victims which is not usually present in the case of victims of other misfortunes. In the case of crime victims, misfortune has not been caused by something which is either beyond the control of other people or at least very difficult to control. On the contrary, it has been caused by the intentional or reckless actions of another person. Arguably, it is this very fact, rather than the material harm caused, that makes crime victimisation such a traumatic experience. The victim of illness or storm damage may suffer physical injury or property loss which far outstrips that suffered by the victim of crime but, unless their misfortune is due to the negligence or worse of other persons, they have not suffered an *injustice* (Lucas 1980). The victim of crime, on the other hand, no matter how slight the material damage incurred, has suffered an injustice and it seems that, if they are to recover fully from their experience, this injustice has to be remedied.

What this means is that it probably matters a great deal to the victim where restitution comes from. To take a simple example, if a person is the victim of a street robbery ('mugging'), there are two different ways in which the damage they incur can be repaired. The victim's community could club together to replace any uninsured property. It might also form a circle of support around the person to help them cope with the practical problems, loss of a sense of personal security, and sense of personal violation which they may experience. On the other hand, if the persons who carried out the robbery could be captured, they could be made to return the property or compensate for its loss, apologise, and answer any questions which the victim may have. The former course of action is probably more efficient as a way of meeting the material needs and even emotional needs of most victims. However, provided the latter course of action is possible, its seems essential to the process of recovery, even though it may be much less efficient as a way of meeting the victim's material needs. Restitution by the offender has a much greater symbolic significance than compensation by the state or community. It helps restore our sense of justice (van Dijk 1985).

This helps explain the finding of empirical studies of victims' attitudes, which point to considerable enthusiasm among victims for reparation from offenders:

> How, then, did victims view state compensation and compensation by offenders? They regarded compensation not as mainly a matter of money or financial assistance (charitable or otherwise), but rather as making a statement about the offence, the victim, and the position that the criminal justice system was prepared to give to the victim. Even the element of payment in proportion to suffering and loss was subordinated to this symbolic function. This was most obvious in victim's enthusiasm for compensation from offenders as part of the sentence of the court.
>
> (Shapland 1984: 144)

What seems clear is that compensation from the community and reparation by the offender have different meanings for victims. The former is important for its material worth and because it can symbolise the community's solidarity with the crime victim (although too often it can symbolise a shift in status from citizen to charity/welfare case). The latter is important because it is understood as redress, i.e. giving back to the victims what they have had taken away from them by the person who has done the taking away. Redress has a moral significance which state compensation does not have.

To say that restitution from the offender to the victim is of particular importance to the process of recovery does not mean, however, that it should be the only means of assisting victims. Also, it must be repeated that relatively few victims will be able to obtain such restitution. A truly victim-oriented system of dealing with crime would therefore start with things like:

- a system of emergency payments for expenses occurred and wages lost in the immediate aftermath of victimisation;

- a system of practical, informational and emotional support for victims; and

- a system of public compensation, organised around principles very different to those which seem to inform current state compensation schemes, to operate as a back up for victims who cannot obtain adequate restitution from the person who committed the crime against them.

In recognition of the fact that victims suffer an injustice which should, if possible, be remedied, serious attempts should also be made to catch the perpetrator(s) and force or persuade them to repair the damage.

Using victims to rehabilitate offenders

If the above argument is accepted, it raises the question of why many proponents of restorative justice place so much emphasis on reparation from the offender to the victim and tend to place relatively little stress on the need for communal reparation. The fact that they do leaves members of victim support groups – who are generally sympathetic towards the idea of restorative justice – in some doubt about whether it really benefits victims (Reynolds 2000). At the heart of these doubts is a suspicion that restorative justice, for all its talk of restoring victims, is still offender-focused and is likely to become more so as it becomes implemented in the criminal justice system. As Teresa Reynolds, head of policy at Victim Support, has put it:

Some criminal justice professionals see restorative justice merely as a tool to prevent re-offending; providing satisfaction to victims of crime is seen as a bonus, not an aim. Will criminal justice professionals 'lose interest' in the victim if the offender cannot be found? Will there be sufficient resources and time to support those who are committed to ensuring that restorative justice initiatives work for victims as well as offenders? Is there a danger that criminal justice professionals will come to see restorative justice programmes as the only option open to victims and overlook their other needs for support?

(Reynolds 2000)

Such doubts are strengthened by the fact that many proponents of restorative justice place considerable emphasis on the benefits of reparation from the offender to the victim *for the offender*. Indeed, since the late 1950s, proponents of restitution have highlighted, as one of its advantages, its effectiveness as a means of reforming criminals. Albert Eglash, an early proponent of restitution, argued:

Restitution is something an inmate does, not something done for or to him. ... Being reparative, restitution can alleviate guilt and anxiety, which can otherwise precipitate further offences.

(Eglash 1958, quoted in Barnett 1977: 293)

Similarly, Gilbert Geis argues:

The process of restitution might create within the offender a sense of the true extent of the harm he had inflicted on another human being. Fiscal atonement could produce in the offender a feeling of having been cleansed, a kind of redemptive purging process, which might inhibit subsequent wrongdoing.

(Geis 1977: 147; see also Baker 1994: 74)

The merits of such ideas will be discussed in the next chapter. What is important here is that the existence of this argument raises the suspicion that this is the core reason why proponents of restorative justice are so attracted to the idea of reparation from the offender, and it explains why they show relatively little interest in other ways of meeting the victim's needs. The campaign for restorative justice, cynics might argue, provides just one more answer to the very conventional question: 'A criminal law exists; someone is convicted of breaking the law. What is to be done to (or with) that person?' (*ibid*). Their particular solution may have the merit of benefiting the victim, but that in itself does not make it a victim-oriented solution. To become truly victim-oriented, the campaign for restorative justice would have to change the question to: A crime has been committed; someone is harmed as a result. What is to be done for that person? Until such a radical shift of perspective occurs, practitioners of restorative justice will remain vulnerable to the charge that they see victims as little more than props in their attempts to rehabilitate offenders (Braithwaite 1999a: 82).

Paternalism towards victims

Restorative justice is remarkable in that it seems to be acceptable to what appear to be two quite opposed tendencies in the politics of criminal justice reform. On the one hand, it seems to be what traditional penal reformers have always sought: a non-punitive, more humane and constructive way of responding to those who break the law. On the other, it seems to be what the more recently formed victims' rights groups seek: an approach which allows and encourages victim participation in the criminal justice process and is guided primarily by a concern to deliver justice to victims. But can it really satisfy victims' demands for justice, while at the same time making the experience of criminal justice a more positive one for offenders?

Many of those outside the restorative justice campaign would find it difficult to see how it is possible to fully meet these seemingly contradictory demands. It tends to be taken for granted that what most victims want is tougher criminal justice for offenders. Victims' rights groups tend to insist that the current system is unjust because it is too lenient with offenders. Given this, the obvious way to meet victims' demands for more justice would be to give them a system which is tougher on criminals. This is not, of course, what proponents of restorative justice offer (although they do insist that restorative justice is not a soft option for offenders). But nor do they say, frankly, the victims cannot have what they want. Rather, they question whether victims, and other members of the public, really want what they say they want (Wright 1989). According to Barnett (1977: 295), the 'social fact' that victims want more severe punishment must be viewed in the light of a lack of alternatives. The real test of victim and public attitudes would be to give them a real choice between punitive and restorative justice, and then see which they choose. He argues that, while we cannot predict the outcome, we cannot assume that victims would opt for punitive justice (*ibid*). Once the advantages of restorative justice become apparent, they may well opt for that. In a similar vein, a frequent theme in the writing of Wright is that the reason victims tend to demand harsh penalties is that punishment is the only route to moral vindication and security offered by the contemporary criminal justice system. If the system made other and better ways of achieving moral vindication and security available, he claims, victims would probably prefer them and would become less punitive (see also Braithwaite 2000: 123–4).

This verges closely on paternalism: victims are told that what they expressly say they want is not really what they want, and that, if they understood their own needs better, they would probably ask for something quite different.[10] Adopting such a paternalistic attitude towards victims is very likely to increase their disempowerment, which Zehr and others say is the heart of the problem. Paternalism is, however, avoidable. It could be argued that what victims are *entitled* to is moral vindication and security. The punishment of offenders is one method of delivering this. However, it is a costly and destructive method both for offenders and for the wider community. Hence, if a less costly and less destructive, but equally effective, method of delivering moral vindication and security such as restorative justice, can be found, victims must accept it, *even if they prefer punishment*. One could try to help victims accept this decision by pointing out that restorative justice may, in fact, have a number of advantages for them over punishment (although such arguments should be used sparingly and with care as they can easily slip into paternalism). This is quite different from telling them that they are in fact getting what they really want (even though they do not know it).

This way of dealing with the issue would avoid a problem which is likely to arise when proponents of restorative justice try to insist that what they are offering is in fact what victims and the public really want. Such claims can be refuted. There is always the possibility of a victim rationally weighing up the choice of punitive and restorative justice and opting for the former. Would proponents of restorative justice then be prepared to concede that the offender should be punished as the victim wishes? If not, it can only be because there are more than the victim's wishes to consider. Putting the argument in these terms does of course mean toning down the rhetorical claims that restorative justice is 'justice for victims and offenders' (Wright 1996a).

Balancing the needs of the victim with those of society

Proponents of restorative justice recognise that crime affects the wider community as well as the direct victim, and that the wider community therefore has a legitimate interest in how it is dealt with. That is, they do not suggest that crime is always purely a private matter:

> Since one cannot ignore the public dimensions of crime, the justice process in many cases cannot be fully private. The community, too, wants reassurance that what happened was wrong, that something is being done about it, and that steps are being taken to discourage recurrence.
>
> (Zehr 1990: 194–5)

But, many proponents do insist that, for all their importance, the public dimensions of crime should not be considered more important than its private dimensions (*ibid*: 195). The latter, many argue, should be our starting point.

Quite what is meant by this is difficult to say, since few proponents of restorative justice spell out exactly what should happen when the private and public interest conflicts. For example, what happens if a person who commits an indecent assault against a relative offers generous restitution, a genuine apology and agrees to undergo therapy, which satisfies the victim who then refuses to testify in a criminal trial. Would it be right to compel the victim to testify if the view of the public prosecutor, after taking all the arguments into consideration, was that the perpetrator of the indecent assault should be convicted and punished in the *public* interest. The reluctance of proponents of restorative justice to provide conclusive answers to such questions, while insisting that crimes should be conceptualised as 'conflicts' which are the property of the parties involved and their local communities (Christie 1977), and that the starting point should be the victim's needs, invites the criticism that they go too far in the direction of 'privatising' crime. The problem with this is that restorative justice could, while remedying the traditional neglect of the victim's interests, result in the neglect of the equally important public interest in the prevention of crime, the maintenance of order, and the minimisation of fear of violation (Ashworth 1986: 111). Finding a way of balancing these interests, in theory and practice, is an important challenge facing those who campaign for restorative justice.

Notes

1 In many European legal systems, victims have traditionally had much stronger rights in the criminal justice process than they have in common law

      countries such as England and the USA (van Dijk 1988: 124).

2 Indeed, for most wrongs which occur in everyday life (e.g. betrayal) there is no legal remedy at all, even though they may cause all the psychological and relational damage which Zehr attributes to crime.

3 Modern states are, of course, beginning to withdraw such claims (Rose 2000: 186; Garland 2001).

4 Barnett (1977: 285) goes a bit further: 'A system of punishment offers no incentive for the victim to involve himself in the criminal justice process other than to satisfy his feelings of duty or revenge. The victim stands to gain little if at all by the conviction and punishment of the person who caused his loss. This is true even of those systems … which dispense state compensation based on the victim's need. The system of justice itself imposes uncompensated costs by requiring a further loss of time and money by the victim and witnesses and by increasing the perceived risk of retaliation'. Brown (forthcoming) goes on to consider, but ultimately reject, Hegel's argument that what punishment restores is not any concrete damage but the victim's (more abstract) rights.

5 Victim impact statements have been introduced in the United States, New Zealand, Canada, Israel, and parts of Australia and Ireland. At the time of writing, steps are being taken to introduce them in the United Kingdom.

6 Barnett uses the term restitution simply to distinguish his proposal from proposals that the *state* pay 'compensation' to the victim (1980: 118). Lawyers should note that, although there are some important overlaps, Barnett's ideas are in many respects distinct from those behind the subsequent emergence of the private law of restitution for unjust enrichment as charted by Virgo (1999).

7 Barnett's argument as to why the forceful imposition of suffering upon offenders is not morally justifiable, but forcing culpable offenders to make good the loss they have caused is morally justifiable, is too complex to explain in detail here. Very basically, he argues from the perspective of a rights thesis in which the offender has an obligation to redistribute that which was unjustly taken, but in which, according to Barnett, it is impossible to find any justification for the imposition of suffering (see Barnett 1980).

8 In his 1980 article, Barnett begins to deal with this issue.

9 Arguably, this is the problem with state welfare systems. State compensation schemes can reinforce rather than assuage the victim's non-involvement and sense of powerlessness, and hence have the opposite of a restorative effect.

10 I owe this point to my colleague, Stephen Brown.

Chapter 5

A restorative approach to offenders

Introduction

In this chapter I present an account of what is distinctive about restorative justice as a way of responding to offenders. I start with Howard Zehr's highly influential presentation of restorative justice as a new paradigm of criminal justice, an alternative to the retributive paradigm which, he contends, has dominated understandings of crime and justice in the West for several centuries (Zehr 1990: chs. 5–6).[1] As we shall see, Zehr's retributive–restorative justice oppositional contrast has recently been criticised by some supporters of restorative justice as both misleading and, for those interested in developing restorative justice, counterproductive (Daly 2000a; Barton 2000). While I share many of the misgivings expressed by such critics, I think there is still considerable value in starting with that contrast. In presenting restorative justice as an alternative paradigm to retributive justice, Zehr made many important criticisms of the latter – especially its obsession with individual guilt. Some important aspects of this critique are in danger of being 'forgotten' by recent proponents and practitioners. Dropping these highly critical elements may give the restorative justice campaign a better chance of influencing government policy on crime. The price to pay for such practical success, however, could be a loss of what is most interesting and challenging about restorative justice.

In setting itself up in opposition to 'retributive justice', the restorative justice movement invites comparison with the campaign for a therapeutic approach to crime, which also launched itself through a trenchant critique of retributive punishment (Johnstone 1996b). However, although there are some overlaps between treatment and restorative justice, many proponents of restorative justice also draw a sharp distinction between therapeutic and restorative responses to offenders. The second section of this chapter will describe the most important differences between the two approaches.

Such attempts to explain restorative justice have been criticised, with some justification, on the ground that they tell us more about what restorative justice is *not* than about what it *is* (Meier 1998: 125). Hence, the following section will move beyond the oppositional contrasts of retributive–restorative justice and therapeutic–restorative justice to present a more positive description of the distinctive features of the restorative response to offenders. Finally, I will return to the question of whether the differences between restorative justice, on the one hand, and retributive and therapeutic justice, on the other, are as sharp as most proponents would have us believe.

Restorative justice as an alternative to retributive justice

Restorative justice is frequently portrayed as a new paradigm of criminal justice, which differs sharply from the dominant paradigm of 'retributive justice' (Zehr 1990). It is important to be clear, from the outset, about how Zehr and others use the term 'retributive justice'. They use it to refer to the framework of values, purposes, outlooks and assumptions which underpin the practice of judicial punishment in Western societies. Many of these values, purposes etc. would be classified by penal philosophers as utilitarian rather than retributive in the strict philosophical sense.[2] When Zehr and most other proponents of restorative justice criticise 'retributive justice', what they intend to attack is the entire social practice of judicial punishment, rather than any more specific retributive rationale for punishing offenders. So, what do they find problematic about this social practice? In this chapter I focus on two aspects of retributive justice which, according to proponents of restorative justice, render it particularly problematic as a response to offenders.[3]

The blame game

According to Zehr, the central activity of retributive justice is fixing blame, or establishing guilt, for a crime which has occurred (*ibid*: 66–74). Retributive justice reflects a more general trait: when something bad has happened, our paramount concern seems to be to attach blame to some individual or group. Retributive justice is obsessed with the question: who should we hold responsible for this crime? Zehr makes numerous criticisms of this preoccupation with fixing blame. Here, from his complex discussion, I will draw out three central criticisms.

First, fixing blame tends to be pursued to the exclusion of equally important concerns, such as determining how the damage caused by the crime should be repaired and how future recurrences can be prevented. This is a familiar critique of retributive punishment: it is too backward-looking or oriented toward the past. It tends to preclude or marginalise forward-looking, future-oriented concerns which require as much if not more attention. Proponents of restorative justice, unlike some other critics of retributive justice, do not argue that addressing the past is unimportant. They do claim that our criminal justice system is too fixated with addressing the past and insufficiently focused on the future.[4]

Second, the enormous hardship and stigma we place on those found legally guilty influences many perpetrators of crime to deny guilt. Those who are found legally guilty are not only liable to judicial punishment, but in addition, they are labelled, often lastingly, as criminals. Criminality becomes an obdurate part of their social identity. As Zehr puts it: 'Guilt adheres to a person more or less permanently, with few known solvents' (*ibid*: 69). Because it is so consequential, the procedure for establishing guilt is governed by elaborate legal definitions and rules, and accused persons are provided with considerable legal safeguards. Those accused of a crime are often advised to exploit these legal niceties and safeguards and to plead 'not guilty' even if, in fact, they were responsible for the commission of an offence. Where this strategy of 'going not guilty' succeeds, and even where it fails, perpetrators of criminal harm are thereby encouraged to see themselves as not guilty in an experiential and moral sense. Their minds become focused on the circumstances which mitigate their blame, and not on their moral responsibility for harming another person. In their efforts to avoid a finding of legal guilt, and the serious consequences of such a finding, they come to see themselves as having no accountability for the crime they have committed. Nor are they encouraged to acknowledge and deal with any subjective moral guilt which they may feel; guilt feelings that can leave them emotionally damaged. Zehr suggests that a system which is less obsessed with fixing blame, and less harsh on those found guilty, will better encourage those who cause harm to others through criminal acts to come forward and acknowledge their responsibility and liability to do something about it.

A third criticism is that the *individualistic* conception of blame which tends to be expressed through retributive justice is so at odds with the way most offenders evaluate their own conduct that it stands little chance of influencing them to accept accountability. In the West, legal guilt is usually interpreted as a product of individual moral failing. The individual found guilty is deemed to be a free moral agent, who had a choice about how to behave, and freely made the unacceptable choice. Zehr argues that this individualistic concept of guilt is completely in conflict with the perceptions of many offenders, who do not see themselves as free agents completely in charge of their own lives. Most see their behaviour as shaped, if not completely determined, by surrounding forces, socio-economic and providential, which they have little capacity to control or resist. Most offenders, according to Zehr, do not really believe that they have the freedom which the law insists they possess.[5]

Zehr's point is not to deny that offenders have responsibility for their behaviour and its consequences, but to argue that the judgement which the law seeks to impose is such a harsh one that most offenders will simply reject it. The gap between the official construction of the offender's behaviour and the offender's own construction is too wide to allow the former to influence the latter. Hence, Zehr suggests, our system of retributive justice fails to encourage offenders to engage with its judgments and to come to terms with their liability for harm which they have brought about. Instead, retributive justice almost obliges offenders to adopt exculpatory strategies as a way of shielding themselves from the severe judgments it seeks to impose.

The pain game

Once blame has been fixed, the concern of retributive justice shifts to ensuring that offenders pay for the suffering they have caused by suffering in return (Zehr 1990: 74–8). It is assumed that each crime creates a debt to society, the size of which can be measured precisely, that this debt can be paid through suffering, and that the amount of suffering due can be calculated and administered with equal precision (Gorringe 1996).

Drawing on Christie (1982), Zehr suggests that we feel uneasy about intentionally hurting others and therefore take steps to distance ourselves from the reality of 'pain law': we delegate sentencing and the administration of penalties to professionals; we try to rationalise what we do by persuading ourselves that its purpose is to deter crime, despite overwhelming evidence that punishment fails to deter;[6] and we disguise what we are doing by calling it 'treatment' or 'corrections'. The reality, nevertheless, is that we have been educated to believe that criminal justice is about suffering and that evil must be curbed by harshness.

Zehr's main problem with punishment, so conceived, is that rather than restoring peace to the community, it reinforces the very attitudes it is meant to keep in check. The message which offenders hear is that those who offend deserve vengeance. This confirms the outlook which often led them to commit crime in the first place. According to Zehr, many crimes are committed by people who see themselves as punishing others for some real or imagined wrong (*ibid*: 77). He also cites evidence on the effects of the death penalty which suggests that far from deterring those tempted to commit murder, it sometimes encourages people to kill since it confirms the attitude that those who wrong us deserve to die.

The suggestion that hurting offenders is not only futile but counter-productive recurs regularly in the discourse of restorative justice. Such arguments are, of course, frequently directed at the prison:

> Prisons are schools for crime; offenders learn new skills for the illegitimate labor market in prison and become more deeply enmeshed in criminal subcultures. Prison can be an embittering experience that leaves offenders more angry at the world than when they went in. The interruption of a career in the legitimate labor market and the stigma of being an ex-con can reduce prospects of legitimate work on completion of the sentence.
>
> (Braithwaite 1999b: 1738)

However, to criticise imprisonment in these terms does not necessarily lead to the rejection of punishment as a response to crime. Such arguments can be, and often are, made by proponents of non-custodial punishments. However, some restorative justice proponents argue that *any* coercive response to offenders can 'backfire'. One reason for this is that attempts to coerce people into doing things they do not want to do, or into not doing things they want to do, often engender 'defiance' (Sherman 1993). As Braithwaite puts it: 'intentions to control are reacted to as attempts to limit our freedom, which lead us to reassert that freedom by acting contrary to the direction of control' (Braithwaite 1999b: 1740; 1999a: 45).[7]

Although it is a more general point, it is worth emphasising again that another reason why retributive justice can have the opposite effect to that intended is that it can lead to stigmatisation (Braithwaite 1989: 16–21). The community's decision to punish the individual 'is a sharp rite of transition at once moving him out of his normal position in society and transferring him into a distinctive deviant role' (Erikson 1962, cited in Braithwaite 1989: 18). This process, according to some, is almost irreversible. Persons labelled 'deviant' find themselves cut off from normal social interaction and consequently seek communality in deviant sub-cultures where their deviant status is viewed as positive rather than negative. Once in a deviant sub-culture, deviants are likely to commit further offences simply to maintain their new deviant status and identity. Braithwaite summarises the idea thus:

> Once a person is stigmatized with a deviant label, a self-fulfilling prophecy unfolds as others respond to the offender as deviant. She experiences marginality, she is attracted to subcultures which provide social support for deviance, she internalizes a deviant identity, she experiences a sense of injustice at the way she is victimized by agents of social control, her loss of respectability may push her further into an underworld by causing difficulty in earning a living legitimately. Deviance then becomes a way of life that is difficult to change and is rationalised as a defensible lifestyle within the deviant subculture.
>
> (Braithwaite 1989: 18)

The restorative alternative to retributive justice: towards an ideal model

Through looking at this critique of retributive justice we can now begin to see, in very broad outline, what an ideal restorative response to offenders might look like.

While it will not ignore the need to assign responsibility for what happened, it will give equal attention to, and perhaps prioritise, the need to determine what should be done to repair the harm caused by the crime and to ensure that further criminal behaviour, by the offender, does not occur. To persuade offenders to admit to the truth, the threat of punishment will be removed, or at least reserved as a last resort. Also, steps will be taken to ensure that those who admit responsibility for a crime are not permanently stigmatised as criminals. Hence, rather than focusing solely on the bad act, restorative justice processes will emphasise the good which exists in all offenders. On the basis that the threat of punishment and the permanent stigma of criminality are removed, restorative justice will regard the need for elaborate legal rules and strong procedural safeguards as much diminished. The legal niceties and protections which are so essential in a punitive system will be seen as less necessary – and indeed an unnecessary hindrance – in a system which is not geared towards inflicting pain but towards reparation and crime prevention.

Those deemed responsible for committing a crime will not be judged as severely as they are in retributive systems. Condemnation of their behaviour as unacceptable to the community, will be mixed with empathy for them as members of the community who have erred. At the same time, it will be made clear that the circumstances which might mitigate their guilt do not excuse their actions and, crucially, do not remove their liability to make amends for the harm they have caused. The moral judgement of restorative justice is neither the harsh one of retributive justice, not the lenient one of those who deny that criminals, being driven by irresistible forces, have any responsibility for their crimes. Rather, the moral judgement of restorative justice reflects the 'ambiguity over guilt' and 'ambivalence about judgement' which we find in everyday moral life (Norrie 1999: 139).

The main reason for insisting on this complex moral judgment is that, in restorative justice, the community's judgment is not simply a prelude to pain delivery, but is intended to perform an educative and re-integrative function. The concern is to persuade offenders to share the community's judgment of their behaviour. For this to happen, the judgment of the community must be one which the offender can accept as reasonable, even if such acceptance is uncomfortable. The judgment must not be one that is so harsh that offenders will simply reject it, and see themselves as victims of unjust condemnation.

The ideal restorative justice system we are envisioning here will refrain from inflicting pain upon offenders, or at least keep pain to a minimum. The notion that offenders must pay for their crimes through suffering is rejected, as is the idea that we can deter crime by threatening those tempted with pain. Imprisonment, in particular, will be rarely if ever used (Cayley 1998). Yet, restorative justice will not be *soft* on offenders. The process of being judged by the community will be discomforting and making amends for what one has done will be burdensome. However, the demands of undergoing a restorative process are quite different from the pain inflicted in the retributive process.[8] One of the reasons for refraining from pain delivery is that it is futile and frequently counterproductive from the point of view of preventing further crime. To prevent further crime, offenders must be reformed. It is assumed that pain of the sort inflicted by retributive justice cannot contribute to the reformation of wrongdoers (on this, *cf.* Moberly 1968: ch. 5).

Restorative justice as an alternative to treatment

Just as most restorative justice advocates want to distinguish restorative justice from retributive justice, many insist on distinguishing it sharply from the therapeutic response to offenders which was favoured by progressive opinion until the early 1970s, when faith in therapy began to wane.[9]

Proponents of therapeutic interventions regard much criminal behaviour as symptomatic of underlying psychiatric disorder (but not necessarily mental illness) and argue that in dealing with offenders our primary aim should be to remedy such disorder, thereby curing them of their propensity to crime. This is generally seen as a task for professionals (psychiatrists, counsellors, therapists, educators, psychologists, etc.) who are regarded as having the expertise required to identify which offenders are suffering from disorders, to determine the nature of the disorder, and to prescribe appropriate forms of intervention (Nokes 1967).

Proponents of restorative justice criticise the therapeutic response to offenders on two main grounds. First, they argue that in focusing on the needs of offenders, while neglecting the needs of those they have harmed, the therapeutic approach adds to the injuries of victims; it is a form of secondary victimization (Bazemore 1996). Second, they contend that therapeutic interventions seldom make a significant positive impact on the behaviour of offenders. This is a standard criticism of treatment and is by no means made only by proponents of restorative justice. However, restorative justice advocates do contribute a fairly distinctive account of why such failure is to be expected. Therapeutic responses, they argue, rest upon a deterministic understanding of criminal behaviour. That is, they see crime as being caused by psychological factors which are beyond the conscious control of offenders (Braithwaite 1989: 9). This 'passive' conception of offenders, it is suggested, encourages them to see themselves as not responsible for their criminal behaviour or the harm it produces.[10] In addition, in treatment programmes offenders tend to be shielded from social condemnation of their behaviour. The professionals who deal with them do not see themselves as being in the business of moral evaluation and condemnatory judgment (Garland 1990: 187). They see their task as involving assessment of the offender against norms of adequate social and psychological functioning, rather than against the community's moral norms (Foucault 1977).[11] Hence, in treatment programmes, offenders are not confronted with the everyday moral judgements of their behaviour, with which they need to be confronted if they are to come to an understanding of the harm they have caused and of their liability to repair it. Without such an understanding, it is claimed, offenders are unlikely to change their ways.

The alternative

This critique again helps us to identify, at a broad level, some central concerns of an (ideal) restorative response to offenders. First, while it is concerned with the healing of offenders, this goal is to be pursued only insofar as it can be made compatible with the goal of achieving justice for their victims. Offenders must be held accountable to victims for the harm they have caused and must make serious efforts to repair such harm before they can expect to have *their* needs attended to. However, as we shall see, it is contended that by holding offenders accountable and encouraging them to make amends for their behaviour we are already beginning to meet their needs.

A restorative response to offenders will seek to influence their behaviour, not through therapeutic techniques, which are based on a passive conception of the criminal, but through 'moralizing social control' based on an active conception of the criminal, i.e. through remonstration based on the assumption that criminals have a choice about how to behave. Offenders will be allowed and encouraged to take personal responsibility for the harm they have caused.

The goals and methods of restorative justice in relation to offenders

I have outlined some important ways in which an ideal restorative response to offenders will differ from a retributive and a therapeutic response. However, as Meier (1998) points out, this is not the same as saying what restorative justice *is*. Hence, I will now look more 'positively' at some characteristic features of the restorative response to offenders. This involves describing the outcomes restorative justice seeks to achieve, regarding offenders, and the methods proposed and used to obtain these outcomes.

Outcomes

The goals of restorative justice regarding offenders seem straight-forward: to get offenders to accept responsibility for their actions and to make amends and to reintegrate (or sometimes integrate for the first time) such offenders into the community of law-abiding citizens.

However, the second of these goals, i.e. reintegration, is a very general ideal which can be interpreted in various ways in practice. Practitioners often espouse a more specific, and quite different, aim of getting offenders to break the habit of crime or at the very least to become less persistent in their offending. But, whether this aim has been achieved can often only be determined some time after the restorative intervention has taken place. Hence, many practitioners have their eyes on much more immediate objectives: to get offenders to take the same attitude of disapproval towards their criminal behaviour as the rest of the community takes and to demonstrate a serious and genuine commitment to avoiding criminal behaviour in the future.

In these ways, the goals of the restorative response to offenders differ little from those pursued for decades or even centuries under the rubric of 'reform' or 'rehabilitation'. However, one of the most significant and distinctive features of some (by no means all) restorative programmes is that they also attend to the need to change the neighbourhood's or community's attitude towards the offender. It is recognised that if offenders are going to be reintegrated into the community, it is not only the offender who will have to make adjustments. The community too must be prepared to make what could be a demanding change. It must shift from shunning and despising offenders to forgiving and re-accepting them (Hadley n.d.). Hence, one of the distinctive aims of restorative justice is to bring about an important shift in social attitudes towards offenders. While ordinary people are expected to become more actively involved in expressing disapproval of crime, they are at the same time expected to become more actively involved in helping offenders who have genuinely repented their crimes to regain a place of respect and esteem within the community (Johnstone 1999).

Methods

One important point about the restorative response to offenders is that the reintegration of offenders into the community is conditional upon their expressing repentance and genuinely committing themselves to a change of ways. Practitioners and programme designers are therefore faced with two sets of problems. The first is how to get offenders truly to repent their behaviour and make such a commitment. The second is how to get the community to reaccept such persons.

Awareness of human consequences   With regard to the first problem, the initial task is to get offenders to understand *entirely* how their behaviour has affected other people. It is frequently argued that many offenders lack awareness of the consequences of their crimes for other people and that it is this lack of awareness which allows them to commit their crimes. If they become more aware of the harm they cause, it is suggested, the majority of offenders will regret their behaviour and avow not to repeat it.

Such claims will strike many as implausible. Surely the burglar, rapist, fraudster and perpetrator of a violent assault are conscious of the harm they cause to other people? Surely it is their indifference to the harm they cause to others, rather than a lack of awareness of the harm, that is the problem? Proponents of restorative justice contend otherwise. They suggest that few people are so lacking in concern for other members of the community as to be wholly indifferent to the effect of their behaviour on them. Most people, including most offenders, care about the plight of others sufficiently to refrain from crime once they are made aware of its traumatic effects.

Let us look closer at this claim. As we have seen, victim studies show that crime affects victims in ways which are not immediately obvious. Crime causes much more than its palpable material harm; it affects people's emotional well-being and social relationships in ways which are far from noticeable. Even people who care very much about the victim frequently fail to appreciate the trauma they suffer. It is hardly remarkable, then, to claim that offenders, especially those who commit property crimes rather than crimes which are more obviously 'against the person', lack awareness of the damage which they do to their victims.

However, the offender's lack of awareness is not attributable only to the fact that the harm caused by crime is seldom self-evident. In addition, it is argued, offenders employ various psychological techniques to shield themselves from an understanding of the full human consequences of their behaviour. Braithwaite draws upon the work of Sykes and Matza (1957) to make this point. They identified 'five techniques of neutralization' which make a 'drift' into a delinquent episode possible. Braithwaite summarises them thus:

> denial of victim ('We weren't hurting anyone'); denial of injury ('They can afford it'); condemnation of the condemners ('They're crooks themselves'); denial of responsibility ('I was drunk'); and appeal to higher loyalties ('I had to stick by my mates').
>
> (Braithwaite 1999a: 47)

Similarly, Zehr writes:

> In order to commit offenses and live with their behavior, offenders often construct elaborate rationalizations for their actions ... They come to believe that what they did was not too serious, that the victim 'deserved' it, that everyone is doing it, that insurance will take care of any losses. They find ways to divert blame from themselves to other people and situations. They also employ stereotypes about victims and potential victims. Unconsciously, or even consciously they work to insulate themselves from the victim. Some burglars even report that they turn photographs toward the wall in homes they burglarise so that they will not have to think of the victims.
>
> (Zehr 1990: 40–1; *cf.* Walker 1994: 148)

It is important to note that, in this quotation, Zehr suggests that techniques of neutralization may sometimes be consciously employed. To the extent that this is true it tends to undermine the point that offenders are unaware of the consequences of their crimes. There is an important difference between consciously shutting one's mind to the consequences and being genuinely unaware, or perhaps only faintly aware, of the consequences. Zehr's point, however, is that, whether consciously or not, many offenders *must* shut their minds to the human costs of their crimes in order to commit them and that if we can confront them with the human costs in such a way that they cannot avoid becoming aware of them, we can prevent much crime.

A complaint which proponents of restorative justice make about the adversarial criminal trial and standard penal response to offenders is that they do little to break through the offender's rationalizations. To the contrary, they often encourage and reinforce them. There are a number of issues here. First, the way the offence is represented in the formal legal process does little to direct the mind of offenders to the consequences of their wrongdoing. Crimes are presented as violations of the interests of the state or the Crown, rather than violations of actual persons (Morris and Young 2000: 13). Also, offences are frequently defined in abstract, archaic language ('you are charged that on or about X in the vicinity of Y you did unlawfully take ... ') which does little to convey to offenders, especially young offenders, the *human* consequences of their actions. Above all, the keeping apart of the victim and the offender, so that they never get to meet face-to-face in an informal setting, means that there are few opportunities for victims to tell offenders directly about the harm they have suffered. The passive, non-participatory role of the offender in the trial process also ensures that formal criminal justice does little to bring home to offenders the reality of the harm they have caused. Furthermore, the very nature of contemporary penal practice, in which the aim of making things unpleasant for offenders is to the fore, encourages offenders to focus on their own plight, rather than that of their victims (Zehr 1990: 41).

In restorative justice, on the other hand, there is a strong emphasis on shocking offenders into awareness of the harm they have caused. This is achieved by having victims tell them personally about how the crime has affected them. Hearing about the human consequences of their behaviour, not from authority figures but from those directly harmed by them, is seen as a way of penetrating the indifference and neutralization strategies of offenders which the formal legal process leaves intact or even fortifies. Morris and Young sum up the differences between the experiences of offenders of a formal trial and a restorative process thus:

> Pre-trial and trial procedures do not engage them [offenders]; they rarely participate directly; they are generally expected to communicate with the court through their lawyer; and they are discouraged from any direct dialogue with the victim. They thus can feel alienated from the process ... Overall, they remain fundamentally untouched ...
>
> Restorative justice processes require more than the presence of the offender: they require their inclusion. They are expected to directly participate in the process, to speak about their offending and matters associated with it, to interact with the victim . . and to contribute to decisions about the eventual outcome. From all this offenders are expected to have a better understanding of their offending and its consequences, to become accountable for the offending in ways which they understand ... The presence of victims also means that offenders' justifications for their offending – 'she could afford it', 'he is insured', and so on – can be challenged.
>
> (Morris and Young: 2000: 17–18)

David Cayley explains such ideas through concrete examples, such as the following from a case in New Zealand where four youths broke into a school, got drunk and accidentally set fire to the school causing enormous damage (Cayley 1998: 172). A Family Group Conference (FGC) lasting three days was organised. On the first day, teachers and parents attempted in vain to upset the offenders by explaining to them the harm their actions had caused (the disruption of the children's schooling and the teachers' work, the need to build temporary

99

classrooms, etc.). The offenders sat through this 'so unmoved, so unemotional' (Matt Hakiaha, youth justice co-ordinator, cited in Cayley 1998: 172). But on the second day a breakthrough occurred:

> And then this young girl walked up with the scrapbook that she had kept in her classroom … About one-half was just burned to a crisp, and the other half was charred. And she came up and sat in front of these four boys … and she said, 'This is all I've got as a remembrance of my brother, because this scrapbook is photos of my family and a photo of my brother, and he died not so long ago, about a year ago, and that's all I've got now.' And then you saw the tears trickling down the faces of these four boys.
>
> (*ibid*)

According to the conference organiser, this was the start of a process in which the boys eventually took 'ownership' of the offence, apologized to all affected by it, gave up their weekends to help build a new playground, and eventually, instead of being permanently stigmatised, were 'looked on as heroes'. They did not come to the attention of the police again (Cayley 1998: 173).

The conference organiser, Matt Hakiaha, provided Cayley with another example which further illustrates the point of making sure that the offenders do not only formally accept responsibility for the crime and the punishment for it, but are made to understand the full human consequences of their behaviour. The case involved a youth, Shane, who stole a car and wrecked someone else's car (*ibid*: 174). At the FGC, Shane quickly accepted responsibility for the offence and apologised to the victim for the harm caused. Had he been processed in the normal way, he would then have received a simple punitive (perhaps a custodial) sentence. But, at the FGC, the victim refused to let him off so lightly. She interceded: 'No, you're going to hear how this has affected me', and went on to explain how she couldn't take her asthmatic daughter to 'emergency', how she couldn't take her son to soccer training, and how she couldn't do her shopping. Hakiaha reports: 'Shane at that stage became a blubbering mess … He started to own the offence *in its entirety*' (quoted in Cayley 1998: 174, emphasis added). The action plan agreed involved Shane giving his car to the victim. Shane, apparently, would have preferred to have gone to prison. Giving up his car was deeply embarrassing, because he had to explain to his friends, who saw his car being driven by the victim, what had happened. This humiliating experience, according to Hakiaha, had a much more salutary affect on his behaviour than a prison sentence would have had.

Exposure to shame and censure   These stories usefully lead on to the next theme: that in order to get offenders to repent their wrongdoing, they need to be exposed to the disapproval of ordinary members of the community (Braithwaite 1989).[12] It could be argued, of course, that the public criminal trial performs this function. However, restorative justice differs significantly from conventional penal practice in the *source* and *mode of transmission* of the message.

With regard to the source, the emphasis is on the message coming not from 'above' (e.g. a dressing down by a magistrate), but from 'the side', i.e. from ordinary people, such as members of the offender's family and 'micro-community', to whom they can relate roughly as equals. In the terms of Nils Christie (1998), restorative justice employs a horizontal rather than pyramidal form of communication. The underlying idea is that disapproval will be more effective when it comes from people whom the offender cares about, and who care about him or her, than when it comes from 'distant' authorities. Restorative justice proponents seldom explain why this is so. One likely reason is that expressions of disapproval are likely to be more effective when they come from those who not only censure but also regularly provide, protect and guide and who are united with the offender through a bond of affection (Moberly 1968: 138). Such persons are unlikely to forget 'the person in the culprit', and hence are likely to express disapproval in a respectful manner and without stigmatizing the offender (*ibid*).

There is also a clear preference in restorative justice for direct verbal forms of communication over less direct methods. However, Braithwaite tends to qualify this by showing that sometimes the communication process is more complex. Often, he argues, attempts to 'move' offenders, by communicating directly with them, fail. However, when victims relate how they have been harmed by the offender's acts, in the presence of people who care about the offender (such as his or her parents), it is the shame of the parents which frequently moves the offender to realise and repent what he or she has done. Braithwaite and others, describing FGCs, have talked of:

> … a shaft of shame crossing the floor of a conference as a victim explains the consequences she has suffered. The offender has learnt a callousness that protects him from experiencing any shame in the face of hearing these consequences. The shield deflects the 'shaft of shame' which then pierces like a spear the heart of the offender's mother, who sobs in consequence. It is the mother's tears which then get behind the offender's emotional defences. Through this indirect emotional dynamic the offender experiences remorse – a

remorse mediated by letting down a mother he loves, indeed by hurting her.

(Braithwaite and Strang 2000: 215;
also Braithwaite and Mugford 1994)

Redemption   A problem with making offenders feel ashamed of their behaviour and of the hurt they have caused, before their family and community, is that they can feel so disgraced that they feel they must leave the family/community for ever. Shaming offenders often has the effect of driving them out of law-abiding society for good, into deviant sub-cultures. It is therefore deemed crucial, by proponents of restorative justice, that shaming be done without so degrading offenders that they turn their back on law-abiding society for good (Braithwaite 1989) and that offenders be offered a way back from shame, a chance to redeem themselves. They can do this, it is suggested, in two ways.

The first is by *expressing* their remorse and shame (Retzinger and Scheff 1996). By showing that they are genuinely ashamed of their behaviour and want to distance their 'true selves' from it, without denying responsibility for the harm they have caused, offenders show that, at a deeper level, they remain part of the law-abiding community and recognize its norms of acceptable behaviour. The transgression becomes a momentary weakness which the offender must accept the blame for and must pay for, but which need not result in his or her permanent disgrace or exclusion from the community. The second mode of redemption is to do something to repair the harm caused by the crime. This idea of reparation now needs to be examined a little more closely.

Reparation   For most proponents of restorative justice, the main point of reparation is to ensure that the harm done by crime is repaired, i.e. it is mainly for the victim's benefit. Some argue, however, that in repairing the harm they have caused, offenders themselves benefit because they are far more likely to be reformed and reintegrated with the community. The process of reparation can produce a reformative and reintegrative effect, it is claimed, in a number of ways. First, through their attempts to repair the harm they have caused, offenders come to realise the true extent of that harm. Hence, reparation helps make offenders aware of the harm they have caused which, as we have seen, is regarded as an all important first step in the reintegrative process. Secondly, by repairing the harm they have done, offenders can help appease the anger and indignation which victims and the public may feel towards them, and may even turn this into respect, thereby paving the way for their reintegration into the community. The example of the boys who burned down a school, but became heroes when they constructed a new playground, is an example. Third, it is argued that repairing the harm can be 'a kind of redemptive purging process, which might inhibit subsequent wrongdoing' (Geis 1977: 147). It is this third idea which I want to explore here.

Geis, the author of the above quotation, does not explain what he means by saying that reparation can be a 'redemptive purging process', and it is difficult to find anywhere in the restorative justice literature a precise account of the process by which making reparation rids the offender of the taint of the crime thereby paving the way for renewed membership of the law-abiding community. This issue has been addressed, however, by Sir Walter Moberly (1968: ch. 7). His work can provide some useful support for the theory of restorative justice, but it also points to ways in which it needs to be developed and perhaps modified. In what follows I will draw loosely on his argument, seeking to draw out its relevance for restorative justice.

Moberly asks: Can a crime ever be annulled? If it can be, can punishment play any role in its annulment? (*ibid*: 186–8). In addressing the first of these questions he starts with the example of a robbery (*ibid*: 188). He points out that the obvious and most perfect way to rectify this wrong is to require the culprit to make simple restitution, i.e. to return what was stolen. However, restitution will often be impossible. The articles stolen may have been consumed, expended or transformed, in which case any attempt to rectify the wrong will have to take the form of compensation rather than restitution. More importantly, the harm caused by crime usually extends far beyond material harm which is relatively easy to rectify. In the case of the robbery, the owner has had to spend time without the goods which, apart from any further material loss this may have caused, is likely to create mental disturbances such as annoyance and anxiety (recall Shane, the car thief). Also, as Zehr (1990: ch. 2) would point out, the manner in which the property was taken – with unjustified force – can create extensive mental trauma. To try to make up for such mental disturbance the robber might pay the owner damages as well as compensation for material loss. But no matter how much they pay, or no matter what else they do, it is not possible to restore the *status quo*, the mental distress suffered in the past can never be undone. All offenders can do is offer victims something which will provide them with consolation for their mental suffering and perhaps ensure that their mental suffering comes to an end.

The problems are similar in principle, but greatly compounded, when the crime involves the infliction of physical injury. The person who punches or stabs another can never un-punch or un-stab them, no matter how much genuine remorse they might later show and no matter how much they might try to compensate the victim (Brown forthcoming). The harm, and the offender's culpability for it, can never be erased. Hence, it seems, at least in the case of serious crimes committed by adults, offenders can rarely if ever fully purge themselves. No matter how much 'reparation' is attempted, the harm done can never be expunged and will continue to create an obstacle to good relations between the offender and the victim. If we add to this the fact that the effects of crime ripple out, harming the whole community as well as the direct victim, it becomes even harder to see how offenders can even compensate for, let alone repair, the damage they cause.

Moberly's response to such objections to the idea of reparation starts with asking: in what does the vileness of crime specially consist? He suggests that what is most loathsome about crime is the moral degradation it does to offenders themselves and the social harm it causes, which consists not so much in the direct suffering caused to others but in 'the lowering of the moral tone, the contagion of evil example and the coarsening, in a hundred subtle ways, of the whole impact of the wrongdoer on his fellows' (ibid: 198). The question, then, for Moberly, is whether these two states of affairs, i.e. the moral ruin of the wrongdoer and social harm, can be so transformed that their total significance is reversed (ibid: 191). He argues that they can. The original situation, disturbed by the crime, can never be simply reproduced (or 'restored'): 'The Wrongdoing has made *some* difference – nothing can alter that' (ibid). But, vitally, there are opposite ways in which offenders can react to their past. There is 'the cowardly course' which is to drift with the tide and continue in wrongdoing. Or, offenders can repent, confess and make such reparation as they can. Taking the latter course, suggests Moberly, modifies the past so far as it is still operative in the offender (ibid). It can help to reverse the moral decay of the offender and arrest and turn round the lowering of the moral tone resulting from the crime.

It follows from the above that the forced punishment of the offender cannot in itself annul a crime. The idea that a crime is wiped out by punishment is a social convention which has much the same status today as duelling had in the eighteenth century and which, like duelling for us, might appear artificial and even ridiculous to future generations (ibid: 194ff). For crimes to be annulled, in Moberly's sense, wrongdoers themselves must voluntarily repent and make such reparation as they can. This does not mean that no coercion can be employed, in order to get the offender to listen to the disapproval of the community and to its demands that they make reparation. Indeed, if we accept Moberly's analysis, we would be doing the offender no favours by refusing to employ such coercion, where they did not spontaneously repent their wrongdoing. But, after this, unless the repentance and reparation is voluntary, it could hardly have the effects Moberly thinks it can produce.

Moberly's argument is of interest because it seems to fit well with the idea of restorative justice and lends it support in an area where it needs such support. But, crucially, Moberly's whole argument rests upon a conception of the harm caused by crime which is different to – and in some ways a challenge to – the conception promoted by many restorative justice proponents. As we have seen, restorative justice proponents often insist that we should conceptualise crime primarily as an act which causes harm to another person. I understand Moberly as arguing that such harm is difficult if not impossible to repair. What can be repaired, however, is the moral harm done by offenders to themselves and to society. Yet, restorative justice proponents tend to suggest that such harm is of secondary importance. It may be that, by thinking more seriously and more rigorously about the idea of reparation, restorative justice proponents will realize that their highly 'privatised' conception of crime is, for all its value in certain respects, a hindrance to a truly restorative justice.

Decertification/circles of support and accountability   So far, we have looked at what offenders must do if they are to pave the way for their reintegration into the community. However, no matter what the offender does, if the community insists that no amount of atonement can make up for the crime and if it refuses to provide the support which many offenders will need to live a normal life in the community, the offender will not be reintegrated. One of the most important aspects of the idea of restorative justice is the attention which it pays to this task of getting the community to change its attitude towards offenders who have confessed, repented and made such reparation as they can.

While restorative justice proponents insist that the victim's and the community's feelings of anger and indignation towards the offender must be regarded as legitimate and that there must be a forum in which these feelings can be expressed, they also insist that there comes a point when anger and indignation must give way to a more forgiving attitude (Hadley n.d.). If offenders are not to be ostracised permanently, the community must follow its censure of the offender with gestures of forgiveness and reacceptance. Shaming, in Braithwaite's terms, must be finite and 'terminated by forgiveness' (Braithwaite 1989: 101). Braithwaite points out that while our society has developed elaborate legal and bureaucratic ceremonies to mark the transition of offenders out of their normal position in society and into the status of criminal, we have no rites to mark a move in the opposite direction. He therefore suggests that we should have ceremonies to decertify people as deviants, i.e. to mark their transition from 'one who has offended' to one who has atoned and is now ready to rejoin normal society.

One of the most interesting practical initiatives, developed to give effect to such ideals, is the 'circle of support', also sometimes known as the 'circle of support and accountability'. Circles of support have been used in Canada and recently in the UK mainly, but not exclusively, for ex-sex offenders (including paedophiles – a group which obviously find reacceptance by the community almost impossible) (Cayley 1998: ch. 16; Hartill 2000; Heise *et al* 2000). The basic idea is that, instead of leaving ex-offenders who have paid for their crime alone, so that they have little choice but to drift back into their old circles and eventually into criminal ways, a group of between four and six people form a circle of support around the ex-offender – the 'core member'. The circle befriends the offender, provides them with appropriate forms of social and practical support, and helps them to become reaccepted by the wider community. The circle also plays a monitoring role, confronting the offender when their behaviour is getting risky, and hence reassuring the wider community that any signs of dangerous behaviour will be picked up. The broad idea is that the circle will enable the offender to live safely in the neighbourhood, while at the same time enabling the neighbourhood to live safely with the ex-offender (Cayley 1998: 303).

The circle of support, which, like many restorative justice initiatives, mirrors informal social control processes, is promoted on the ground that it is actually more dangerous to isolate and ostracise 'sex offenders' and others generally considered a danger to the community, than it is to befriend them and allow them to be part of the community. The danger which such people potentially represent is better checked and controlled when the person is living openly in the community than when the person is driven underground and forced to conceal their past.

An alternative to punishment or an alternative form of punishment?

I started this chapter by following Zehr (1990) and contrasting restorative justice with retributive justice. However, some recent writers, most markedly Daly (2000) and Barton (1999; 2000), argue that to present restorative justice as an alternative to retributive justice is misleading and counterproductive (see also Zedner 1994). Without going into all the details of what is a complex debate, I deal here with certain aspects of it which are essential to a proper understanding and assessment of restorative justice. I look, very briefly, at whether the notion of a paradigm break between retributive justice and restorative justice is sustainable and at whether it is useful, for promotional purposes, to insist upon presenting restorative justice as an alternative to retributive punishment.

In certain respects, the image of retributive justice, which proponents of restorative justice criticize, is a caricature. This is particularly so when retributive justice is characterised as 'an elaborate mechanism for administering "just" doses of pain' (Zehr 1990: 75). It is, of course, quite true that in 'retributive justice' the immediate intention is to make things unpleasant for the offender. However, restorative justice proponents tend to imply that, in retributive justice, hurting offenders is either the whole *raison d'être* of punishment, or is intended as a crude form of deterrence.

There can be no doubt that many of those who advocate and support the idea of inflicting pain upon offenders do conceive of it in such terms. Others, however, advocate and seek to justify the practice of pain delivery in quite different terms. For example, classic exponents of a retributive theory of punishment, such as Immanuel Kant and Georg Hegel, defended the imposition of pain upon criminals as necessary to restore a metaphysical state of right which the criminal act had upset (Doyle 1969; Sorrell 1999; Brown forthcoming). Others retributivists see the imposition of pain as being the only way or the best way of expressing our indignation at cruelty or injustices which have been perpetrated, and they see indignation as quite distinguishable from the emotions underpinning revenge:

> Indignation against wrong done to another has nothing in common with the desire to avenge a wrong done to oneself.
> (T. H. Green, cited in Moberly 1968: 83)

Most relevant of all, proponents of a moral education theory of punishment such as Jean Hampton (1984) and Herbert Morris (1981), regard the pain caused by punishment as neither an end in itself nor a simple disincentive to criminal actions, but as a method of conveying a larger message: that the offender's behaviour was morally wrong and should not be done for that reason (Hampton 1984: 212). Moreover, they contend that the prime beneficiaries of this educative process are offenders (and potential offenders) themselves, should they listen to the message, since they will gain moral knowledge.[13] Proponents of the moral education theory usually insist that if the imposition of pain is to perform its educative purposes, it must be done in accordance with retributivist principles, i.e. the pain must be shown to be deserved.

Among the latest in this line of penal philosophers who view retributive punishment as a (potential) communicative, educative and reintegrative act is Anthony Duff (1999a, 1999b). He argues that the proper aim of punishment should be to communicate censure and hence contribute to the offender's moral reform. Punishment should also, on his account, reconcile offenders with their victims and communities, and repair the damage to relationships which crime causes. The aim of punishment, he writes:

> should ideally be to bring the criminal to understand, and to repent, the wrong he has done: it tries to direct (to force) his attention onto his crime, aiming thereby to bring him to understand that crime's character and implications as a wrong, and to persuade him to accept as deserved the censure which punishment communicates – an acceptance which must involve repentance.... by undergoing such penitential punishment the wrongdoer can reconcile himself with his fellow citizens, and restore himself to full membership of the community from which his wrongdoing threatened to exclude him.
>
> (Duff 1999a: 51–2)

According to Duff, if punishment is to perform these functions, the current style of punishment needs to be altered, with less emphasis on highly coercive and exclusionary sanctions such as imprisonment, and more on community-based communicative sanctions, involving reparation, of the kind which proponents of restorative justice recommend:

> Such communicative punishment is best exemplified, not by the kinds of long prison sentence which loom so large in penal discussion; nor by the fines which, though the penalty of choice for very many offenders, are usually ill-suited to this communicative purpose: but by such 'punishments in the community' as community service orders and probation (as well as by 'mediation' schemes whose aim is to bring the offender to recognise the nature and implications of what she has done, and thus make material or symbolic reparation for it).
>
> (Duff 1999a: 53)

Duff, along with Hampton and Morris and proponents of a reintegrative theory of punishment, such as Reitan (1996), are much closer in their thinking to proponents of restorative justice than they are to the likes of Thomas Carlyle, who justified punishment by appealing to the virtues of revenge and the natural hatred of scoundrels (Moberly 1968: 82), and to those who believe that the surest way of preventing crime is to make criminals suffer. Yet Duff and like-minded thinkers remain convinced that retributive punishment must be part of our response to offenders. They see the goals of retribution and restoration as compatible and even suggest that retributive punishment is essential to the achievement of restorative justice (Daly 2000).

It is quite clear, then, that many of those who advocate and support the practice of retributive punishment do not see pain delivery as an end in itself, nor as a crude form of deterrence, but regard it as an essential component (but only one component) of a more constructive, educative and reintegrative process. So, if the paradigm of retributive justice is to be rejected, it must be rejected simply on the grounds that it involves inflicting pain upon offenders. Those retributivists who are willing to inflict a minimal amount of pain upon offenders and to combine this with more positive educative and reintegrative measures must be condemned alongside those who take delight in making scoundrels suffer intense pain for their misdeeds and those who think that longer and harder prison sentences are the only solution to the crime problem.

Many proponents of restorative justice do seem to adopt such a position. They write as if any intentional infliction of pain upon offenders is to be expunged from our criminal justice system. Restorative justice is presented as an alternative to punishment; an alternative which eschews any intentional imposition of pain. Hence, restorative justice is distinguished sharply from even the most constructive versions of retributive justice.

However, if we subject the discourse of restorative justice to more rigorous scrutiny, the impression that it eschews intentional imposition of pain is revealed as, at best, wishful thinking. It is quite clear that undergoing a restorative justice process can be painful for offenders. Indeed, proponents of restorative justice are much concerned to reassure politicians and the public that it is not a soft option, that offenders will find it demanding. As we saw earlier (in the case of Shane), the fact that some offenders experience the restorative process as more arduous than a prison sentence is advertised as a point in its favour. More generally, most restorative justice processes aim to instil feelings of shame in offenders, and there can be no doubt that shame is a painful feeling (Nathanson 1992; Johnstone 1999). So why do proponents of restorative justice believe that, unlike the retributivists, they are not playing the pain game?

A common answer to this question is that of Lode Walgrave (2000: 166–7, 179). He concedes that restorative interventions may be painful. However, he insists that restorative interventions are not punishments because 'the pain is not deliberately inflicted' (*ibid*: 179). This seems disingenuous. Walgrave might be on sound ground when he states that, in restorative justice, the imposition of pain is 'subordinated to the aim of restoration' (*ibid*: 167). But this does not mean that pain is not deliberately inflicted. If pain is an inevitable, or even highly probable, consequence of restorative interventions, then (unless one adopts a perversely narrow interpretation of the term 'deliberately') somebody who purposely puts an offender through a restorative process, thereby causing them pain, deliberately inflicts pain on them. Whether causing pain is their primary intention, or something they desire, is immaterial. Or, at the very least, as we have seen, many supporters of retributive punishment could argue, with equal plausibility, that causing pain is not their primary aim nor something which they desire.

If both retributive punishment and restorative justice involve the deliberate imposition of pain, then the claim that there is a sharp distinction between them fails (to the extent that the distinction is drawn by reference to pain). Restorative justice, as Daly (2000) and others suggest, might be more accurately presented as an alternative form of punishment, rather than an alternative to punishment (see also Duff 1992). Daly argues, further, that there are practical advantages to dropping the retributive-restorative justice oppositional contrast (2000: 41). She sees the emphasis in restorative justice discourse on abandoning punishment for restorative justice as counterproductive. Offenders will treat the claim that they are not being punished (and hence do not need protection from unwarranted or excessive punishment) as hypocritical. Victims might see it as a denial of the validity of the 'retributive emotions' – such as indignation and resentment – which they feel towards the offender. And, the community might see it as trivialising crime. Hence, she maintains, there would be much to gain from recognising and portraying restorative justice as a more constructive use of the power to punish, rather than as something quite different from punishment.

An alternative to treatment?

We have seen that, as well as drawing a sharp distinction between retributive and restorative justice, many restorative justice proponents maintain with equal vigour that there is a sharp difference between restorative and therapeutic responses to offenders. Again, the image of treatment which proponents of restorative justice reject is largely a caricature. What they tend to attack is a highly 'medicalised' model of penal treatment, in which experts attempt to cure offenders of their criminal tendencies through psychiatric treatment and other techniques. What proponents of restorative justice seem to find most problematic about the 'treatment paradigm' – apart from the fact that it does little or nothing to meet the needs of victims – is that it assumes the offender to be a 'passive object' in need of expert intervention (Bazemore 1996: 40). Hence, an important point of contrast is that, in the restorative process offenders are required to play an active role and are expected to accept responsibility for their acts and for making reparation.

As I have argued elsewhere, many proponents of therapeutic interventions into the lives of offenders themselves reject such a highly medicalised model of treatment (Johnstone 1996a; 1996b). What they tend to prefer are socio-therapeutic programmes in which offenders are encouraged to play a highly active role, rather than remain passive recipients of expert help, and to develop a sense of personal responsibility for their behaviour. If we examine these programmes and the assumptions which underpin them in detail, it becomes quite clear that they overlap in many ways with restorative interventions and that the two processes are more complementary than incompatible. Moreover, it is arguable that, in many cases, the goal of reintegrating offenders into the law-abiding community has a better chance of being achieved if both therapeutic and restorative interventions are employed, in a coordinated programme, rather than if we rely upon one to the exclusion of the other.

Notes

1 Zehr's argument that the retributive understanding of justice, which we tend to take for granted, is in fact just one paradigm (and one that is increasingly unable to solve our problems) is modelled on Thomas Kuhn's famous study *The Structure of Scientific Revolutions* (1970) and Leshan and Margenau's less well-known, *Einstein's Space and Van Gogh's Sky: Physical Reality and Beyond* (1982). Kuhn challenged the then conventional notion that science was a continual accumulation of knowledge, suggesting instead

that it consisted of a series of peaceful interludes interrupted by revolutions in which one way of constructing reality was replaced by another. Kuhn's work focused on the physical sciences but was enormously influential in the social sciences and beyond. Before Zehr, Barnett (1977) described restitution as a new paradigm of criminal justice.

2 In penal philosophy it is common to distinguish utilitarian justifications of punishment from retributive justifications. In the former, punishment is deemed to be justified – despite its morally problematic features – if it is shown that it will produce a good (usually prevention of crime) which outweighs the pain it causes. Philosophical retributivists, on the other hand, insist that the coercion involved in punishment is justified only if it is shown that it is deserved and consistent with respect for the offender as a rational being (see Moberly 1968; Duff and Garland 1994).

3 Zehr defines the retributive paradigm by reference to six assumptions:
    1. crime is essentially *lawbreaking*;
    2. when a law is broken, justice involves establishing *guilt*;
    3. so that just deserts can be meted out;
    4. by inflicting *pain*;
    5. through a *conflict* in which *rules* and intentions are placed above outcomes.
    [6] '… the state, not the individual, is defined as victim'.

    (Zehr 1990: 81, italics in original).

    In this chapter, I deal with assumptions 2, 3 and 4.

4 See Shearing (2001) for an interesting discussion of past-oriented and future-oriented responses to crime. Shearing suggests that restorative justice is appealing because it both fits with the future-oriented logic of risk-focused security found in much private policing and 'acknowledges the importance of symbolically reordering the past' (214).

5 See Norrie (1999) for an illuminating account of the ambiguities inherent in Western notions of legal and moral guilt.

6 For a challenge to this claim that deterrence does not work – a claim which has become just as much a conventional wisdom as its counterpart – see Wilson (1983: ch. 7).

7 William Connolly makes a similar point in a very different way in an essay on 'The desire to punish', where he discusses how an authoritative prohibition can help to crystallise, shape, stimulate and inflame the very desire to do what is prohibited (Connolly 1995: 50).

8 Later, we will ask how sustainable this distinction actually is.

9 See Johnstone (1996) and Sim (1990) for studies of the therapeutic interventions of criminal justice.

10 Strictly speaking, a deterministic understanding of human behaviour does not automatically imply that individuals are not responsible for their behaviour (see Glover 1970). However, it is commonly assumed, especially by critics of human science, that to explain is to excuse, and restorative justice proponents are not unusual in falling into this trap.

11 Norms of adequate social functioning can and frequently do incorporate (disguised) moral judgments, but that is a different issue.

12 This theme will be explored in more detail in the next chapter.

13 For a criticism of this theory see Shafer-Landau (1991). It should be made clear that proponents of a moral education theory of punishment do not contend that punishment, as currently practised, performs the function of moral education. Their position is a penal reformist one, i.e. they contend that if punishment is to function as moral education, we need to reform our penal institutions, and even the wider social context in which they operate, in fundamental ways. Nor is it suggested that punishment is essential to moral education in general. According to Hampton it is only essential when we are trying to teach someone that something which they did was wrong (1984: 225).

Chapter 6

Shame, apology and forgiveness

Jason Temple, 17, watches his 68-year-old victim, Annie Brook, from across the room. This is the first time they have met since he snatched her handbag in the local shopping mall. Temple's mother, Brook's daughter and a probation officer are also there.

Brook tells Temple how she felt violated by his crime. He, clearly upset and shocked by coming face-to-face with the consequences of his actions, apologises, offers to do supervised voluntary work at a local retirement home, and outlines his plans for retraining for a job.

This is the process of restorative justice, given pride of place in this year's Crime and Disorder Act.

(D. Lee, 'Time to say Sorry', *The Guardian*, 1 December 1998)

Introduction

In this chapter I develop some of the themes introduced earlier by look-ing more closely at some of the emotional dynamics of the restorative justice process, focusing specifically on restorative cautioning (the form in which restorative justice is best known in the UK). I focus on what Retzinger and Scheff (1996) call the 'core sequence' of the restorative justice process: the communication of shame followed by a ritual of apology-forgiveness. In their efforts to set in train the core sequence, practitioners have been guided to a considerable degree by John Braithwaite's theory of reintegrative shaming (Braithwaite 1989; Braithwaite and Mugford 1994). However, while Braithwaite is certainly interested in promoting and shaping restorative justice programmes, he also has a much broader concern: to bring about a fundamental change in our mode of social control, a change which, in turn, requires a transformation of public attitudes and feelings towards crime and criminals. Hence, Braithwaite's theory is interesting because it links restorative justice practice with a much broader concern to transform social arrangements for keeping order. Braithwaite's work shows us that to look at crime through a restorative lens involves much more than supporting a new set of professionally organised programmes for dealing with the aftermath of criminal incidents. Adopting a restorative perspective means undergoing a fundamental change in our personal commitments to order and in the way we personally relate to criminals. I will suggest, therefore, that to assess the case for restorative justice, we need to move beyond the standard questions which have hitherto dominated the research agenda (does it work? is it cost effective? etc.). We need to ask whether the attitudinal shifts with which restorative justice programmes are articulated are feasible and desirable.

Restorative cautioning vaiovanie

In the UK, one of the main applications of restorative justice so far has been as a new method of delivering police cautions to youth offenders (Young and Goold 1999; Paterson and McIvor 1999). 'Restorative cautioning', as it is accordingly sometimes known, was 'trialled' in the UK by the Thames Valley Police and is now being implemented in many British police forces. In these forces, arrestees who could be sent to court are, in cases deemed appropriate, given the option of receiving a restorative caution. They are invited to take part in a restorative conference – a meeting attended by the offender(s), members of the offender's family, the victim(s), members of the victim's family or other supporters, and a trained restorative justice facilitator (usually, but not always or necessarily, a police officer).[1] The general aims of the conference are:

- to confront offenders with the consequences of their unacceptable behaviour;

- to get them to understand what it was about their lifestyle, company, habits etc. that led them to offend;

- to commit themselves to changing their lifestyle etc. so that there is less risk of them reoffending;

- to persuade them to apologise to their victims and to agree to a reparative action plan.

- to give victims a chance to express their feeling about what happened and to meet the offender; and

- very gently, to encourage victims to take some first steps towards forgiving offenders.

The psychological routes of restorative conferencing

The interaction which takes place at a restorative cautioning conference is directed by a conference facilitator, whose key role is to ensure that the meeting achieves a restorative outcome. In their training it is emphasised that to do this they need to be aware of the 'psychological routes' along which they should take the offenders and the victims. One of the first objectives of the conference is to alter the mind-set of the offenders by making them experience 'trauma from shame'. This is to be achieved, not through direct attempts to embarrass or humiliate them, but by making offenders relate their story of the criminal incident to the other participants and by having victims tell offenders about how the incident has affected their lives. Crucially, however, the offender is not left in this traumatised state. At a certain stage, the shaming process is terminated and the objective shifts to 'uplifting' the offender. As the conference script (which facilitators are supposed to use as a rough guide) states, the mood shifts 'from negative to positive'. This is achieved through making it clear that it is 'the criminal behaviour which [is] the focus of shaming, and not the offenders themselves' (Young and Goold 1999: 133) and by giving the offenders a power which they do not have in the conventional criminal justice process: the power to do something to help repair the harm they have caused. Offenders are given an opportunity, and encouraged, to apologise to their victims and to others who have been harmed by their behaviour, such as their parents. They are then invited to offer to do something to repair the harm they have caused and to commit themselves to changing their life so that they become less at risk of reoffending. For example, they might offer to pay for damage they have caused, undergo therapy for drink or drugs problems, change their friends, report everyday to their teacher (if they are at school), or make serious efforts to find a job (if they are unemployed).

It is worth re-emphasising that acts of apology and reparation are intended for the offender's benefit, as well as for the benefit of the victim. Through showing remorse, saying sorry, and accepting responsibility for repairing their harm, offenders pave the way for their reintegration into the community of law-abiding citizens. They distance their true selves from their criminal actions, confirming that they are in essence good people, whilst at the same time accepting responsibility for their 'unacceptable' behaviour. The victims and others affected by the crime can advance the offender's journey towards reintegration by offering gestures of forgiveness, reconciliation, and reacceptance into the community.

These processes are also intended for the benefit of victims. In the restorative conference, those affected directly by a criminal act have a chance to meet offenders face-to-face and to tell offenders directly how their behaviour has affected them. This, it is claimed, has a number of benefits. Victims usually enter a restorative conference traumatised by their experience. At the conference, they are uplifted in several ways. The revelation of the full story of 'their crime' gives them cathartic release. Their face-to-face meeting with the offenders helps dissolve many of the dreadful images which they had conjured up in their minds. Their participation in the process by which it is decided what is to be done helps them recover a sense of power which they might have lost as a result of their victimisation. And, they obtain a sense of closure by having the opportunity to forgive those who have harmed them.

Symbolic reparation: the core sequence

The psychological dynamics of the ideal restorative conference are explained by Suzanne Retzinger and Thomas Scheff (1996) in a paper which is used in training courses for conference facilitators. They distinguish two processes that occur in a conference: material reparation and symbolic reparation. By material reparation they mean the settlement agreed to by the parties – the offer and acceptance of a clearly specified amount of compensation or reparative work. By symbolic reparation, they mean the less visible process by which the social bond between the offenders and the victims is repaired and restored. This process consists of what they call a 'core sequence':

> the offender first clearly expresses genuine shame and remorse over his or her actions. In response, the victim takes at least a first step towards forgiving the offender for the trespass.
>
> (*ibid*: 316)

Retzinger and Scheff warn against attaching too much importance to achieving a material settlement. Symbolic reparation, they state, is much more important. Indeed, without symbolic reparation, it may be difficult to achieve agreement about material reparation. Yet, symbolic reparation is very difficult to achieve. It depends upon 'the emotional dynamics of the meeting and the state of the bonds between the participants' (*ibid*). In particular, symbolic reparation depends upon 'shame dynamics':

> Symbolic reparation will occur to the extent that shame and related emotions are evoked and acknowledged by the participants. On the other hand, symbolic reparation will not occur to the extent that shame and related emotions are denied. ...
>
> If the offender can come to the point of 'sharing and communicating' shame, instead of hiding or denying it, the damage to the bond between the offender and other participants may be repaired. ...
>
> Disguised and denied shame inhibits the participants from repairing the bonds between them; it therefore blocks symbolic reparation.
>
> (*ibid*: 318–9)

The idea of reintegrative shaming

[handwritten annotation: RJ use R.S to prevent Criminal from reoff.]

Restorative cautioning is often understood and represented by practitioners as a type of 'reintegrative shaming' ceremony (Young and Goold 1999). As the publicity material of one police force puts it: 'Restorative justice uses "shaming principles" to intervene in the cycle of committing crimes and, hopefully, put a stop to perpetual reoffending' (Webster 1999). This conception owes much to the highly influential work of Braithwaite (1989), to which I will now turn.[2]

Shaming has long been recognized and employed as a method of crime control. Our penal system has traditionally relied as much upon shame as upon pain to deter criminals. Many traditional penal sanctions, such as the pillory, the chain-gang and public floggings, were intended to be both shameful and painful. The underlying rationale has been expressed thus:

> That the offender is subjected to the rejection and contempt of society serves as a deterrent; the thought of the shame of being

caught and of the subsequent conviction is for many stronger than the thought of the punishment itself.

(Andenaes 1974: 78, cited in Braithwaite 1989: 59)

According to Braithwaite, this close link between punishment and shaming has been broken: 'the recent history of Western punishment practices has amounted to a systematic uncoupling of punishment and public shaming' (Braithwaite 1989: 59). This, in fact, is overstating matters. Explicit shaming sanctions have indeed largely been abolished or fallen into disuse (although, as we shall see, they are reappearing). But, as Braithwaite himself clearly recognises, the shamefulness of criminal conviction and punishment has been maintained in other ways. Our criminal justice system is still an institution which humiliates, and being convicted of a crime – or even suspected – is for the majority of citizens a source of deep embarrassment, at the very least (Feinberg 1994). However, subject to these qualifications, Braithwaite is correct to point to the decline of shaming sanctions as a central element in the modernization of judicial punishment.

This 'uncoupling of shame and punishment' is generally celebrated as progress. To an extent, Braithwaite agrees with this assessment, although he differs from many others in what he finds most problematic about shaming penalties. Commonly, shame sanctions are denounced as cruel, as an affront to the dignity of offenders, and as inconsistent with the values of a civilised society (cf. Whitman 1998). For Braithwaite, the additional and primary problem is that such sanctions are counter-productive as a method of crime control. The rejection and contempt to which offenders are subjected is so complete that they can never regain their honour and the respect of others. Offenders become outcasts and turn into enemies of society. While the threat of shaming may deter many from a life of crime, the actual carrying out of the threat frequently converts those shamed into career criminals. For many, the shame is so total that the only way they can survive it is to invert the standards of law-abiding society and turn their status into a sign of honour.

Howard Zehr, in an interview with David Cayley, put it like this:

The shame that our criminal justice system reflects is a stigmatizing shame. It says that ... what you did is bad, but you are also bad, and there's really nothing you can do ... You will always be an ex-offender. So, what do you do? You find other people who have been shamed also, and you hang out together. You convert shame into a badge of respect. ...

[Zehr goes on to discuss a 'lifer' who told him:] 'I remember my first arrest. I rode through my community in the back of that police car, and it was the proudest moment of my life. I had become a man'.

(Zehr, cited in Cayley 1998: 236)

Braithwaite, however, departs from the general tendency of 'progressive opinion' to condemn shaming sanctions completely. He suggests that while shame *could* have the effect of so degrading and mortifying offenders that they are forever driven out of law-abiding society into criminal sub-cultures, it need not have that effect. It is possible, claims Braithwaite, to shame without stigmatizing. Shaming can be combined with efforts to reintegrate the offender into society. Hence, although it is 'a dangerous game' (Braithwaite 1989: 12), we can get the benefit of shaming without its harmful effects.

Crucially, Braithwaite claims, we need to shame. Attempts to control criminal behaviour through coercion and violence simply provoke counterviolence. Attempts to control crime through what Feinberg (1994: 73–4) would call 'mere penalties' – i.e. 'pricetags' attached to unwanted behaviour which are intended to discourage it but do not express the outright condemnation of the community – have limited value for controlling crime. Without the ability to ensure that almost every offence is penalized, people who do not have what Hampton (1984: 210) calls an 'ethical incentive' to refrain from the unwanted behaviour will simply act like the rational opportunists the penalties assume them to be, i.e. they will make an instrumentally rational calculation of the risks and potential gains and will frequently conclude that the advantages of committing the crime outweigh the risks involved.

Shaming, then, is a tool which, according to Braithwaite, we cannot do without:

The key to crime control is cultural commitments to shaming in ways that I call reintegrative. Societies with low crime rates are those that shame potently and judiciously; individuals who resort to crime are those insulated from shame over their wrongdoing.

(Braithwaite 1989: 1)

However, as this quotation indicates, we must draw a crucial distinction between disintegrative or stigmatizing shaming and reintegrative shaming. We must avoid the former but develop the latter:

The crucial distinction is between shaming that is reintegrative and shaming that is disintegrative (stigmatization). Reintegrative shaming means the expressions of community disapproval ... are followed by gestures of reacceptance into the community of law-abiding citizens. ... Disintegrative shaming (stigmatization), in contrast, divides the community by creating a class of outcasts.

(*ibid*: 55)

How, according to Braithwaite and like-minded thinkers, do we ensure that wrongdoers are exposed to reintegrative shaming? First, it is necessary to revive the willingness and capacity of citizens to shame wrongdoers. We must dispel the permissive fallacy that crime and other forms of social deviance are simply expressions of healthy human diversity or part of the growing-up process which must be permitted and tolerated to the greatest degree possible. Such a permissive attitude emaciates the sense of right and wrong and virtually encourages crime. We must also dispel the attitude that crime control is a task which can be left entirely in the hands of the state and its professional bodies, such as the police and the judiciary. State control must be supported by and indeed subordinated to *social* control. People must recognise that 'much misbehavior occurs outside the influence of these agencies and must be confronted and controlled through informal means available to the community' (Kennedy 1990: *xi*). In particular, ordinary people must be exhorted to shame wrongdoers, if not directly then at least indirectly. We must revitalise the habit of 'listening to and participating in secretive gossip directed at others' (Braithwaite 1989: 76). The social value of what is often denounced as a nasty custom must be recognised: it is through the mechanics of gossip that healthy consciences are formed (*ibid*: 75–9).

On the other hand, however, we must ensure that shaming is done in such a way that it does not stigmatize wrongdoers. While we must make people ashamed of their wrongdoing, we must do so in a way which allows people to retain, or at least regain, the respect of the community. We must therefore entrust the task of shaming to those who have a relationship of care with the offender. Such persons are likely to see the good in wrongdoers, as well as the bad, and will be able to express fierce indignation without ever forgetting that they are dealing with a valued member of the community. We must also ensure that shaming ceremonies are followed by efforts to reconcile the offender with the community. Shaming must be followed by forgiveness. Reintegrative shaming is distinguished from stigmatization:

by (a) a finite rather than open-ended duration which is terminated by forgiveness; and (b) efforts to maintain bonds of love and respect throughout the finite period of suffering shame.

(Braithwaite 1989: 101)

Promoting reintegrative shaming is largely a matter, then, of exhorting ordinary people to recognize and accept their responsibility for crime control. The policy implication is that ordinary citizens must be urged to change their attitudes and behaviour in fundamental ways. They must commit themselves to shaming wrongdoers, while at the same time committing themselves to forgiving and re-embracing those offenders who admit their responsibility, express their shame, and avow to make amends and submit to whatever measures the community deems necessary to assure public safety.

At the same time, there are certain social conditions which seem conducive to cultural processes of reintegrative shaming: communitarianism and interdependency (Braithwaite 1989: ch. 6). Reintegrative shaming is most likely to prevail in 'close-knit societies where people confront each other on a relatively equal footing' (Cayley 1998: 274). Failing that, it is most likely to thrive in a society which 'combines a dense network of individual interdependencies with strong cultural commitments to mutuality of obligation' (Braithwaite 1989: 85). It follows that, as well as exhorting people to engage in reintegrative shaming, we should also seek to create such social conditions. Whether we in the modern West have anything resembling such conditions, whether it is possible to create such conditions, and whether such a society is one that we would want to live in, are some of the key questions surrounding Braithwaite's theory.

To the extent that restorative justice is informed and influenced by Braithwaite's theory, these questions are also highly pertinent to our assessment of it. As indicated, the theory of reintegrative shaming has had a significant impact upon the practice of restorative conferencing. Yet, at the same time, it is clear that the theory does not lead to conferencing alone. Rather, it has implications for the way the whole problem of crime control is understood and tackled by our society and for the way we relate to crime and criminals. Braithwaite's theory helps us see how restorative justice fits into broader visions of social control. Any audit of restorative justice should involve an examination of the feasibility and desirability of the broader pattern of social control with which it is articulated.

Some questions about shaming

There are important questions about whether the social conditions of modern society are conducive to shaming offenders. These questions are almost identical to those addressed in chapter three – about whether modern societies are sufficiently communitarian to make the recreation of ancient conceptions of conflict resolution viable – so we need not examine them here. What I want to focus upon here are some ethical questions about the practice of shaming offenders.

As we have seen, 'progressive opinion' deems shaming to be morally problematic for a number of reasons. Braithwaite's theory deals with the objection that, because it is stigmatizing, it is counterproductive from the perspective of crime control. However, this is not the problem which is uppermost in the minds of most of those who are perturbed by the idea of shaming wrongdoers. Rather, objections to shaming are usually based on two rather different considerations. One is that shaming is considered an affront to the dignity of offenders. Another is that a revival of shaming, while it might render us more secure, will result in oppressive conformity. We need to ask whether these criticisms are warranted and, if so, whether they apply not just to Braithwaite's ambitious ideas about reviving reintegrative shaming but also to the more moderate Braithwaite influenced attempts to shame specific offenders in restorative conferencing. I will also discuss a criticism suggested by Whitman (1998) in an illuminating essay on shame sanctions. He rejects the standard criticisms of shaming punishments, but insists that such punishments are wrong for an entirely different reason: they incite the public to behave irrationally.[3]

Shame and dignity

In the 'early modern period' (c. 1500–1800), sanctions such as the pillory, the stocks, the ducking stool and branding were an important part of the penal repertoire (Sharpe 1990: 19–27; Whitman 1998:1055–66). In fact, before the early nineteenth century, the main objective of punishment for lesser offences was to mock and humiliate offenders before their neighbours (Thompson 1992: 480). Outside of the formal penal system, the practice of shaming deviants from certain social norms, through rituals such as 'rough music' in which a gathering of neighbours would ridicule and antagonize deviants through making a harsh discordant noise by clashing pots and pans, blowing horns and yelling and hissing, was an important part of European popular culture (*ibid*: 467–531;

Ingram 1984). Such 'punishments' frequently had devastating effects as those subjected to them were often so mortified that life within their communities became intolerable.

In contemporary Western societies, such sanctions, like those involving the infliction of corporal pain, virtually died out by the middle of the nineteenth century. They survive only in countries which tend to be regarded by members of contemporary Western society as less civilised, at least in their penal methods, than ours.[4] Participation in the public mockery and humiliation of offenders came to be viewed as plebeian and distasteful. Ironically, to partake in such activities itself became shameful.

However, in recent years, shame sanctions have made a bit of a comeback (Whitman 1998; Karp 1998; Garvey 1998; Book 1999). We need only a brief description of modern shaming punishments to see why so many commentators find them morally repugnant. They consist of the fanciful, ostentatious penalties which, until fairly recently, would have been proposed only in coarse popular discourse. To be sure, the courts are not (yet) ordering people to be publicly flogged, dunked or branded, but in the USA, offenders are being sent out in chain-gangs and courts are making orders: 'requiring offenders to wear shirts describing their crimes, publishing the names of prostitutes' johns, or . . . making offenders sit outside public courthouses wearing placards' (Whitman 1998: 1056). People caught shoplifting have been required to march in front of the store with a sign reading, 'I STOLE FROM THIS STORE' (Garvey 1998: 734). Convicted sex offenders have been required to put a notice on their house doors and on any car they drive reading: 'DANGEROUS SEX OFFENDER – NO CHILDREN ALLOWED' (*ibid*: 735). And, offenders have been required to give a shaming speech, approved by the court, on the steps of the local courthouse (*ibid*: 736).

Proponents of restorative justice would, of course, draw a sharp distinction between such penalties and the sort of shaming practice which they advocate and support. Indeed, they are as condemnatory as anyone else of modern judicial shame penalties:

Can these forced shaming practices be considered reintegrative and healing? The answer, of course, is no. Indeed, they appear to be a throwback to the kinds of public shaming that were standard practice in the English colonies of the United States throughout the seventeenth century.

(Sullivan *et al* 1998: 12)

We can accept that there is a significant distinction between judicial shame penalties and the reintegrative shaming advocated for and practised in restorative conferences. But, is the gulf between them as wide as exponents of restorative conferencing would like to believe?

We need to be quite clear about the terms in which the distinction between shame punishments and reintegrative shaming is drawn. It is drawn mainly by reference to what *follows* the shaming process. For Braithwaite, what makes shame sanctions stigmatizing rather than reintegrative is not their cruelty or viciousness. Rather, it is the fact that 'degradation ceremonies *are not followed by* ceremonies to decertify deviance' (1989: 101 emphasis added). Hence, Braithwaite states: 'Reintegrative shaming is not necessarily weak; it can be cruel, even vicious' (*ibid*). Braithwaite is quite clear that the concern for reintegration should take nothing away from the process of shaming; rather the processes of forgiveness and reconciliation commence after the shaming process is complete: 'Shaming and reintegration *do not occur simultaneously but sequentially*' (*ibid*: emphasis added).

However, other proponents of restorative justice seem to differ from Braithwaite on this point. They argue that there is another crucial difference between shame punishments and restorative shaming: in the latter shame is produced, not as a result of deliberate degradation ceremonies, but as an incidental effect of victims explaining to the offender, in front of a small group of people, how the offender's behaviour has harmed them.[5] This certainly absolves some proponents of restorative justice from the charge that they are advocating cruel practices. The problem is that, given the participatory nature of restorative justice, there can be no guarantee that, once there is an emphasis on getting offenders to experience and express shame, shaming will be done in the approved manner. In restorative justice, the victim and other members of the community have considerable control over what happens. They may use this to engage in humiliating, degrading practices which some professional proponents of restorative justice would not approve of. As we saw in chapter three, there are reports of restorative justice processes resulting in sanctions quite similar in content to those ordered by courts. For example, there is a case where a young offender was made to wear a T-shirt emblazoned with 'I AM A THIEF' (Braithwaite 1999a: 97).

Of course, any process is likely to miscarry in one or two cases. We should not condemn the whole idea simply because it goes wrong occasionally. We need to find out how significant this danger is. How likely is it that restorative conferences will become forums for the degradation and humiliation of offenders?

Despite the proliferation of research projects evaluating restorative justice programmes, such issues have received relatively little serious attention in the literature. A notable exception is Young and Goold's study of restorative police cautioning in Aylesbury (1999). They found that the police officers who invariably acted as facilitators of restorative conferences were committed to ensuring that criminal *behaviour* was the focus of shaming, rather than the offenders themselves, and that offenders and others were treated with respect. On the other hand, they found that, in order to impress upon offenders how serious their behaviour was, what were often fairly minor offences tended to be 'talked up', i.e. the harm caused was exaggerated as were the possible penal consequences of such behaviour for the offenders. This propensity, Young and Goold suggest, tended to undercut the conscious efforts made to avoid stigmatisation.

It is also likely that humiliation can occur without the facilitator being aware of it. In some research which I have undertaken into the perceptions and experiences of citizens who have participated in restorative conferences, I came across a case in which the offenders (youths aged 14–15) and their parents felt deeply humiliated by the presence, at the conference, of the victim's son, who attended the conference as the victim's 'supporter'. The victim's son was the same age as the offenders, was acquainted with them, and there had been some bad feeling between them. The offenders and their parents felt that the victim's son was there simply to make fun of them, during what was already a traumatic and embarrassing experience. It was the mere presence of this person at the conference that was humiliating, rather than anything he said or did. Or rather, subtle remarks and gestures by the victim's son, which would have appeared relatively trivial to the facilitator who was unaware of the background of bitter feelings between the main protagonists, were experienced by the offenders and their parents as deeply insolent, and led them to experience the process as a 'degradation ceremony', in a way which escaped the attention of the facilitator (Garfinkel 1956; *cf*. Braithwaite and Mugford 1994).

From the little evidence available, all we can say at the moment is that there is a not insignificant danger of restorative conferences becoming the degradation ceremonies which their proponents seek to distinguish them from, and that restorative justice proponents, in general, tend to underestimate that danger.

Shame and cultural conformity

Another reason why the idea of shaming offenders – even if this is done while retaining respect for them and is followed by efforts to reintegrate them – makes people uneasy is that they tend to identify shaming with a culture of oppressive conformity (Cayley 1998: 282). To explain why many people feel this way and to assess the extent to which their distaste for shaming is warranted, we need to look, albeit very briefly, at some key themes in the history of attitudes toward shame and shaming.

The use of shaming as a method of inducing conformity with social norms is by no means confined to the criminal justice system. In the wider society, shaming, often through much more subtle techniques, is an important form of social control. However, in modern times, attitudes towards shaming have varied considerably, and many have tried to eliminate not just the practice of shaming but also the very sense of shame.

The Victorian era was perhaps the heyday for shaming as a method of regulating thought and conduct (Lynd 1958; Nathanson 1992). Among the upper and middle classes, in particular, a sense of shame played a central role in the control of conduct and lifestyle. A range of methods were used to make people suffer the various degrees of the emotional discomfort we call shame whenever highly detailed and intrusive norms of respectability and decency were transgressed. Knowledge of this kept most people from such transgression. Moreover, shame had such a social presence that it conditioned the thoughts and behaviour of people even when they were shielded from the gaze of others.

By the end of the Victorian era, cultural radicals were launching a scathing critique of the notion of shame. Shame became depicted as a repressive mechanism, an obstacle to liberty and self-actualisation (Schneider 1977: *xiii–xiv*). People were urged to divest themselves of shame in order to realise their true humanity. Freud was at the forefront of this attack. He urged first his patients, and then all of us, to become less prudish, more frank. In the name of mental health and self-realisation we had to stop being ashamed of our sexuality, we had to stop being too embarrassed to talk about things like money (*ibid*: 92–108).

This highly negative attitude towards shame has since become a mainstay of the discourse of human freedom and self-expression. Feminists, in particular, have tended to view shame as a tool of oppression, a mechanism of keeping women in their place:

Shame … has been used as a tool by men to mould women into dependence and obedience. Women, in the main, conformed because to do otherwise often left them penniless, without the status of a wife or the protection of respectability.

> Stigma still operates. Read the tabloids every day. The 'shame' of the unmarried mother and the divorcee may have dissolved but the 'shame' of the working mother has not totally dissipated.
>
> (Roberts 1998)

Such criticisms have succeeded in shifting attitudes. Whilst the experience of shame has by no means disappeared, the contemporary estimate of shame is for the most part negative (Schneider 1977: *xiii*). Four decades ago, Helen Lynd wrote:

> The word shame – or talk of being ashamed of ourselves – does not occur as frequently in conversation today as it did ... We do not verbally 'shame' our children... We strive for self-enlightenment.
>
> (Lynd 1958: 19)

A few decades later, the project of expunging shame from our discourse and consciousness seems even further advanced.

Or, at least it did until quite recently. We can regard the current interest in reintegrative shaming as a clear attempt to revive shame – to place it back at the centre of our lives. For instance, Braithwaite's work can be read as a straightforward attempt to revive Victorian notions, values, moralities and practices, which seemed to have long been left behind. In his first major statement of the theory, Braithwaite appeared to draw some mischievous pleasure from the fact that his advocacy of shaming was jarring to modern sensibilities. In the preface to *Crime, Shame and Reintegration* he announces: 'The present book is about a concept which was at the height of its popularity in the Victorian era – shame' (1989: *viii*). Later in the same paragraph he states: 'An old-fashioned concept like shame is perhaps uncomfortable for contemporary scholars to use in thinking about crime'. And, he refers to his work as 'a decidedly Victorian analysis of crime'.

Given such an introduction, Braithwaite could hardly be surprised to find that people who identify themselves as 'progressive' or 'liberal-minded' tend to be turned off by the notion of reintegrative shaming. C. Schneider wrote in 1977 (and the words still have some truth today): 'Most contemporary radicals view the political and social consequences of shame as inherently conservative, if not reactionary' (Schneider 1977: *xiv*). While proponents of restorative conferencing might see reintegrative shaming as a progressive alternative to incarceration and pain delivery, the moment they mention 'shaming' they arouse suspicion amongst contemporary 'cultural progressives' who have internalised a highly negative estimation of shame and shaming.

Yet, as Schneider notes, not all radicals decry shame. Schneider's work is an attempt to retrieve and push forward, *in the name of radical sociality*, a more positive assessment of shame (but not necessarily of shaming). He argues that our sense of shame arises from, and plays a vital role in sustaining, our interdependency and mutual involvement.[6] We do not, as critics of shame tend to assume, possess isolated identities; our nature is communal. This mutuality does not, as radical individualists might maintain, limit our independence, rather, it is the primary condition of human freedom (Schneider 1977: 137). But to live together in community, we need mechanisms to protect us from complete exposure. Our sense of shame is what provides this protection. Shame protects that which is private from public intrusion, thereby allowing certain valuable activities and relationships to flourish, while maintaining our essential sociality. Hence for Schneider:

> Shame ... reminds us of the deep mutual involvement we have with one another. The recovery and acknowledgement of such interrelatedness would lead us back from our pursuit of the path of an autonomous individualism. Our discomfort with shame reflects our lack of comfort with the reality of our interdependence. The determination to cast off shame in our culture is grounded in our distorted and distorting individualism. The point is not to throw out shame and enthrone autonomy; but to recover an appropriate sense of shame and of the mutuality that is its foundation.
>
> (*ibid*: 138)

How does this bear on the debate about the value and acceptability of shaming in restorative conferencing? If restorative conferencing is to continue to employ the notion of reintegrative shaming which many proponents regard as central to it, it will be necessary to convince critics that a revival of shaming will not lead to an emotionally crippled society in which diversity cannot be tolerated and human expression is stifled. It will be necessary to show that, despite Braithwaite's imprudent references to Victorian analyses of crime and his description of shame as an old-fashioned concept, restorative conferencing is not an attempt to revive Victorian values and to put them to work in contemporary criminal justice.[7] Rather, it will be necessary to link reintegrative shaming to a more progressive vision of community and a more progressive moral theory.[8] Schneider's work is one resource for constructing such a progressive vision of reintegrative shaming. His work potentially challenges the notion that instilling people with a sense of shame is emotionally crippling and oppressive. As we have seen, he contends that the radical critics of shame have failed to appreciate its more positive side, and this is because they themselves adhere to an inadequate understanding of social identity and of the inter-connectedness of self and society. If we adopt a more radical sociological perspective, (not social determinism but a perspective which sees human identity as inherently social) a sense of shame appears both necessary and valuable.

Shaming as a politically questionable practice

In his critical analysis of modern shame sanctions in the USA, James Whitman (1998) rejects the standard arguments against such penalties: that they can never work in the modern Western world and that they are in some way inordinately cruel. The most compelling arguments against shame sanctions, he contends, have little to do with the way they deal with offenders, more to do with the way they deal with the public. Shame sanctions involve the government delegating part of its law enforcement power to the public. They involve turning certain types of offenders, especially sex offenders, commercial offenders and young offenders, over to ordinary members of the public to be judged by 'the established norms of public opinion' and subjected to whatever the public imagines is an appropriate degree of censure.

Part of the rationale for this delegation of law enforcement is that the public may be more effective in enforcing some norms than is the state. 'Official justice' is often too abstract and too distant from many types of offenders for its censure to make much of an impact upon their attitudes towards criminal behaviour. On the other hand, when people close to the offender express their disapproval, and explain the real human consequences of crime to them, they often have considerable influence (Garvey 1998).

For Whitman, however, the delegation of some law enforcement to the public is motivated by more than a concern for effective enforcement. It is also an attempt to change public norms. Whitman argues that the decision to involve the public in shaming offenders is part of an attempt to nudge prevailing views, about sexual morality, commercial morality and petty criminality, in a more moralistic direction, or at least to consolidate what had previously been a more vague and less effective consensus. Put more crudely, shame sanctions are an attempt to stir up public indignation – to create or enhance an impression that something is wrong and that the public ought to feel annoyed about it.

Whitman considers this development to be unhealthy and highly dangerous: the government is delegating its law enforcement responsibilities to a fickle and volatile populace; it is rousing dark sentiments and playing upon the irrational urges of the public; it is inciting the public to act in an undisciplined, unthinking way; it is indulging in a politics of the dark and volatile, a politics which represents a great threat to the democratic rule of law (1998: 1087–92). Hence, for Whitman, the core objection to shame sanctions is less that they are unacceptable as penal methods, more that they are questionable as political or cultural practices.

How much of this analysis applies to restorative conferencing? Restorative conferencing clearly involves delegation of responsibility for handling offenders to some members of the public, including victims and their supporters. And this is justified on the grounds that offenders are more likely to be influenced by such people, than they are by a formal justice process. But it is also clear that, at least in Braithwaite's highly influential accounts of reintegrative shaming, the value of the practice lies as much in its capacity to produce 'deep cultural changes' as it does in its capacity to reform individual offenders (Braithwaite 1998: 54). He argues that certain types of crime, such as domestic violence and white-collar crime, have persisted because they have enjoyed immunity from public disapproval. While formally defined as crimes, official justice can do little to control them whilst it is unsupported by strong public condemnation of such behaviour. With such support, on the other hand, the potency of official sanctions is increased, but they also become less necessary. Widespread public disapproval makes crime unthinkable for the vast majority of citizens. It keeps crime off our menu of ways to solve our problems. However, public disapproval of some forms of crime clearly needs to be aroused, and for Braithwaite, getting people to participate in the (reintegrative) shaming of offenders is the way to arouse it.

For Braithwaite, reintegrative shaming is clearly a social as well as a penal practice. Hence, Whitman's analysis of the political import of shame sanctions is applicable to the shaming that occurs in restorative conferencing, as well as to judicial shame penalties. Braithwaite and other proponents of restorative conference would no doubt argue, however, that Whitman's highly critical assessment is either wrong or applicable only to the disintegrative shaming on which he focuses. In restorative conferences, it could be argued, the public are invited to take part, not in an undisciplined ritual of public humiliation of offenders, but in a restrained and sober practice in which shaming is part of a broader process designed to condemn the wrongful behaviour but also to reintegrate the offending person into the community. Participation in such a process is less likely to awaken dark sentiments and irrational urges, more likely to produce a sober and constructive response, in which it is made clear that the offender's behaviour is unacceptable, but where this is done in a reasoned and reasonable way.

This, at least, is how proponents of restorative conferencing might respond. So far, they have not addressed such issues. Debate so far has tended to dwell on the efficacy of restorative shaming as a way of reforming offenders, and on its acceptability as a way of dealing with offenders. The issue of whether restorative shaming is acceptable as a way of dealing with the public has received little or no attention.

Apology and forgiveness

I turn now to the second part of Retzinger and Scheff's 'core sequence', the ritual of apology-forgiveness (1996: 316). As we have seen, this ritual plays a central role in the process of reintegrative shaming. It is crucial to the success of restorative conferencing that authentic apology, forgiveness and reconciliation take place. If they do not, and the offender has successfully been shamed, the outcome of the restorative conference process is likely to be stigmatisation and outcasting of offenders, rather than their reintegration. However, in insisting that rituals of apology and forgiveness should play a central role in our processes for dealing with offenders, proponents of restorative justice are also making an ethical challenge to our culture. In what follows I look very briefly at the nature of this ethical challenge and at some possible responses to it.

There was a time when it was considered acceptable to hate the criminal and when this attitude was strongly reflected in the treatment of offenders (Murphy and Hampton 1988). During the twentieth century, this attitude came to be regarded, at least by 'progressive opinion', as reactionary and distasteful. We prided ourselves on having outgrown that sort of thing. We regarded ourselves as civilised enough to show emotional restraint when confronted with the criminal and even to pity and feel sympathy for people who, perhaps due to some personality disorder or problem, might not really have been able to help what they did.[9] But in recent years there has been a retreat from this sympathetic attitude (Garland 2001). It has become more acceptable, and perhaps even more fashionable, openly to express anger, indignation or at least frustration with criminals, and our penal policies increasingly reflect this.

The call to incorporate rituals of apology-forgiveness into our criminal justice systems can be seen as an attempt, not only to recover the recently lost trend towards a more forgiving attitude to wrongdoers, but to move us much further than we have ever been along the road towards what its proponents see as a more generous, more mature and more constructive emotional response to criminals (Gorringe 1996). Proponents of restorative justice, while not denying either the legitimacy or even the usefulness of the resentment which people often feel towards criminals, insist that there comes a point when resentment becomes counterproductive. At that point, a shift from resentment to forgiveness is required if the justice process is to have positive outcomes.[10]

Some doubts about forgiveness

The most obvious question to ask about this advocacy of apology and forgiveness is whether it is realistic. Apology and forgiveness may work well as ways of healing rifts and settling disputes amongst people who are closely bound together, and who are eager to maintain and repair these bonds when they are threatened by some misdeed.[11] But many would regard it as over-optimistic to expect it to work between offenders and their victims in contemporary Western societies, in all but the smallest proportion of cases. Many offenders have too little in common with their victims to be able to share their view of the offence. Furthermore, few victims are saintly enough to be able to waive '*quid pro quo* justice' (Moule 1998: *x*). Consequently, we might well get offenders and victims to go through the motions of apology and forgiveness, but the ritual might not mean much to them.

However, the question of how realistic this ideal is should not, despite its importance, monopolise the debate. It is also important to ask about the desirability of the ideal. Such questioning has not been much evident in the debate about restorative conferencing, nor in the wider debate about restorative justice. This is no doubt because forgiveness, unlike shaming, seems indisputably to be a virtuous practice. We may doubt that it is possible in all cases to forgive those who have wronged us, but few question the ethical desirability of forgiveness.

As was the case with shame, however, the consensus is not complete. Classical deterrence theorists, such as Cesare Beccaria and Jeremy Bentham, regarded forgiveness of offenders as a vice, because it undermined the certainty of punishment and therefore encouraged crime (Moberly 1968: ch. 2). However, others have presented more complex ethical arguments in favour of seeing forgiveness, at least in some circumstances, as more of a vice than a virtue (Roberts 1995; Lang 1994; Murphy and Hampton 1988). For example, for Jeffrie Murphy, the passion of resentment defends the value of self-respect and a too ready tendency to forgive 'may be a sign that one lacks respect for oneself'

(Murphy and Hampton 1988: 16–7; *cf.* Murphy 2000). He accepts that forgiveness heals and restores and that without it 'resentment would remain as an obstacle to many human relationships we value'. He contends, however, that while, 'forgiveness may indeed restore relationships, … to seek restoration at all cost – even at the cost of one's very human dignity – can hardly be a virtue' (*ibid*: 17). For Murphy forgiveness is virtuous only where it is consistent with self-respect and respect for others as moral agents, and in compliance with certain other moral principles (*ibid*: 19).

Space does not permit a more detailed account of this more wary attitude towards forgiveness. However, from the little that has been stated, it should be clear that Murphy and others raise issues which are crucial to an adequate estimation of the value and acceptability of restorative conferencing. Restorative conferencing, and other measures designed to deliver restorative justice, promote as virtuous and constructive a particular way of feeling about offenders: we should try to give up our negative feelings about them (which does not mean condoning their actions); we should stop hating and desiring revenge; we should, (provided the offender offers reparation) forgive them. Such forgiveness is a central part of informal dispute settlement in many communities (Estrada-Hollenbeck 1996). Proponents of restorative conferencing aim to set up mechanisms within or on the borders of the formal criminal justice system which will facilitate such forgiveness processes. This is a noble ideal. But in assessing it, it is not enough to ask whether it is practical. Also, and perhaps primarily, it is important to ask whether, and in what circumstances, encouraging forgiveness is ethically appropriate. This involves recognising that there are some circumstances in which it may not be – that there are circumstances when, despite offers of apology and reparation, it is morally right to withhold forgiveness.

Notes

1 In the discourse of restorative cautioning it is common to refer to arrestees as 'offenders', although they have not been convicted, on the ground that they have admitted the offence to the police, such admission being a condition of their being deemed suitable for the conferencing option.

2 The debt to Braithwaite is acknowledged explicitly in publicity material for restorative conferencing schemes produced by the Restorative Justice Consultancy for the Thames Valley Police; see, for example, Thames Valley Police (1997: 10 and 18). From my own conversations with police officers

involved in developing and running restorative cautioning schemes, it is clear that Braithwaite's ideas are a major influence. On the other hand, few have even heard of the work of Christie (1977), which is much cited in 'academic' literature as one of the foundational works of the restorative justice movement (e.g. von Hirsch and Ashworth 1998: 302).

3 In what follows my concern is simply to describe some ethical issues concerning shaming and to point to some directions which the debate might fruitfully take. A rigorous analysis of these issues is well beyond the scope of this book.

4 See Whitman (1998: 1055–6), who provides a brief account of the use of shame as a penal method around the World today. On the use of the concept of 'civilization' in conventional stories of penal progress see Garland (1990: 214–215) and Pratt (2000).

5 Martin Wright, personal communication.

6 Space does not permit anything more than the crudest summary of what is a very complex and detailed argument.

7 For the kind of critique this invites, see Watts (1996).

8 Braithwaite and others do attempt to link restorative justice with the political theory of republicanism (Braithwaite and Strang 2000; Walgrave 2000; *cf.* Braithwaite and Pettit 1990).

9 Even those who are old-fashioned enough to retain a belief in evil tend towards the view that evil people are that way because they themselves are suffering from some deep unhappiness. On the partial medicalization of criminality, see Johnstone (1996).

10 But in the discourse of restorative justice, in order to obtain forgiveness, offenders must apologise. Through apologising, offenders acknowledge they have done wrong, accept responsibility for the harm they have created, express remorse and show they want forgiveness (Tavuchis 1991: *vii*; Roberts 1995). By apologising, the offender demonstrates 'that he takes (roughly) the same position of moral disapproval of the offense as the offended one takes' (Roberts 1995: 193).

11 On the sociology of apology see Tavuchis (1991).

Chapter 7

Mediation, participation and the role of community

Introduction: handling criminal conflicts

A basic goal of the restorative justice campaign is to establish new forums and processes to which many criminal cases currently dealt with by conventional criminal justice forums and processes can be diverted either at the pre-trial or sentencing stage. One of the key distinctive features of these new forums and processes is that they are intended to promote restorative outcomes, such as reparation of harm to people and relationships, healing of victims, and reintegration of offenders. However, restorative justice also differs *procedurally* from the conventional criminal justice process. In order to introduce the most important of these procedural differences, it is useful to think of crime in the way proposed by proponents of restorative justice, i.e. as a conflict.[1] In many crimes, one person has harmed another, directly or indirectly, through a wrongful act. The injured parties – the direct victim and others indirectly harmed – seek redress for this wrongful harm. They may want retributive punishment or they may want restitution or reparation, but in either event, there is a conflict between two or more parties. How is this conflict to be handled?

Conventional criminal process

In the conventional criminal justice process, such conflicts are frequently taken to court. A group of professionals – police and prosecutors – prepare and present the case against the suspect, on behalf of the victim and community. Usually, the suspect will also be represented by a professional lawyer. A neutral third party (such as a magistrate or judge/jury) has the power to decide which party wins. If the suspect wins, i.e. if he or she is found 'not guilty', the process comes to an end. Those seeking redress, if they wish to continue, must do so through other processes (for example, if they have the resources, they might initiate a private law action for damages against the suspect). If the prosecution wins the case, i.e. the offender is found 'guilty', the neutral third party (the magistrate or judge, but not the jury) then decides what the offender must undergo or do in order to pay for the crime and in order to protect the public.

The offender might be sentenced to spend some time in prison, to comply with a probation order, to pay a fine to the state, to pay restitution to the victim, to undertake reparative acts, or to do community service, or to some combination of these. The decision-maker has considerable discretion in sentencing (Norrie 1993: ch. 10; von Hirsch and Ashworth 1998). In using this discretion, sentencers are guided by: legal statutes, which lay down maximum and sometimes minimum sentences which may be imposed for an offence; standards set in similar cases in the same jurisdiction; and (increasingly) sentencing guidelines. Sentencers will usually attempt to impose a sentence which they think is consistent with those imposed in similar cases, proportionate to the seriousness of crime, and necessary for public protection. In deciding what sentence to impose, sentencers frequently consult with other professionals (such as probation officers, social workers, and psychiatrists). Also, there may be some negotiation and bargaining behind the scenes between the lawyers representing the offender and those representing the state, which can result in an 'agreed' sentence to be proposed to the sentencer.

Throughout the whole process the parties to the conflict – the victim, offender and the community – usually remain passive, silent and uninvolved (although, as we have seen, there are strong moves towards giving victims a more active role and an effective voice within the sentencing stage of process). For the most part, the conflicting parties are confined to the role of onlookers. They tend to be represented by lawyers and other professionals who decide which arguments to use, which facts to present, etc. If the parties to the conflict become involved at all, they usually do so as witnesses to the alleged crime, in which case they simply answer questions put to them by lawyers (i.e. they will not present arguments). The disputing parties play no role in making the key decisions, which are imposed from above, by the neutral third party.

Restorative process

Proponents of restorative justice tend to accept that if the suspect denies responsibility for the alleged offence, the case must be dealt with in the conventional way. They argue, however, that if at any stage the offender admits involvement and responsibility (but not necessarily legal guilt), the question of what should be done about the matter should be decided through a very different procedure. Instead of a neutral third party deciding what the offender should undergo or do to pay for the crime and ensure public safety, such matters should be decided through an informal, consensual and participatory procedure. The key distinctive features of this procedure are as follows.

First, although there is still a relatively neutral third party involved,[2] the power and role of that party changes. Instead of having the power to decide what the offender should undergo or do, his/her role changes to facilitating the 'primary stakeholders' in the conflict to reach a mutually acceptable decision about what the offender should undergo or do. The third party's role is to mediate or facilitate, rather than to decide. The key decisions are made by the 'primary stakeholders' in the conflict, i.e. the victim, the offender and their respective support groups.

It is important to note that in some actual programmes, the agreement must be approved by a judge, who therefore has the power to veto decisions considered to be not in the public interest or significantly out of line with public standards of justice. But most restorative justice proponents feel that such judicial interference should be kept to a minimum. Although they accept that the state, representing the general public, has a legitimate interest in the outcome of a criminal case and that it may in extreme cases be necessary to interfere with the decision reached by the primary stakeholders, they tend to insist that the decision reached by the primary stakeholders should rarely be overruled.[3]

A second way in which the restorative justice process differs is that the 'sentencing' decision is not made by reference to legal rules, precedents, sentencing guidelines, etc. Rather, the sentence can be anything which the primary stakeholders find mutually acceptable as a way of repairing the harm caused by the crime and ensuring the safety of the community. For example, if the victim of an assault wants an apology and £100 compensation, and the community thinks the perpetrator should also agree to being 'curfewed' at night and to meeting regularly with a circle of support and accountability, and the offender finds these proposals acceptable, then from a restorative justice perspective, this is what should happen. The fact that, in a similar case, the offender was sent to prison for one year is immaterial. So is the fact that the court might think that the offender needs to go to prison in order to protect the public. It is assumed that the community *which knows the offender* is in the best position to judge how much of a threat the perpetrator represents and how likely it is that certain measures will succeed in controlling him or her.

A third distinguishing feature of the restorative justice process is that the primary stakeholders represent themselves. Professional lawyers are usually not involved in the process, and if they are the ideal – from a restorative justice perspective – is to keep them in the background. The parties to the conflict make their own arguments, introduce whatever facts they feel are relevant, express their feelings about the matter, etc. Ideally all of the primary stakeholders play an active, participatory role. They are at the centre of the action rather than onlookers in a game played by lawyers and other professionals.

The dialogue is not, however, completely unstructured. Usually, especially in Family Group Conferencing, there is a script, designed by restorative justice experts to help ensure that restorative outcomes are achieved, which facilitators are expected to follow, either to the letter or in spirit. Following the script the facilitators will commence the process by: introducing the parties; telling everyone that 'we are here to focus on what X (the offender) did and the effects of X's unacceptable behaviour, not to judge whether X is a good or bad person; ask first the offender and then the victim to tell what happened; ask X whom they think was harmed by their actions; ask X if they want to say anything to the others, etc. (Real Justice 2000).

Other differences

From these basic differences, other important differences follow.

- In conventional criminal justice, matters are decided in a courthouse, a special place reserved for deciding legal disputes. Restorative justice usually takes place in non-specialised settings, such as a room at a police station, in a school or in a community centre.

- Conventional criminal justice is highly formal. In restorative justice formality is kept to a minimum, reflected in the way people dress, address each other and so on.

- In conventional criminal justice the dialogue has an air of technicality about it; in restorative justice, all the dialogue consists of ordinary language which everybody involved can understand.

- Conventional criminal justice is designed to keep the offender and victim(s) apart and to curb emotional expression. In restorative justice, offenders and victims engage each other directly and positive attempts are made to encourage the expression of feelings (Morris and Young 2000). There is a great deal of crying, hugging, expressions of love and upset, etc. Part of the preparation for the process includes ensuring that there is a box of tissues to be passed around. Whereas conventional criminal justice can seem cold and detached, restorative justice can seem sentimental.

The rationale for the restorative justice *process*

Why do proponents of restorative justice prefer this restorative justice process to the conventional criminal justice procedure? This is a matter over which there is some confusion. I suggest that it is crucial to distinguish between two quite different rationales for the restorative justice process.

1. The process is seen as better suited than conventional criminal processes for achieving restorative goals, such as reparation of harm, reconciliation of conflicting parties, and public safety.

2. The process is seen as having the potential to achieve a range of other goals, including: increasing the participants' sense of personal efficacy and power; increasing the capacity of parties locked in conflict to 'recognise' the other party; and increasing the confidence, capacity and inclination of ordinary members of the community to resolve their own disputes and keep their own order.

It is crucial to realise that this second set of rationales exists. It is also important to realise that, for some proponents, this second set of rationales is more important than the first set. That is to say, for some, reaching a mutually acceptable agreement and improving relationships between conflicting parties is less important than empowering individuals, promoting recognition and increasing the capacity of communities to handle their own conflicts. Crucially, some would argue that a restorative justice process is preferable to a conventional criminal process even if it fails to result in an agreement about reparation, or even if an agreement reached seems to reflect punitive values and concerns rather than restorative values and concerns (Barton 2000). On this view, even if restorative justice processes start resulting in punitive outcomes, they should not be overruled and the process should still be supported and encouraged. The important fact is that it empowers primary stake-holders, strengthens communities, etc.

Achieving restorative goals

It should not be taken for granted that a restorative justice process is necessary in order to achieve restorative outcomes. A conventional criminal justice process can result in an offender being ordered to pay restitution to the victim, or to undertake community service to repair the harm the crime has done to the community (Walgrave 1995), or to submit to measures designed to monitor his or her behaviour. Indeed, in the UK, the term restorative justice is frequently applied to programmes in which reparation is emphasised, but in which there is little evidence of a restorative justice process. Hence, we need to ask why a restorative justice process is regarded by most proponents as more suited than conventional criminal processes for achieving restorative goals.

To discern the claimed advantages of a restorative justice process, it is useful to consider what might result if we attempt to achieve restorative objectives through a conventional criminal justice process. To do this I will consider a hypothetical, but common enough, scenario: two youths have pleaded guilty to robbing a bag from a woman in a street – the bag contained £20 cash, some credit cards, various keys, a driver's licence, toiletries and some other personal items. Suppose the magistrate (a progressive, reflective practitioner who has heard about the good which can result from reparative sentences) decides that, as this is their first conviction, instead of imposing a purely punitive sentence he or she will order the offenders to write a letter of apology to the victim and pay her £50 compensation, the money to be earned by working in a community service programme in which offenders wash police cars for re-muneration. How likely is it that this order will result in the victim being healed, the offender reintegrated, further offending prevented, and the parties being reconciled? Proponents of restorative justice would say something like the following.

The first question is whether the order will be complied with. Proponents of restorative justice claim that people are far more likely to do things they have agreed to do, than to do things which they have been ordered to do, and that default levels are therefore likely to be lower in restorative justice than in conventional criminal justice. But suppose that, in this case, the offenders have complied with the order. Will this result in repair of harm, etc.?

Let us look at the scenario, first from the victim's perspective. Will the letter of apology and the money repair the harm she has suffered? And will she experience justice? To answer these questions we have to look at the harm she may have suffered.

As we saw in chapter four, studies of the victim experience suggest that this victim will have suffered considerable shock in the immediate aftermath of the incident. Following that, she will have had a great deal of trouble and expense. She will have had to get new locks fitted, obtain new keys, cancel credit cards and have them reissued, apply for a replacement driver's licence, claim insurance, etc. In addition, she may have been affected in less obvious ways; for example, she may have been planning an important trip abroad the next day, but had to cancel it. Once all these practicalities are taken care of some longer-term psychological effects will set in. She may feel nervous about walking in the street. She may feel upset that some personal items have been handled by thieves and discarded in some unknown place. She may also worry that the offenders will seek revenge because she gave a statement to the police which led to their arrest and conviction. These anxieties may affect her work and private relationships, and so on.

By way of reparation she has received a letter of apology which the offenders were *ordered* to write and £50 (which she may have to deduct from her insurance claim). She will probably regard these as wholly inadequate compensation for the trouble and trauma she has suffered. Nor will they do anything to put an end to the anxiety which she continues to suffer. Indeed, she may now feel bitter about the fact that the persons who caused her all this harm have got off so lightly. She may feel that rather than receiving justice from the criminal justice system, she has received a further insult.

The direct victim is not, of course, the only person who will have been harmed by this offence. Along with other offences, this robbery will have contributed to a general feeling of insecurity and to a lowering of the moral tone of the community. It also sets a bad example for other youths. However, the reparation order will do little to reassure members of the community that they will be safer or to improve the moral atmosphere.

Let us turn now to the offenders? Will the carrying out of this order render them less likely to reoffend? Will it help them to become reintegrated into the community of law-abiding citizens? As we saw in chapter five, to achieve these goals they would have to made aware of the extent of the harm their actions had caused, their rationalizations for their behaviour would have to be penetrated, they would need to be exposed to the disapproval of people whose opinion of them mattered, and they would have to undertake reparative acts voluntarily in order to redeem themselves.

The court case, conviction and reparation order are unlikely to achieve any of these things. The more likely outcome is that that will feel relieved that they have got off fairly lightly this time. Their brush with the law may lead them to avow not to commit further offences for the purely prudential reason that they might receive a heavier penalty next time. On the other hand, their relatively soft punishment may encourage them to risk further crimes. Nevertheless, despite receiving a light sentence, their conviction for a serious crime will result in them being socially identified as criminals. This will result in them being shunned by many respectable members of their community. Other offenders, however, may now be willing to welcome them into their sub-cultures, as people who have proved themselves.

Now let us look at some of the things that might have happened, according to its proponents, if once the offenders had admitted the crime they had been dealt with through a restorative justice process. The victim would have had an opportunity to explain to the offenders how the crime had affected her life and she would have been able to express her feelings about the matter. She might have heard the offenders express remorse and offer what seemed like a genuine apology. She might have heard the offenders *offer* to pay compensation and to work hard to earn the money to do so. She might have heard the offenders reassure her that they bore her no grudge and that they would not be causing her any further trouble. She might have heard people who care about the offender scold them harshly and offer to exercise closer supervision over them, yet at the same time reveal information about their circumstances and character which would put the offence in a somewhat different light. She will have had the opportunity to accept or refuse the apology and/or offer of compensation, to explain her decision, and to propose some different resolution. She might have felt that she had considerable control within the process and over the outcome. All of these things, as we saw in chapter four, could make a significant contribution to her recovery from the experience of being victimised.

The offenders, on hearing from the victim about the harm they had caused, in the presence of people whose opinion of them mattered to them, might have experienced shame and remorse. They may have felt an urge to apologise without being ordered to do so. They may have offered to do something (perhaps more than ordered by the judge) to make up for the harm they had caused. The fact that the offer of reparation was their idea, rather than something they had been ordered to do, might have made them feel good about themselves, because they were voluntarily doing something to repair harm rather than cause it. Their expressions of genuine remorse, accompanied by strong efforts to make amends for their wrongdoing, might have earned them the respect of law-abiding members of the community and perhaps even of the victim. All of this, combined with the support and monitoring of family members and other people who cared about them, might have led them to reform themselves, not because they were afraid of the legal consequences should they be caught again, but because they realised that crime is morally unacceptable. All of this, it is claimed, might make the community feel more secure and might help repair the sense of moral order which had been damaged by the crime.

Moral development and the strengthening of community

Pointing to the advantages, or even the necessity, of a restorative justice process for achieving restorative goals is the most common way of seeking to justify such a process. However, running through the discourse of restorative justice is the suggestion that the restorative justice process is a desirable way of handling criminal conflicts because it has the potential to engender moral growth and a sense of community. The restorative justice process, on this view, is to be preferred not just because it is the best way of achieving restorative goals such as reparation of harm and reduction of reoffending, but because it can reap the opportunities for moral development and community-building which criminal conflicts provide us with.

It should be emphasised that this vision of the potential of restorative justice processes is seldom proposed as their primary justification and indeed, is seldom clearly articulated.[4] Nevertheless, the idea is important enough to warrant consideration in more detail.

Conflicts as opportunities

To identify what, following Bush and Folger (1994), I will call the 'transformative potential' of restorative justice processes, it is necessary to question some common assumptions about what conflict is and what the ideal response to conflict should be (*ibid*: 81). It is often taken for granted that conflict between members of a community is abnormal – a temporary disruption of a normal state of equilibrium and harmony – and a bad thing.[5] Accordingly, it is presumed that conflicts should be solved quickly and conclusively, thereby restoring peace and harmony.

Such assumptions are challenged by some proponents of restorative justice, most notably Christie (1977; 1982: ch. 11). Christie suggests that conflicts between members of a community should be viewed as 'something of value, a commodity not to be wasted' (1982: 93). Indeed, he suggests, we should cultivate conflicts (1977: 1). Conflicts should be viewed less as problems, more as opportunities. For example, Christie stresses the opportunities conflicts provide for 'norm-clarification', i.e. for understanding and deciding the precise meaning, range and appropriate application of a particular norm or law (1977: 8).

For Christie, if such opportunities are to be taken advantage of, we need to rid ourselves of the assumption that conflicts should be resolved as quickly as possible. Instead, conflicts should ideally give rise to a more protracted 'political' debate, in which the whole community participates, and in which there are no exclusionary rules preventing people from introducing facts and arguments which they consider relevant (*ibid*). To the objection that there might be no end to such a debate, Christie responds by suggesting that maybe there ought to be no end (*ibid*). Indeed, he questions whether we should be concerned at all to solve conflicts:

> ... it is important not to presuppose that conflict ought to be solved. The quest for solution is a puritan, ethnocentric conception. ... Conflicts might be solved, but they might also be lived with ... maybe participation is more important than solutions.
>
> (1982: 92–3)

Crucially, if people are to exploit the opportunities provided by conflicts, they must not delegate their handling to professionals or as Christie also puts it, they must not let the state 'steal' their conflicts. It is only by handling conflicts themselves that people can seize the opportunities which they provide. It is through participation in the handling of conflict that we acquire the ability for norm-clarification and other arts of citizenship.

Christie's work has been an important influence on the campaign for restorative justice (e.g. Cayley 1998: ch. 10). However, it is very important to realize that most restorative justice proponents do not go nearly as far as Christie in viewing criminal conflicts as valuable com- modities.[6] Most would regard 'criminal conflicts' as serious problems in need of solutions. Their arguments are mainly about the type of solution required, rather than about whether conflict is good or bad or about whether resolution is really necessary and desirable. Nevertheless, many proponents of restorative justice would agree with a much more moderate version of Christie's argument. Whilst they certainly see criminal conflicts as bad things, they also seem, at times, to recognize that they do create opportunities for learning and developing and for growing stronger. And, in line with Christie, they think that if these opportunities are to be seized, the primary stakeholders in the conflict must play a leading role in deciding how they should be resolved.

For Christie, the most important opportunity provided by conflict is that for norm-clarification. This idea, however, has quite radical implications (in terms of politicising criminal law) which, when they become clear, are unlikely to appeal much to most mainstream advocates of restorative justice.[7] However, Bush and Folger (1994), who share many of Christie's radical ideas about conflict, emphasise rather different opportunities provided by conflict, opportunities for *empowerment* and *recognition*. Their views are, I think, likely to be more attractive to mainstream proponents of restorative justice.

Empowerment and recognition

Bush and Folger argue that mediation processes (of which restorative justice would be an example) have the unique potential, albeit largely unfulfilled, to generate empowerment and recognition. They suggest that a mediation process should be regarded as successful if it produces empowerment and recognition, even if it fails to result in a (reparative) agreement and even it fails to improve relationships between conflicting parties. However, they also suggest that when mediators work for empowerment and recognition, they usually also achieve a mutually acceptable agreement between disputing parties and some degree of reconciliation.

What do Bush and Folger mean by empowerment and recognition? And, how are these effects to be achieved through mediation of conflicts? Empowerment occurs when a person realizes and strengthens their 'inherent human capacity for dealing with difficulties of all kinds by engaging in conscious and deliberate reflection, choice and action' (1994: 81). Recognition occurs when a person realizes and strengthens their 'inherent human capacity for experiencing and expressing concern and consideration for others, especially others whose situation is "different" from one's own' (*ibid*). Alternatively:

> Empowerment is achieved when disputing parties experience a strengthened awareness of their own self-worth and their own ability to deal with whatever difficulties they face, regardless of external constraints. Recognition is achieved when, given some

degree of empowerment, disputing parties experience an ex-
panded willingness to acknowledge and be responsive to other
parties' situations and common human qualities.

(ibid: 84-5)

Bush and Folger argue that developing and integrating these inherent
human capacities is the essence of human moral development (ibid:
81-2).

Crucially, they argue, conflicts provide us with opportunities for
developing and integrating these capacities. They give each party a
chance to become conscious of and to enhance their own resources for
addressing substantive concerns and relational issues. They give each
party the opportunity to develop and use self-reliance (ibid: 82). Further,
each party in a conflict is confronted with 'a differently situated other
who holds a contrary viewpoint' (ibid). Hence, each party has the
opportunity to experience and communicate understanding of and
concern for the other, despite diversity and disagreement:

> Conflict thus gives people the occasion to develop and exercise
> respect and consideration for others. In sum, conflicts embody
> valuable opportunities for both dimensions of moral growth,
> perhaps to a greater degree than most other human experiences.

(ibid: 82)

Given that conflict provides us with these opportunities, the
productive response is not to try to resolve it as quickly as possible.
Rather, it is to utilize the opportunities which conflicts present to
transform the parties as human beings. Conflicts ought to be used to
actualise the intrinsic capacity for strength of self and for relating to
others which humans possess. Conflicts should be used to 'transform
individuals from fearful, defensive, or self-centred beings into confident,
responsive and caring ones' (ibid: 82-3).

According to Bush and Folger, one way of harvesting such opportunities is to handle them through a process of mediation. However,
whilst such moral development may sometimes occur by chance within
a mediation process, in order to maximise the chances of it occurring,
achieving it should be the conscious and primary goal of the process.
Mediation processes should be designed, primarily, to take full advantage of the opportunities for fostering moral growth which conflict
presents. The main goal of mediation processes should be not to bring
about agreements and improve relationships between the parties, but to
change the parties as persons for the better (ibid: 82-3). As Bush and

Folger put it, the objective of mediation should be, not to improve the parties' situation from what it was before, but to improve the parties themselves from what they were before (*ibid*: 83).

How do we design mediation processes to maximise the chances of achieving empowerment and recognition? First, these terms must be defined as concretely as possible, so that the phenomena can be recognized when they occur. Accordingly, Bush and Folger provide a long list of quite precise indicators of empowerment and recognition (*ibid*: ch. 4). They go on to present some very detailed and concrete discussion of how mediators can recognize and take transformative routes as they arise during mediation (*ibid*: ch. 5). Such advice does not lend itself to easy summary, but at a more general level, they suggest that mediators should avoid thinking of their role as being to solve people's problems, to resolve their disputes, and to meet the needs of both parties to a conflict. Instead, they should: encourage parties to define their problems and goals in their own terms; help parties to decide for themselves how, and even whether, they should settle their conflict; help parties to identify and employ whatever personal resources they have which will help them address their problems and achieve their goals; and provide parties with 'a nonthreatening opportunity to explain and humanize themselves to one another' (*ibid*: 20).

Even more generally, Bush and Folger suggest that mediators should not think that there is an optimal solution to the conflict between the parties, which they, as professionals, can identify and steer the parties toward. Mediators should instead use their capacity for assisting human interaction to allow the parties themselves to identify and deal with their problems in their way, even if, in the mediator's view, they fail to identify the core of the real problem and they come up with solutions which are likely to be ineffective or even not in their interests. In other words, Bush and Folger suggest that mediators should seek to maximise the participants' ownership of their conflict. To achieve this the mediators must recognise that the point of the process is not to get better solutions but to morally develop the conflicting parties.

Before drawing out some implications of this argument for the development of restorative justice (which, we should remember, had its roots in, and is still very much about, victim-offender mediation), it is necessary to explain that Bush and Folger's ambitions extend well beyond the reform of the practice of mediation. Through restructuring mediation, so that it achieves its transformative potential, they believe that it is possible to contribute to the creation of a better humanity and a better society. This is because, when people are changed for the better through mediation, the interactions they have with others – in their families, businesses, neighbourhoods and institutions – will in turn be altered. Hence:

> The effects of mediation reach beyond the settlement of particular disputes and have a cumulative impact on the larger social arenas in which daily interactions unfold in our society.
>
> (*ibid*: *xv–xvi*)

So, developing a transformative approach to mediation 'would support and further a progressive shift in human consciousness' (*ibid*: 230).

The approach to mediation which Bush and Folger advocate is driven by a particular view of human nature and society, which they call a 'relational worldview' (*ibid*: 229; cf. Burnside and Baker 1994). What is at stake, then, for Bush and Folger, is not simply a choice between two styles of mediation. Rather, that choice reflects a more fundamental choice between an individualist worldview, in which satisfying individuals' needs and desires is the ultimate goal and value, and a relational worldview, in which 'the most important value is trans-formation, the achievement of human conduct that integrates strength of self and compassion towards others' (Bush and Folger 1994: 242).[8]

The potential of restorative justice

It must be re-emphasised that Bush and Folger are discussing potential rather than actuality. Their view is that the mediation movement has largely failed to fulfil its potential to change people for the better in the midst of conflict. Whilst mediation was initially conceived as a transformative process, over recent decades it has increasingly been understood and practiced as a settlement-producing, problem-solving technology. As a result, mediation has more and more failed to respond to opportunities to promote empowerment and recognition. Bush and Folger's book is not a description of mediation as it is currently practiced, but an attempt to alter radically the goals and practices of mediation.

To turn to restorative justice (a particular form of mediation), it is arguable that it is in much the same position as mediation in general. It is increasingly understood as a technique for (a) bringing about agreement which, if complied with, will result in the harm caused by crime being repaired and the likelihood of the offender reoffending being reduced and (b) improving relationships between the victim and offender. The emphasis is on making the situation better for victims and offenders. The success of restorative justice interventions is increasingly measured in terms of the extent to which they satisfy the needs of victims, turn offenders away from criminal careers, and produce some degree of reconciliation. Certainly, a restorative justice process which failed to result in an apology and reparation agreement, which failed to improve the offender's behaviour in subsequent months and years and failed to make any improvement in relationships between victim and offender, would be regarded as completely unsuccessful.

This relatively 'narrow' vision of the potential of restorative justice is not completely unchallenged. Within the restorative justice movement there is an undercurrent – albeit one which is rarely articulated or vocally proclaimed – which does emphasise the goal of moral development of parties in conflict. And, behind this, there is some emphasis in restorative justice on promoting a relational worldview. This is perhaps most pronounced in some of the essays in Burnside and Baker's edited collection, *Relational Justice* (1994).[9] But by and large, restorative justice is increasingly being thought about and practised as a valued technology for facilitating collaborative, integrative problem-solving and satisfying the needs of parties affected detrimentally by criminal incidents. The question of whether it is successful is being asked by reference to those relatively limited ambitions.

If we applied Bush and Folger's analysis, we might instead measure the success of restorative justice, not by reference to whether it achieves its declared goals, but by reference to whether it fulfils its true potential to instill in people caught up in social conflict the power to solve problems themselves, a sense of control over their own lives, and an ability to see their adversaries as real persons with real human needs. Restorative justice arguably has the potential to do far more than provide a satisfactory way of dealing with some crimes and to turn some young offenders away from a life of crime. It may have the potential to make an impact on the sense of disempowerment that is rampant in modern societies, and which lies behind much of the crime problem and the problematic punitive and exclusionary response to it (Garland 2001). It is arguable that, to the extent that restorative justice fails to realize this potential – which is recognized by many of its proponents – we should regard it as failing. At the moment, however, it is seldom evaluated against such high standards. Instead, experiments in restorative justice are being assessed and presented as great successes because they purportedly achieve some much more limited, albeit useful, goals. By Bush and Folger's standards, restorative justice has lowered its sights and reduced its ambitions.

The role of community

As we have seen, a key distinctive feature of the restorative justice process is that it involves the primary stakeholders in the handling of their own conflict. But who are the primary stakeholders? In early experiments in victim-offender mediation the tendency was to assume that they were the direct victim and offender. However, many who were sympathetic towards the ideas of restorative justice which arose from these experiments nevertheless criticised such victim-offender mediation for being too 'private' and for failing to involve the community (Zehr 1990: 256).[10] Whilst there was some emphasis on community justice in the rhetoric of the victim-offender mediation movement, in practice community involvement was limited to some lay people serving as volunteer mediators.

One of the important features of later experiments which are now included under the rubric of restorative justice – such as family group conferences and sentencing circles – is that they involve a larger number and wider range of people in the process as stakeholders. FGCs include immediate and sometimes extended family members of offenders, family members and other 'supporters' of victims, and others such as youth advocates and police officers. Sentencing circles, which have so far been used almost exclusively in cases involving aboriginal offenders, further extend the range of actors involved. A wide range of 'interested community members' are invited to take part, and do take part, in the sentencing circle. Of all the main forms of restorative justice, sentencing circles (perhaps along with 'circles of support and accountability') can lay the largest claim to being expressions of community justice.

Despite these developments, the idea of involving the community in the process by which criminal conflicts are handled has remained largely a distant ideal. Shortly, I will look briefly at some ideas which have been proposed for closing the gap between ideal and actuality. First, though, it is necessary to look briefly at what proponents of restorative justice hope to achieve by involving the community, however it is defined, in the process.

The rationale for community involvement

Again, there are two quite different rationales for community participation in restorative justice processes and these correspond to the justifications for participation of victims and offenders in the process. First, it is thought that the offender's community is the entity with the most power to influence the offender to repair the harm he or she has caused and to refrain from further anti-social behaviour and also an entity which can provide support which offenders will need in their efforts to go straight. The community, that is to say, is a key resource for achieving restorative goals. Second, however, involving the community in the handling of criminal conflicts between its members is seen as a way of *empowering* communities in something like the Bush and Folger sense, i.e. developing its inherent capacity to regulate itself. For some, involving members of the community in the handling of criminal conflicts is a way of strengthening the community (Kurki 2000: 267). As Cayley, drawing on Christie, puts it:

> Community … is made from conflict as much as from cooperation; the capacity to resolve conflict is what gives social relations their sinew. Professionalizing justice 'steals the conflicts,' robbing the community of its ability to face trouble and restore peace. Communities lose the confidence, their capacity, and finally their inclination to preserve their own order. They become instead consumers of police and court 'services,' with the consequence that they largely cease to be communities.
>
> (Cayley 198: 168)

Such arguments provide a way of responding to those critics who contend that, since restorative justice requires the existence of a sense of community, and since such a sense is lacking in modern society, restorative justice in modern society is a pipedream (see chapter three). According to some proponents, the very lack of opportunities for meaningful lay participation in the criminal justice process is one of the reasons why we have such weak communities. Involving local residents in the handling of criminal conflicts is one way of revitalizing a sense of community among neighbours (Christie 1977: 12). The weaker our communities, the more we need to involve them in the justice process.

Community involvement: the reality

Such is the ideal; but, how do we translate it into an actuality? Fostering lay participation in the criminal justice process is not simply a matter of making opportunities for participation available. People must be persuaded to become involved. In modern societies, where the majority of people tend to divide their time between work and leisure, with little time left for civic duty, getting a representative range of people to volunteer for any civic duty is difficult enough. But getting people to become involved in doing criminal justice poses extra difficulties. Criminal justice is usually seen as being about punishment or, as Nils Christie puts it, 'pain delivery'. Many citizens may prefer not to be directly involved in such pain delivery because they fear the repercussions for themselves and because they do not want to see themselves as participants in or accomplices to the infliction of pain (although this may be changing, *cf.* Garland 2001). Hence, we prefer to delegate such tasks to professionals, to be carried out in private away from the public gaze (Garland 1990: 216*ff*). This is not just because we have not got the time, but also and perhaps primarily because we have not got the inclination to perform such tasks ourselves (Christie 1982: 104). Restorative justice proponents claim, of course, that restorative justice is not about pain delivery. But, as indicated in chapter five, the claim is not completely persuasive; so long as it takes place within a criminal justice context, restorative justice is likely to be perceived as being about doing unpleasant things to people who have themselves done unpleasant things.

Advocates of restorative justice are increasingly identifying community participation and development as essential elements of restorative justice (Kurki 2000: 267). Yet it is clear that in practice, most restorative justice programmes (outside of aboriginal communities) have not only failed to encourage wide community involvement, but have failed to address seriously the issue of what role the community should play in the programme and how community participation is to be fostered (McCold 1996: 90). I will conclude this chapter by looking at some of the few attempts to think through aspects of these problems with any degree of rigour.

Operationalising the notion of community involvement

One attempt to analyse the role of the community in restorative justice is that of McCold (1996). McCold does not seem quite clear about what the rationale of community involvement is. He starts by depicting the community as a secondary victim of crime. The community as victim has needs arising out of the commission of a crime and hence an interest in how it is dealt with. The community seemingly has a *right* to participate in the criminal justice process as a stakeholder. At the same time, the community seems to have a *duty to assume responsibility* for the resolution and prevention of crime (*ibid*: 90). It cannot leave these tasks to statutory agencies as these are unable to prevent the never-ending supply of victims and offenders. This idea is neatly expressed by Leslie Kennedy:

much misbehavior occurs outside of the influence of these agencies and must be confronted and controlled through informal means available to the community. The informal processes of mediation and conflict management practised by the community outside of the courts are important ways of reducing these problems.[11]

(Kennedy 1990: *xi*)

Having argued that restorative justice programmes require community involvement, McCold goes on to attempt to determine what counts as 'community' for the purpose of restorative justice. Although, in my view, he fails to provide a satisfactory answer, he does make a very important point. He argues that within the restorative justice paradigm, 'community' cannot be defined *'a priori'*; rather, what counts as community depends on the nature of the conflict. For purposes of restorative justice, the relevant community does not exist independently of the conflict, it is brought into being by the conflict. Hence, the definition of a community in any particular case will depend on things like the level of harm inflicted, the relationships of the victim and offender, and the 'aggregation' represented. McCold gives the following examples:

Consider a dispute between two young siblings. The boundary of the community whose interest is at stake is limited to the family. Should the conflict exist between married partners and the injury involve physical harm, the boundary of the interested community widens to include, at the least, other non-primary family members and associates. Where the conflict is between ambassadors from differing countries, the scope of the community at stake is on a much different scale.

(McCold 1996: 91–2)

One of the problems with this argument is that we cannot determine, simply by looking at the nature of the conflict, where the boundary of the community whose interests are at stake should be drawn. For example, with what McCold calls 'normal stranger crime', the relevant community could be the entire nation (at least), since arguably every single such crime makes some contribution to the general fear of crime in the nation as well as causing other social harm. Yet, in any modern nation, it would clearly be impractical to involve directly in a criminal justice case every individual affected indirectly by the crime (even allowing for modern means of communication such as the internet). This seems to take us back to the conventional criminal justice view that the community should be represented in the criminal justice process by the public prosecutor(s). But then the community is not directly involved in the process and – to the extent that direct community involvement is a defining feature – we do not have restorative justice.

McCold deals with this dilemma by suggesting that the boundaries of community be drawn quite narrowly, to encompass only those with a direct concern in a particular dispute:

> it seems prudent to consider the minimal necessary boundary of community as that limited to parties with a direct stake (need and responsibility) in the specific conflict.
>
> (*ibid*: 92)

Unfortunately, this does not take us any further; in trying to decide who has a 'direct stake' we are back with our original problem. Community, so defined, clearly includes what McCold calls the 'personal com-munities' of the victim and the offender, i.e. 'those individuals who know and are personally involved in the lives of the victim and/or the offender' (*ibid*). But, McCold does not want to restrict the 'community' to such personal communities. He also wants to include what he calls the 'local community'. However, his definition of 'local community' is simply lifted from a dictionary:

> a social group of any size whose members reside in a specific locality, share government, and have a common culture and historical heritage.
>
> (Stein 1979: 272, quoted in McCold 1996: 92)

It is difficult to see how this conceptual definition helps solve the practical problem of determining who has the right and the responsi-bility to take part in the process by which a specific criminal conflict is handled. It is hardly surprising that McCold (in my view) fails to solve this problem, as there can hardly be an objective answer to the question of who has a direct stake in the outcome of a particular conflict. Rather, the issue seems inherently contestable.

For this reason, the question of who constitutes the community for a specific conflict is best subordinated to the questions of what the responsibilities of the community are and what role it might and should play in a restorative criminal justice process. According to McCold, when a crime occurs:

> The responsibilities of local communities are to (1) act immediately to protect victim and offender; (2) hold offenders accountable and

insist on active involvement of interested parties in the resolution process; (3) provide the local resources for victim and offender to seek their healing; (4) provide local education and serve as a model for peaceful resolution processes; and (5) seek the systemic sources of recurring conflicts and encourage amelioration at their etiological source.

(McCold 1996: 96)

What I think this means is that, for McCold, creating a system of restorative justice means much more than creating alternative forums and processes for the resolution of conflicts which would otherwise be dealt with by conventional criminal justice forums and processes. Rather, it means that the group of people he identifies as the local community should undertake responsibility for reducing levels of crime and victimization within them without resorting to coercion and violence and for ensuring that whenever crime and other forms of antisocial behaviour do occur within the community, they meet with a restorative response. Not all individuals within the community will take part in the process by which specific conflicts are resolved, but part of the task of the local community is to 'insist' that those who should take part (presumably the 'personal communities' of victims and offenders) do take part. The campaign for restorative justice, then, is no longer confined to developing and promoting restorative alternatives to conventional modes of sentencing and punishment. It entails an attempt to relocate the work of crime control and criminal justice, shifting it from state agencies to the local community (Garland 2001: 123–4; cf. Kurki 2000), and at the same time attempting to ensure that, in carrying out these tasks local communities are guided by restorative values, such as reintegration and healing, rather than by retributive values. In trying to specify the role of the community within restorative justice processes (narrowly defined), McCold ends up by radically expanding the ambitions of the restorative justice campaign.

Building community support

Even if we agreed with McCold and others, that a comprehensive restorative response to crime involves much more than the creation of new forums to which sentencing decisions can be diverted – that it also involves engaging 'the community as a resource for reconciliation of victims and offenders and as a resource for monitoring and enforcing community standards of behaviour' (Pranis 1998: 1) – we would still be left with our initial problem of how to get the community involved in such a project. Indeed some, who are generally supportive of such views, nevertheless urge caution, on the ground that proponents of restorative justice may be making enormous demands of local communities, without addressing the problem of the resources which local communities will need to meet these new demands. Tony Marshall states:

> As with any initiative that invokes 'community' it is necessary to think about what this may actually involve. Neighbourhoods differ in their capacities to support potential offenders in their midst. Programmes that seek to tap into community support may therefore be tapping into something that hardly exists. In the more broken communities, resources and education may be needed to be committed for restorative justice programmes to work. Otherwise there is the danger that such programmes will increase the burden of expectation and involvement of local people and groups to a level they cannot sustain. Initiatives like conferencing, therefore, may need to be introduced gradually and in parallel with the development of other community programmes.
>
> (Marshall 1998: 30)

Restorative justice, then, is not the cheap alternative it is sometimes assumed to be. Because it is grounded in community involvement it can only be implemented with community support (Pranis 1998: 1). Before we can expect that, we need to put resources into developing our 'killed neighbourhoods' (Christie 1977).

If the resources for developing 'broken communities' were made available, what else would need to be done to secure 'grass-roots commitment at the local level' (Pranis 1998: 2)? Among those to address this issue is Kay Pranis, a restorative justice planner in the Minnesota Department of Corrections (ibid). She sets out some basic principles which should guide those concerned to promote restorative justice. Her argument seems to be addressed mainly to people working in criminal justice agencies, since she thinks that restorative justice programmes and projects are only likely to be established if such agencies take the initiative. This creates a problem for Pranis, in that such agencies tend to be very hierarchical and not well-suited to grass-roots participation. Hence, she suggests, such agencies must overcome their natural tendency to implement programmes through a top-down authoritarian process. They must provide leadership, without usurping the power of other participants (ibid: 1–2). In particular, they must recognise that there is no single blueprint for building a restorative system. Rather, the

157

method of building a restorative system must itself be decided through a collaborative, participatory process in which the stakeholders in such a system determine what is to be done: 'The process of implementing restorative approaches must model the principles themselves' (*ibid*: 2). State agencies should, then, articulate the vision of restorative justice, disseminate information, provide support and technical assistance, establish pilot programmes and monitor outcomes to ensure fairness etc. Yet, they must at the same time ensure that stakeholders remain in control of the processes themselves. For example, 'at all times the leading agency should resist the urge to develop detailed plans unilaterally because that might supplant the development of plans based on the participation of all the stakeholders' (*ibid*: 2).

Pranis also argues that a shift towards restorative justice is most likely to occur if it forms part of a much broader shift in our social institutions. Restorative justice is likely to make sense to people when it parallels their experience in other core social institutions. So, the chances of attracting community support for restorative justice are highest when authority in our families, our schools and our workplaces becomes less centralised and hierarchical, more dispersed and egalitarian. Also, restorative justice is most likely to thrive when we abandon fear, coercion and violence as ways of influencing and motivating people in other areas of life, and when we rely more on the power of relationships.

In the remainder of her paper, Pranis outlines a whole range of strategies for building community support for restorative justice, including: public education, especially using stories of real experiences, theatre pieces, etc; being prepared to provide technical support once people show an interest in developing schemes; and using basic community organizing skills such as finding your natural allies in the community, avoiding becoming identified with a particular political label and listening to those who disagree.

Pranis offers much excellent advice for those keen to promote community-based restorative justice. More cynical commentators might, however, suggest that the community is most likely to get involved in criminal justice issues when, as is increasingly likely, it feels that it must. When the state decides that it is no longer interested in 'stealing' our conflicts, when the option of wholly delegating criminal conflicts to professionals no longer exists, the community is left with the ownership of its conflicts and all the burdens such ownership involves. Whether the community will respond to calls to think and act restoratively, or whether it will adapt to such a situation in a less benevolent way, remains to be seen (*cf*. Garland 2001).

Notes

1 The conflict model of crime has been criticised on the ground that many crimes do not involve a conflict (von Hirsch and Ashworth 1998: 302; *cf.* Marshall 1988: 38ff). In this chapter I use the conflict model for purposes of exposition only. I do not make any claims about the extent to which this model is useful for 'constructing' crime. For purposes of exposition, I will also assume a simple situation in which one person (the suspect or offender) has allegedly harmed another person (the victim), and that this act has an indirect impact upon others (the community). Many actual crimes, of course, involve multiple perpetrators and multiple direct victims (or no direct victims), and the line between direct and indirect victims can be very blurred.

2 Where police officers or other criminal justice agents act as facilitators of restorative conferences, as they frequently do in restorative cautioning schemes, the idea that the facilitator is a neutral third party is clearly stretched to the limits of credibility.

3 For differing views on this crucial issue see the essays in Strang and Braithwaite (2000), comparing, in particular, Mason (2000) with other essays such as Barton (2000).

4 Such a vision is clearly articulated in Bush and Folger's work on the community mediation movement (1994). The community mediation movement was one of the original sources out of which the campaign for restorative justice emerged and the two movements continue to overlap significantly. What follows draws upon the work of Bush and Folger, along with that of Nils Christie and some classic writings on participation (see Johnstone 2000).

5 For more detailed discussion of the nature of conflict see Marshall (1988: 30*ff*) and (Kennedy 1990).

6 See Zehr (1990: 182*ff*) for a more cautious use of such ideas. It is important to stress that Christie's radical views on conflict are *not* shared by most proponents of restorative justice, because some critics of restorative justice take Christie's radical ideas as their main target (e.g. von Hirsch and Ashworth, 1998: ch. 7), although this may be changing as John Braithwaite's vision becomes more and more influential.

7 The core mainstream writers are identified in chapter one, note 1.

8 Bush and Folger also differentiate the relational worldview from an 'organic worldview', which is driven by the value of collective welfare (1994: ch. 9).

9 However, terms such as 'relational justice', as currently employed, are ambiguous in a way which reflects the more general tension which we have been discussing. It can simply mean improving the relationship between disputing parties. Or, it can mean transforming the justice system so that it promotes a relational world, in Bush and Folger's sense. Similarly, whilst there is much emphasis in restorative justice discourse on 'empowerment' of stakeholders in a conflict, this is often understood simply as giving them

more power *within the process*, which, as we have seen, can be regarded as essential for the achievement of restorative goals. However, giving the parties more power within the process is not at all the same as using the process to empower them as human beings, in the Bush and Folger sense.

10 Herman Bianchi was one prominent critic. Zehr states:

> In the early days . . . Herman Bianchi chided us that the approach was too individualized and private. Many cultures are accustomed to addressing their conflicts and problems within larger family and community contexts, he said. They would find the simple one-on-one diads of a victim-offender encounter too isolated.
>
> (Zehr 1990: 256)

Bianchi's own vision of an alternative model of dealing with crime is outlined in his book *Justice as Sanctuary* (1994).

11 Note that proponents of restorative justice do not suggest that direct victims of crime have a similar responsibility. The position is that they have a right to be involved in the process, but should not be pressurised into taking part. Hence, the community is in a different position to the direct victim. It has the right to take part (as a secondary victim), but also a responsibility to take part. It is never quite explained from where that responsibility arises. Some show quite convincingly that it is prudent for the community to take responsibility for the handling of criminal conflicts (Cayley 1998), but that is not the same as showing that it has a duty to take part. See Garland (2001: 124–7) on the responsibilisation strategy in recent crime policy. See Braithwaite and Strang (2000) for an attempt to provide a link between republicanism, as a normative ideal for how society should be organised, and restorative justice.

Chapter 8

The future of restorative justice

Introduction

Throughout this book I have focussed mainly on the campaign for a systemic shift from punitive to restorative criminal justice as the routine response to crime. I have looked at how such a shift would affect the goals, techniques, procedures and values of criminal justice. The main priority of criminal justice would change from making offenders pay for their crimes through suffering to ensuring that they repaired the harm, both material and symbolic, which they had caused. Reducing re-offending and enhancing public safety would still be central concerns, but the methods of achieving such goals would change. Instead of isolating offenders and seeking to deter them through threats of punishment, a restorative criminal justice would hold offenders accountable to those they had harmed, subject them to the disapproval of people who care about them, establish circles of support and accountability around them, and attempt to restore repentant offenders to full membership of the law-abiding community. Restorative criminal justice would differ significantly in its 'sentencing' procedures from conventional criminal justice: in place of formal courthouse justice it would use informal, participatory, consensual, community-based mediation of conflicts. Behind all this, there would be a shift in the values which guide and are expressed through the practice of criminal justice. A restorative criminal justice would be 'about healing rather than hurting, moral learning, community participation and community caring, respectful dialogue, forgiveness, responsibility, apology and making amends' (Braithwaite 1999a: 6; *cf.* Consedine 1999).

As well as trying to describe the central distinguishing characteristics of a restorative criminal justice, I have indicated some of the areas where the vision of restorative criminal justice is vague or positively contested. Is the overriding concern to heal victims or is it to deal more constructively with offenders? What role, if any, can and should punishment or pain delivery play in a restorative criminal justice? Is the main point to replace retributive outcomes with restorative outcomes, or to empower the 'primary stakeholders' in a criminal conflict? Just how much control should victims and other primary stakeholders have over the outcome? Is the ambition simply to create a better way of dealing with crimes which have been committed, or is it to bring about some broader and deeper change in humanity and society (better people, stronger communities)?

I have also raised and briefly discussed some questions concerning the possibility and desirability of a systemic shift from punitive to restorative criminal justice. Is restorative criminal justice feasible, as the routine response to crime, in modern societies with their eroded sense of community and/or fragmentation into conflicting communities (Norrie 1999: 136–7)? Does the idea of a restorative criminal justice presuppose quite different public attitudes towards offenders than those which prevail and are likely to prevail (or would a shift to restorative justice itself help shift punitive attitudes)? Is it naïve to suppose that once victims and victimised communities hear about the success of experiments with restorative justice they will then lose their appetite for harsh retributive justice? Would people feel safe, and would they be safe, if restorative justice were to become the routine response to crime? Would a shift from punitive to restorative criminal justice actually make things worse for many offenders, by eroding their procedural safeguards and subjecting them to the wrath of a fickle and aroused public which has been urged to shame them? Will it disturb the relatively safe relationship between offenders, the state, victims and communities which our current system has achieved? Will it frustrate the goals of creating 'principled sentencing' and if so does it matter? Will it contribute to a process of net-widening, and if so would that necessarily be a bad thing?

I believe that, given how recently it is that the concept of restorative justice has become familiar outside a small group of reformers and academics (Bazemore and Walgrave (1999: 1), and given the uncertainty and disagreement which still exists about what a restorative criminal justice would look like (McCold 1998), such an exploration of the meaning, feasibility and desirability of a system-wide shift from punitive to restorative criminal justice is of considerable value.

Nevertheless, I do not imagine that such a change is likely to occur. If there is anything we can know with relative certainty from a study of the history of criminal justice reform it is that visions of a radically different system, while they may have enormous reformative influence, are seldom if ever fully realized. To imagine that they will be is to ignore the fact that there are simply too many other forces – institutional, political, cultural, social and economic – shaping criminal justice discourses, institutions and practices (Garland 1990; 2001). So what is likely to occur? In attempting a brief answer to this question I do not propose to speculate freely about the future. Rather, I will simply point to one or two possibilities which are already becoming apparent.

Implementing restorative justice: the paths less likely

To explain what is happening and what is likely to continue happening, it is useful to start by looking at what is not happening. A useful starting point for such a discussion is Howard Zehr's *Changing Lenses*, in which he discusses a number of 'blueprints' for system-wide implementation of restorative justice (1990: ch. 11).

A modified civil procedure

One blueprint involves dismantling the existing system of criminal justice and replacing it with a restorative system (*cf.* Bianchi 1994). This restorative system would be modelled, not on criminal law, but on the existing structure of civil law in which the focus is on settlement and restitution rather than punishment, degrees of responsibility or liability are recognized, and disputing parties remain central stage and retain significant power. This model would not necessarily abolish the concept of crime and deal with what we now call crimes as *torts*, i.e. private wrongs. Rather, a crime/tort distinction would be maintained and hence there would still be a separate system for dealing with crimes. This system would employ a modified civil procedure, in which some of the procedural safeguards and, presumably, many of the police powers found in the current criminal justice system would feature. Also, although he omits to state it, Zehr would clearly want a system in which – to a much greater extent than in current civil law – mediation had replaced litigation as the normal way of resolving disputes.

The relationships between the criminal law system and the civil law system are complex, and the boundaries between them are by no means as clear as is often supposed (Epstein 1977). Hence, current legal structures could support the emergence of a 'hybrid' system for dealing with much that we currently call crime, without there necessarily being a formal abolition of criminal justice and its replacement by a new system based on a modified civil procedure. However, the bulk of conventional criminal cases, currently dealt with by the regular criminal justice system, look likely to continue being dealt with in the conventional way. There are few signs of a restorative criminal justice system being created along the lines of this model.

A parallel track

A second model is that, instead of thinking in terms of dismantling criminal law, we might simply establish a separate restorative justice system which would serve as an alternative to it. Such a system would refuse to deal with conflicts which were in the criminal justice process. Hence, victims and offenders might agree to take a conflict to the restorative justice system instead of to the formal criminal justice system. Bianchi (1994) claims that there are historical precedents for such a parallel track model: state justice and church justice in mediaeval times. In addition, the neighbourhood justice system established by the San Francisco Community Board would serve as a more contemporary model (Merry and Milner 1993).

The possibility of such a development should not be dismissed too lightly. As well as the historical and contemporary examples mentioned, it is clear that the majority of conflicts which could be taken to criminal justice are in fact dealt with 'privately', sometimes according to restorative justice principles (Hulsman 1986). The more formal development of a system of restorative justice could make this option more attractive. The obvious drawback, of course, is that without a body with police powers to bring suspects to justice and to enforce 'sanctions' – where community persuasion had clearly failed – such a system would be incapable of dealing effectively with many crimes.

Parallel but interlinked tracks

The limitations of the second model could be overcome by a system, based on Japanese law, in which a separate restorative justice track was created but was linked to and interdependent with the formal criminal justice system (Zehr 1990: 217–20; cf. Haley 1995). As in the Japanese system, few cases would proceed to the end of the formal criminal justice track. Instead, at an appropriate stage, they would be shunted aside to the alternative restorative justice track. Crucially, the factors influencing the decision to divert would be much broader and different from those which tend to influence diversion schemes in contemporary Western criminal justice. The seriousness of the crime and the existence of psychiatric or medical problems would continue to be important factors. But so too would things like the willingness of the offender to acknowledge guilt, express remorse and to repair harm, and the victim's willingness to accept apologies and restitution and to offer forgiveness (Zehr 1990: 218).

To be workable, such a system would clearly require an understanding of and commitment to the principles of restorative justice on the part of those operating the formal criminal justice system. It would also require certain cultural conditions, apparently existing in Japan but much less evident in the West: a considerable willingness on the part of offenders to confess and take responsibility, and a willingness on the part of victims to accept restitution, to forgive those who have harmed them provided they express remorse, and to play a more active role in criminal justice decision-making processes.

John Haley, who has done most to bring this model to the attention of the West and to highlight its merits, acknowledges that its success is due to the cultural context and it should not be expected that such a model could be transported to a very different culture. Nevertheless, he argues that we have much to learn from it. Zehr summarises his ideas thus:

> While the Japanese pattern is obviously tied to Japanese culture, … we have much to learn from that example. It suggests intriguing possibilities for linking formal and informal, adversarial and non-adversarial, systems. The Japanese model suggest a place for the formal machinery of justice and for the state while leaving space for restoration and giving victim and offender an enlarged role. While the West cannot simply imitate this model, it suggests that justice might be both personal and formal.
>
> (Zehr 1990: 220)

To those who are persuaded that there is a strong case for using restorative justice to a much wider and deeper extent than is currently the case, but who see the complete abolition of formal punitive justice as unfeasible and/or undesirable, this third model has considerable appeal. Yet, I do not see the creation of such a model as very likely. Largely, this is because there is an alternative fate for restorative justice which seems far more likely and may already be in progress: piecemeal incorporation of restorative justice programmes, ideas and techniques into the formal criminal justice complex.

The implementation of restorative techniques

Restorative juvenile justice?

One likely development, already underway, is that restorative justice will become increasingly prominent in the response to youth crime, but remain much more peripheral in the response to adult crime. One reason for this is that the response to youth crime has long been differentiated from the response to adult crime, but the traditional welfarist rationale for this distinction is becoming increasingly hard to sustain. Traditionally, the need for a separate system for dealing with young offenders – with its own courts, custodial institutions, sentencing regimes, etc. – has been based on the assumption that, in responding to juveniles who offend, the care and protection of the offender is just as important as the need to punish offenders and protect the public. Such welfarist concerns play a role, of course, in the treatment of many adult offenders (Garland 1985), but they are much less prominent in the response to adult crime.

Today, as part of the more general decline of the rehabilitative ideal, the welfarist justification for a separate response to youth crime is under threat. Hence, the options are either to abandon the relatively clear distinction between the response to youth crime and that to adult crime, or to find another rationale for youth criminal justice (Bazemore and Walgrave 1999). Those policy-makers and practitioners who are opposed to the former course need to adopt a new and persuasive rationale for continuing to maintain a distinction which is already well established (although the gap between adult and youth criminal justice is growing smaller). They are increasingly finding restorative justice attractive as this new rationale, since it allows them to respond positively to growing demands that young offenders be held responsible for their actions and not be let off lightly, yet at the same time it allows them to retain an emphasis on the welfare of the young offender, to which many remain committed. Hence, the response to youth crime is fertile ground for the development of restorative justice, because it allows considerable movement towards a moralising and responsibilising response to young offenders, without altogether abandoning welfarist concerns. But, to suggest that the prospects for implementing restorative justice are greatest in the area of youth crime is not to suggest that the prospects are particularly good. Even in the area of youth crime it may be difficult for restorative justice to gain a strong foothold, given the more general drift towards punitive segregation.

It is crucial to realize, however, that to implement a restorative juvenile justice without a corresponding development in the response to adult crime, is already seriously to distort the original vision of restorative justice. This is because the distinction between the response to youth crime and that to adult crime is drawn by reference to the age of the offender. Hence, the sharp distinction is possible only if one focuses on offenders to the near exclusion of victims. But, for many proponents, especially early proponents such as Barnett (1977) and Zehr (1990), the central theme of restorative justice was that meeting the needs of victims should be the primary concern of society in the aftermath of a crime. The crucial argument for restorative justice was that it outperformed punitive justice as a way of meeting the needs of victims for justice and healing. Yet, if we look at the development of restorative juvenile justice from the victim's perspective, we find that getting one's needs for restitution, empowerment and symbolic reparation met is strongly influenced by the purely fortuitous factor of whether one's offender happens to be a juvenile or an adult.

A small-scale response to minor crime

Another possibility is that restorative justice programmes will be developed within the criminal justice system as a small-scale response to minor crimes. Crimes regarded as not sufficiently serious for a full-scale penal response, yet too serious to be dealt with through a simple police caution, would then be diverted to restorative justice programmes. Such a development would allow the criminal justice system to step up its response to minor crimes which individually seem trivial but collectively constitute a major social problem, without overloading the deep end of the penal system. Such a development could be attractive to those charged with running the penal system, as it would help solve a pressing practical problem. It could also be sold to proponents of restorative justice, on the ground that once restorative justice gets a foothold in the system, its benefits will soon become apparent and it will become increasingly used for more serious cases.

Nevertheless, from a restorative justice perspective, there are clear limitations and dangers with such a development. For those who believe that restorative justice is a more effective and more just way of dealing with all crime, no matter how serious, to create the impression that it is only suitable or most suitable for minor crimes is to miss and distort its message. Moreover, the campaign for restorative justice would fail to achieve its objective of marginalising the use of punishment and replacing it with restorative justice. Instead, punishment would probably be used almost as widely as before, while restorative justice would probably be used to 'widen formal control over very minor crimes that previously were ignored by the criminal justice system' (Kurki 2000: 241).

Incorporation of restorative justice ideas and techniques into penal interventions

Another strong possibility is that some of the ideas and techniques promoted by campaigners for restorative justice will be taken up within the penal system, but as part of interventions which are not in any broader sense about restorative justice. For example, the idea of getting offenders to repair harm might be taken up, but without adopting a restorative justice procedure and without much thought being given to the question of what would benefit victims. Ideas of shaming offenders might be taken up, but without any corresponding emphasis on reintegration. Or, the idea of victim–offender mediation might be taken up, but without an emphasis on achieving restorative outcomes. Restorative justice will then become a source of useful ideas and techniques to be used in the fight against crime, especially youth crime, but without any fundamental change in the character or focus of the criminal justice system.

The examples could go on and on, but perhaps enough has been said to indicate that restorative justice could well be implemented – and is probably already being implemented – in ways which are far from true to the original vision (Zehr 2000). Many proponents of restorative justice are very aware of such possibilities and of the dangers involved. However, such awareness may not be sufficient to prevent much diluted and distorted versions of restorative justice being implemented. To use the language of Zehr (1990), those who planted the seed of restorative justice may not be the ones to cultivate it. Others, less apprehensive about the dangers involved in implementation and less anxious about remaining true to the original vision, are likely to take over this task. There is no copyright to the term 'restorative justice' and, of course, those who think that, despite the inevitable compromise and self-restraint required, it is important to cooperate with the criminal justice system – to talk its language and to help it pursue its goals – in order to ensure official sponsorship, referral of cases, resources and so on, have an important argument on their side. As a senior government official put it at a meeting with restorative justice activists which I attended in 1999, the alternative is to remain a movement of high ideals but little practical impact on the system. At a time when governments are becoming friendly to restorative justice (*cf.* Quin 1998), those interested in promoting restorative justice should, the argument runs, be prepared to demonstrate that they can help the government achieve its aims of reducing crime and the fear of crime. In such a climate the warnings of 'founding fathers', such as Howard Zehr, will still, out of respect, be heard, but are less and less likely to be heeded. It seems appropriate, then, to give Zehr the last word on this matter:

> As reforming visions are made operational, they tend to be diverted (or subverted) from their original intents. Sometimes they end up serving purposes quite opposed to their original intent.
>
> (Zehr 1990: 232)

Restorative justice and the pattern of penal control

How might the rise of restorative justice affect the overall pattern of penal control? It should be clear from the above that it all depends upon the precise way in which restorative justice is implemented. For instance, a system-wide shift to restorative justice – whatever form it took – would have a very different impact upon the pattern of penal control than would a piecemeal incorporation of restorative ideas and techniques into strategies for dealing with juvenile offenders and minor crimes. Crucially, however, the differences are not just quantitative. If restorative justice became the governing principle of criminal justice, routinely replacing conventional penal interventions which would be used only where restorative justice repeatedly failed, its impact would probably be qualitatively different than it would be if it became just one more weapon, in an increasingly diversified arsenal, to be used in the war against youth crime.

A systemic shift to restorative justice would amount to a fundamental shift in our manner of viewing and responding to crime. This shift might not be as radical as some penal abolitionists, such as Hulsman (1986), would like to see, and it may fall short of the vision of transformative justice proposed by some, such as Sullivan and Tifft (1998), but, for better or worse, it would nevertheless involve a significant change in the way criminal justice is calculated and in the definitions and assumptions which govern the way we think about and act upon crime (Pavlich 1996; Zehr 1990).

A more piecemeal incorporation of restorative ideas and techniques could, at best, soften the harshness of the overall criminal justice system, and give the restorative justice movement a foothold in the system from which it could slowly grow. On the other hand, there is a danger that such piecemeal incorporation could result in restorative justice becoming a cheap supplement to repressive justice, to be 'used only to clean up the easy cases at the margins of the system and having little effect on the treatment of the main body of cases' (Cayley 1998: 359). Worse still, restorative justice might become the means through which the criminal justice system expands its reach, intruding deeper into the domain of petty crime, incivility and disorder, without changing its approach to more serious crimes.

The future of restorative justice research

All of this suggests the need for a much broader and more radical research agenda than that which is currently dominant. Governments, which are showing increasing interest in restorative justice as a set of techniques which can be used to help them achieve their goals – reducing crime rates, intervening into the problems of quasi-criminal disorderly behaviour, and reducing the fear of crime and disorder – are increasingly sponsoring research designed to test just how effective (and how cost-effective) restorative justice can be in achieving such goals, as well as in providing consumers of criminal justice services with customer satisfaction. Without denying the importance of such research, I would argue that there is a pressing need for the more rapid development of other lines of critical inquiry, not restricted by such governmental concerns and interests.

There is a need to understand much more about how the implementation of restorative justice, in various forms, might alter our patterns of crime control and the meaning of doing criminal justice and there is a need to articulate and address a whole range of ethical issues raised by the emergence of restorative justice. Important questions about how restorative justice might impact upon our human rights and civil liberties and about how it might unsettle long-standing constitutional arrangements (and with what effects) are beginning to be addressed rigorously by some legal scholars and penal philosophers, such as von Hirsch and Ashworth (1998: ch. 7; *cf.* Ashworth 1993). However, we need to inquire also into the implications of restorative justice practices such as restorative shaming for human freedom, asking in what ways do such practices impinge upon people's lives and with what sorts of effects. More generally still, we might seek a better identification and analysis of the conceptions of personhood, social relations and justice which underpin and inform the project of restorative justice, as well as exploring the way restorative justice links up with broader themes such as the reassertion of emotionality in law (Laster and O'Malley 1996; Freiberg 2001). Another important topic for research is the relationship of restorative justice to the development of risk-focused security within criminal justice (Shearing 2001). Also, we need to identify and investigate the conceptions of and assumptions about expertise and authority which permeate restorative justice discourses and practices.

This is not, of course, an attempt to set out a comprehensive agenda for future research into restorative justice. I have merely tried to identify some areas of investigation which I think are interesting and important, but are currently underdeveloped. Others, no doubt, will identify other interesting and important lines of inquiry. My point is simply that, however much we might welcome restorative justice, as a refreshing and in many ways heartening challenge to the drift towards a strategy of punitive segregation, we must never forget that it involves the exercise of power by some people over others, and that there is an urgent need for critical investigation of the nature, limits, problems and dangers of such exercise of power.

Appendix to Chapter 3

The theological roots of judicial punishment

The rather simplistic 'conspirational' account of origins of state punishment relied upon by most proponents of restorative justice (described in chapter three) is supplemented by some proponents with a much more complex account of how, around the eleventh and twelfth centuries, new theological doctrines, themselves influenced by legal concepts, helped give criminal law a new status and crime a new moral meaning (Berman 1983; Bianchi 1994; Gorringe 1996; Cayley 1998: ch. 7). A key event, according to such accounts, was the papal revolution which began in 1073, when Pope Gregory asserted the autonomy and supremacy of the Christian church in society and the supremacy of the pope within the church. Previously, the church was decentralised and the lines between church and society, and between secular and sacred authority were blurred. The papal revolution 'gave birth to the modern state, the first example of which, paradoxically, was the church itself' (Berman 1983: 113), an 'independent, hierarchical public authority executing its own laws through its own administrative machinery' (Cayley 1998: 127).

A crucial development occurred early in the twelfth century, when the clergy claimed a special responsibility for the care of souls and regulation of society, which involved the right to make new laws (*ibid*). This was innovative in that, until this time, it had been assumed that law was 'codified custom', i.e. it was embedded in social life. Now, law became conceived as a bureaucratic creation with its own internal logic. This new conception of law had a profound influence on the meaning of crime. Previously, crime had been conceived as a wrong done by one person to another which created an obligation to pay restitution to the injured party. Customary law tended to be confined to providing a framework for deciding matters such as what counted as a crime and how much restitution was due. Now, crime became reconceived as a violation of the law of the church/state which, although a bureaucratic creation, was also (somewhat contradictorily to the modern eye) represented as reflection of divine law (Gorringe 1996: 13ff). This had two crucial implications. First, the church/state, rather than the person harmed, became defined as the party offended against and the party entitled to exact the price of the crime. Hence, the church/state claimed the right to prosecute crimes. The criminal 'trial' was no longer a contest between two approximately equal parties overseen by the central power; rather it was a battle in which the might of the church/state was pitted against the individual offender. The second implication was that crime took on a profound moral significance which it previously had lacked. It was no longer simply a violation of another person; it was a violation of God's will incurring the wrath of God which had to be appeased. The restitution which might satisfy the direct victim of a wrong was wholly inadequate as a means of placating God. Since God's status was infinitely higher than even the highest of humans, and since it was well established that the amount of expiation due was determined mainly by the status of the party offended against, the criminal lawbreaker had to atone through suffering.

But why suffering? And how was the amount of suffering required to put things right to be determined? According to such accounts, to find answers to questions like these we need to look at two developments in religious doctrine associated with the papal revolution. First, a doctrine of purgatory emerged, involving a new conception of sin (*ibid*: 129*ff*). Previously sin was conceived as a condition of estrangement from the Christian community. Acts of penance were required as signs of repentance, as a prelude to rituals of reconciliation (Cosgrave 2000). In the new doctrine of purgatory, sin was conceived more 'legalistically' as specified wrongful acts and desires. For each specific sin, depending on its gravity, an appropriate period of purgatorial suffering was prescribed which, once served, could expiate guilt. Accordingly, in order to determine the amount of purgation required it became important to assess the precise gravity of each sin and the precise degree of moral guilt of each offender. This involved an examination of both the class of the sinful act and the degree of evil intent accompanying it. This doctrine of purgatory, itself drawn from legal notions and discussions, in turn provided a cultural space within which the judicial punishment of criminals could seem more and more divinely ordained and self-evident.

The second new doctrine to have a profound influence on penal practice was the 'satisfaction theory' of the Atonement (Gorringe 1996). In the eleventh century the church, drawing on legal notions, began to teach that God had required the sacrificial death of His son to make satisfaction for human sinfulness (Cayley 1998: 132–4). The fact that Christ assumed the guise of a criminal and was punished through a legal procedure paved the way for this legalistic understanding of the crucifixion, but in turn it was easy to make the reverse journey and to develop the notion that offenders must suffer as Christ did to atone for their sins. The emerging institution of judicial punishment influenced understandings of the Atonement, which in turn lent judicially imposed suffering a new authority, allowing it to be represented and understood as an analogue of divine justice (Gorringe 1996).

Over the centuries, crime eventually became seen as distinguishable from sin, and state criminal law became distinct from church law and gained dominance over it. The institution of judicial punishment has largely, but by no means completely, disowned its religious origins, representing itself as a purely secular institution performing purely practical functions in modern society. However, some advocates of restorative justice argue that the very structure and cultural meaning of judicial punishment is determined by its complex relation with medieval religious doctrines. If we no longer find these religious doctrines appropriate, and many modern theologians reject them, we should also question the continued relevance of the institution of judicial punishment (Gorringe 1996).

References

Alder, J. and Wundersitz, J. (eds) (1994) *Family Conferencing and Juvenile Justice: The Way Forward or Misplaced Optimism* (Canberra: Australian Institute of Criminology).

Andenaes, J. (1974) *Punishment and Deterrence* (Ann Arbor: University of Michigan Press).

Ashworth, A. (1986) 'Punishment and Compensation: Victims, Offenders and the State', *Oxford Journal of Legal Studies*, 6:1, pp. 86–122.

Ashworth, A. (1993) 'Some Doubts about Restorative Justice', *Criminal Law Forum*, 4:2, pp. 277–99.

Baker, N. (1994) 'Mediation, Reparation and Justice', in Burnside, J. and Baker, N. (eds) *Relational Justice: Repairing the Breach* (Winchester: Waterside Press), pp. 71–82.

Barnett, R. (1977) 'Restitution: A New Paradigm of Criminal Justice', *Ethics*, 87, pp. 279–301.

Barnett, R. (1980) 'The Justice of Restitution', *American Journal of Jurisprudence*, 25, pp. 117–32.

Barton, C. (1999) *Getting Even: Revenge as a Form of Justice* (Illinois: Open Court).

Barton, C. (2000) 'Empowerment and Retribution in Criminal Justice', in Strang, H. and Braithwaite, J. (eds) *Restorative Justice: Philosophy to Practice* (Aldershot: Ashgate/Dartmouth), pp. 55–76.

Bauman, Z. (2000) 'Social Uses of Law and Order' in Garland, D. and Sparks, R. (eds) *Criminology and Social Theory* (Oxford: Oxford University Press), pp. 23–45. [also available in *The British Journal of Criminology*, 40:2, Spring 2000].

Bazemore, G. (1996) 'Three Paradigms for Juvenile Justice', in Galaway, B. and Hudson, J. (eds) *Restorative Justice: International Perspectives* (Monsey, NY: Criminal Justice Press), pp. 37–67.

Bazemore, G. and Walgrave, L. (eds) (1999) *Restorative Juvenile Justice: Repairing the Harm of Youth Crime* (Monsey, NY: Criminal Justice Press).

Berman, H. (1983) *Law and Revolution: The Formation of the Western Legal Tradition* (Cambridge, MA: Harvard University Press).

Bianchi, H. (1994) *Justice as Sanctuary: Toward a New System of Crime Control* (Bloomington: Indiana University Press).

Blagg, H. (1997) 'A Just Measure of Shame: Aboriginal Youth and Conferencing in Australia', *British Journal of Criminology*, 37:4, pp. 481–501.

Book, A. (1999) 'Shame on You: An Analysis of Modern Shame Punishment as an Alternative to Incarceration', *William and Mary Law Review*, 40, pp. 653–86.

Braithwaite, J. (1989) *Crime, Shame and Reintegration* (Cambridge: Cambridge University Press).

Braithwaite, J. (1993) 'Shame and Modernity', *British Journal of Criminology*, 33:1, pp. 1–18.

Braithwaite, J. (1994) 'Thinking Harder About Democratising Social Control', in Alder, J. and Wundersitz, J. (eds) *Family Conferencing and Juvenile Justice: The Way Forward or Misplaced Optimism* (Canberra: Australian Institute of Criminology), pp. 199–216.

Braithwaite, J. (1998) 'Reducing the Crime Problem: A Not so Dismal Criminology', in Walton, P. and Young, J. (eds) *The New Criminology Revisited* (Houndmills: Macmillan), pp. 47–63.

Braithwaite, J. (1999a) 'Restorative Justice: Assessing Optimistic and Pessimistic Accounts', *Crime and Justice: A Review of Research*, 25, pp. 1–127.

Braithwaite, J. (1999b) 'A Future Where Punishment is Marginalized: Realistic or Utopian?', *UCLA Law Review*, 46, pp. 1727–50.

Braithwaite, J. (2000) 'Survey Article: Repentance Rituals and Restorative Justice', *Journal of Political Philosophy*, 8:1, pp. 115–31.

Braithwaite, J. and Mugford, S. (1994) 'Conditions of Successful Reintegration Ceremonies: Dealing with Juvenile Offenders', *British Journal of Criminology*, 34:2, pp. 139–171.

Braithwaite, J. and Pettit, P. (1990) *Not Just Deserts: A Republican Theory of Criminal Justice* (Oxford: Clarendon Press).

Braithwaite, J. and Strang, H. (2000) 'Connecting Philosophy and Practice' in Strang, H. and Braithwaite, J. (eds) *Restorative Justice: Philosophy to Practice* (Aldershot: Ashgate/Dartmouth), pp. 203–20.

Brown, S. (forthcoming) 'Punishment and the Restoration of Rights', *Punishment and Society*.

Burnside, J. and Baker, N. (eds) (1994) *Relational Justice: Repairing the Breach* (Winchester: Waterside Press).

Bush, R. and Folger, J. (1994) *The Promise of Mediation: Responding to Conflict through Empowerment and Recognition* (San Francisco: Jossey-Bass Publishers).

Bussmann, K. (1992) 'Morality, Symbolism, and Criminal Law: Chances and Limits of Mediation Programs', in Messmer, H. and Otto, H. (eds) *Restorative Justice on Trial* (Netherlands: Kluwer), pp. 317–26.

Cayley, D. (1998) *The Expanding Prison: The Crisis in Crime and Punishment and the Search for Alternatives* (Cleveland, OH: Pilgrim Press).

Christie, N. (1977) 'Conflicts as Property', *British Journal of Criminology*, 17:1, pp. 1–15.

Christie, N. (1982) *Limits to Pain* (Oxford: Martin Robertson).

Christie, N. (1993) *Crime Control as Industry: Towards Gulags, Western Style?* (New York: Routledge).

Christie, N. (1998) 'Between Civility and State', in Ruggiero, V., South, N. and Taylor, I. (eds) *The New European Criminology: Crime and Social Order in Europe* (London: Routledge), pp. 119–24.

Clarkson, C. (2001) *Understanding Criminal Law* (3rd edn.) (London: Sweet & Maxwell).

Cohen, S. (1985) *Visions of Social Control: Crime, Punishment and Classification* (Cambridge: Polity Press).

Connolly, W. (1995) *The Ethos of Pluralization* (Minneapolis: University of Minnesota Press).

Consedine, J. (1999) *Restorative Justice: Healing the Effects of Crime*, revised edition (Lyttelton, New Zealand: Ploughshares).

Cooper, R. (1995) 'Lawyers as Peacemakers: Our Navajo Peers could Teach Us a Thing or Two about Conflict Resolution', *American Bar Association Journal*, p. 6.

Cosgrave, B. (2000) 'Confession: How it Developed', *Word*, 49:3, pp. 25–7.

Cotterrell, R. (1999) *Emile Durkheim: Law in a Moral Domain* (Edinburgh: Edinburgh University Press).

Cragg, W. (1992) *The Practice of Punishment: Towards a Theory of Restorative Justice* (London: Routledge).

Daly, K. (2000a) 'Revisiting the Relationship between Retributive and Restorative Justice', in Strang, H. and Braithwaite, J. (eds) *Restorative Justice: Philosophy to Practice* (Aldershot: Ashgate/Dartmouth), pp. 33–54.

Daly, K. (2000b) 'Restorative Justice: The Real Story' (paper presented at the Scottish Criminology Conference, Edinburgh, 21–22 September 2000, revised version available online at http://www.gu.edu.au/school/ccj/kdaly.html).

Davies, C. (1994) 'Crime and the Rise and Decline of a Relational Society', in Burnside, J. and Baker, N. (eds) *Relational Justice: Repairing the Breach* (Winchester: Waterside Press), pp. 31–41.

Dignan, J. (2000) 'Overview of Current Research' in Restorative Justice Consortium (ed.) *Restorative Justice from Margins to Mainstream* (London: Restorative Justice Consortium).

Doyle, J. (1969) 'Justice and Legal Punishment', in Acton, H. (ed) *The Philosophy of Punishment: A Collection of Papers* (London: Macmillan), pp. 159–71.

Duff, R. A. (1992) 'Alternatives to Punishment – or Alternative Punishments?', in Cragg, W. (ed.) *Retributivism and its Critics* (Stuttgart: Franz Steiner), pp. 44–68.

Duff, R. A. (1999a) 'Punishment, Communication, and Community' in Matravers, M. (ed.) *Punishment and Political Theory* (Oxford: Hart Publishing), pp. 48–68.

Duff, R. A. (1999b) 'Penal Communities', *Punishment and Society*, 1:1, pp. 27–43.

Duff, R. A. and Garland, D. (1994) 'Introduction: Thinking about Punishment', in Duff, R. A. and Garland, D. (eds) (1994) *A Reader on Punishment* (Oxford University Press), pp. 1–43.

Durkheim, E. (1933) *The Division of Labour in Society* (translator W. Halls) (London: Macmillan).

Eglash, A. (1958) 'Creative Restitution: Some Suggestions for Prison Rehabilitation Programs', *American Journal of Correction*, 40.

Elias, R. (1993) *Victims Still: The Political Manipulation of Crime Victims* (Newbury Park: Sage).

Epstein, R. (1977) 'Crime and Tort: Old Wine in Old Bottles', in Barnett, R. and Hagel III, J. (eds) *Assessing the Criminal: Restitution, Retribution and the Legal Process* (Cambridge, MA: Ballinger Publishing).

Erikson, K. (1962) 'Notes on the Sociology of Deviance', *Social Problems*, 9, pp. 307–14.

Estrada-Hollenbeck, M. (1996) 'Forgiving in the Face of Injustice', in Galaway, B. and Hudson, J. (eds) *Restorative Justice: International Perspectives* (Monsey, NY: Criminal Justice Press), pp. 303–13.

Feinberg, J. (1994) 'The Expressive Function of Punishment' in Duff, R. A. and Garland, D. (eds) (1994) *A Reader on Punishment* (Oxford University Press), pp. 71–91.

Findlay, M. (2000) 'Decolonising Restoration and Justice: Restoration in Transitional Cultures', *Howard Journal of Criminal Justice*, 39:4, pp. 398–411.

Foucault, M. (1977) *Discipline and Punish: The Birth of the Prison* (translator A. Sheridan) (London: Allen Lane).

Freiberg, A. (2001) 'Affective versus Effective Justice: Instrumentalism and Emotionalism in Criminal Justice', *Punishment and Society*, 3:2, pp 265–78.

Fry, M. (1951) *Arms of the Law* (London: Victor Golancz).

Fry, M. (1959) 'Justice for Victims', *Journal of Public Law*, 8, pp. 191–4.

Galaway, B. and Hudson, J. (1996) (eds) *Restorative Justice: International Perspectives* (Monsey, NY: Criminal Justice Press).

Garfinkel, H. (1956) 'Conditions of Successful Degradation Ceremonies', *American Journal of Sociology*, 61, pp. 420–4.

Garland, D. (1985) *Punishment and Welfare: A History of Penal Strategies* (Aldershot: Gower).

Garland, D. (1990) *Punishment and Modern Society: A Study in Social Theory* (Oxford: Clarendon Press).

Garland, D. (2000) 'The Culture of High Crime Societies: Some Preconditions of "Law and Order" Policies', *British Journal of Criminology*, 40:3, pp. 347–75.

Garland, D. (2001) *The Culture of Control: Crime and Social Order in Contemporary Society* (Oxford: Oxford University Press).

Garland, D. and Sparks, R. (2000) 'Criminology, Social Theory, and the Challenge of our Times', in Garland, D. and Sparks, R. (eds) *Criminology and Social Theory* (Oxford: Oxford University Press), pp. 1–22. [also available in *The British Journal of Criminology*, 40:2, Spring 2000].

Garvey, S. (1998) 'Can Shaming Punishments Educate?', *University of Chicago Law Review*, 65, pp. 733–94.

Gath, D. (1969) 'The Male Drunk in Court', in Cook, T., Gath, D. and Hensman, C. (eds), *The Drunkenness Offence* (Oxford: Pergamon Press), pp. 9–26.

Gehm, J. (1992) 'The Function of Forgiveness in the Criminal Justice System', in Messmer, H. and Otto, H. (eds) *Restorative Justice on Trial* (Netherlands: Kluwer), pp. 541–50.

Geis, G. (1977) 'Restitution by Criminal Offenders: A Summary and Overview', in Hudson, J. and Galaway, B. (eds) *Restitution in Criminal Justice* (Lexington, MA: Lexington Books), pp. 147–64.

Giddens, A. (1991) *Modernity and Self Identity* (Oxford: Polity Press).

Glover, J. (1970) *Responsibility* (London: Routledge & Kegan Paul).

Gorringe, T. (1996) *God's Just Vengeance* (Cambridge: Cambridge University Press).

Graef, R. (2000) *Why Restorative Justice?: Repairing the Harm Caused by Crime* (London: Calouste Gulbenkian Foundation).

Hadley, M. (n.d.) *Forgiving the Unforgivable: The Limits of Restorative Justice?* (Pamphlet printed by Springhill Enterprises HMP, Bucks. HP18 0TH).

Haley, J. (1995) Victim-Offender Mediation: Lessons from the Japanese Experience', *Mediation Quarterly*, 12:3, pp. 233–48.

Hampton, J. (1984) 'The Moral Education Theory of Punishment', *Philosophy and Public Affairs*, 13:3, pp. 208–38.

Hartill, R. (2000) 'Circling Paedophiles', *The Guardian*, 13 December [also available in *The Friend*, 5 Jan. 2001].

Heise, E., Horne, L., Kirkegaard, H., Nigh, H., Derry, I. and Yantzi, M. (2000) *Community Reintegration Project: Circles of Support and Accountability* (revised edn.) (Mennonite Central Committee/Correctional Services Canada).

Home Office (1996) *The Victim's Charter: a Statement of Service Standards for Victims of Crime* (London: Home Office).

Hudson, J. and Galaway, B. (1996) 'Introduction' in Galaway, B. and Hudson, J. (eds) *Restorative Justice: International Perspectives* (Monsey, NY: Criminal Justice Press), pp. 1–14.

Hulsman, L. (1986) 'Critical Criminology and the Concept of Crime', *Contemporary Crises*, 10:1, pp. 63–80.

Ingram, M. (1984) 'Ridings, Rough Music and the "Reform of Popular Culture" in Early Modern England', *Past & Present*, 105, pp. 79–113.

Ivison, D. (1999) 'Justifying Punishment in Intercultural Contexts: Whose Norms? Which Values?', in Matravers, M. (ed.) *Punishment and Political Theory* (Oxford: Hart Publishing), pp. 88–107.

Jackson, M. (1988) *The Maori and the Criminal Justice System*, vol. 2 (Wellington, NZ: Dept. of Justice).
Jacob, B. (1977) 'The Concept of Restitution: An Historical Overview' in Hudson, J. and Galaway, B. (eds) *Restitution in Criminal Justice* (Lexington, MA: Lexington Books), pp. 45–62.
Johnstone, G. (1991) 'Between Permissiveness and Control: Community Treatment and Penal Supervision', *Law and Critique* 2:1, pp. 37–61.
Johnstone, G. (1996a) *Medical Concepts and Penal Policy* (London: Cavendish).
Johnstone, G. (1996b) 'Towards a Revised Image of the Therapeutic Approach to Offenders', *Law and Critique*, 7:2, pp. 193–216.
Johnstone, G. (1999) 'Restorative Justice, Shame and Forgiveness', in Mair, G. (ed.) *Criminal Justice – Liverpool Law Review*, 21: 2–3, pp. 197–216.
Johnstone, G. (2000) 'Penal Policy Making: Elitist, Populist or Participatory?', *Punishment and Society*, 2:2, pp. 161–80.
Johnstone, G. (2000b) 'Restorative Justice: The Emotional Challenge', in The Howard League (ed.) *Citizenship and Crime* (London: The Howard League for Penal Reform), pp. 6–8.
Johnstone, G. and Bottomley, K. (1998) 'Introduction: Labour's Crime Policy in Context', *Policy Studies*, 19:3–4, pp. 173–84.

Karp, D. (1998) 'The Judicial and Judicious Use of Shame Penalties', *Crime and Delinquency*, 44:2 (1998), pp. 277–94.
Kennedy, L. (1990) *On the Borders of Crime: Conflict Management and Criminology* (New York and London: Longman).
Kuhn, T. (1970) *The Structure of Scientific Revolutions*, 2nd edn., enlarged (Chicago: University of Chicago Press).
Kurki, L. (2000) 'Restorative and Community Justice in the United States', *Crime and Justice*, 27, pp. 235–303.

Lang, B. (1994) 'Forgiveness', *American Philosophical Quarterly*, 31:2, pp. 105–117.
Laqueur, T. (2000) 'Festival of Punishment', *London Review of Books*, 22:19 (5 October), pp. 17–24.
Laster, K. and O'Malley, P. (1996) 'Sensitive New-age Laws: The Reassertion of Emotionality in Law', *International Journal of the Sociology of Law*, 24, pp. 21–40.
Leshan, L. and Margenau, H. (1982) *Einstein's Space and Van Gogh's Sky: Physical Reality and Beyond* (New York: Collier Books).
Lucas, J. (1980) *On Justice* (Oxford: Clarendon Press).
Lynd, H. (1958) *On Shame and the Search for Identity* (New York: Harcourt, Brace & Company).

Marshall, T. (1988) 'Out of Court: More or Less Justice', in Matthews, R. (ed.) *Informed Justice?* (London: Sage), pp. 25–50.

Marshall, T. (1998) *Restorative Justice: An Overview* (available online at http://ssw.che.umn.edu/rjp/Resources/Resource.htm).

Marshall, T. (1999) 'Message from the Chair', in *Restorative Justice Consortium: The First Year (Annual Report 1999)* (unpublished).

Mason, A. (2000) 'Restorative Justice: Courts and Civil Society', in Strang, H. and Braithwaite, J. (eds) *Restorative Justice: Philosophy to Practice* (Aldershot: Ashgate/Dartmouth), pp. 1–9.

Masters, G. and Roberts, A. (2000) 'Family Group Conferencing for Victims, Offenders and Communities' in Liebmann, M. (ed) *Mediation in Context* (London: Jessica Kingsley Publishers), pp. 140–54.

McCold, P. (1996) 'Restorative Justice and the Role of Community' in Galaway, B. and Hudson, J. (eds) *Restorative Justice: International Perspectives* (Monsey, NY: Criminal Justice Press), pp. 85–101.

McCold, P. (1998) 'Restorative Justice: Variations on a Theme', in Walgrave, L. (ed.) *Restorative Justice for Juveniles: Potentialities, Risks and Problems for Research* (Leuven: Leuven University Press).

McCold, P. (1999) *Restorative Justice Practice – The State of the Field 1999.* (available online at http://www.realjustice.org/Pages/vt99papers/vt_mccold.html).

McCold, P. and Wachtel, B. (1998) 'Community is Not a Place: A New Look at Community Justice Initiatives', *Contemporary Justice Review,* 1:1, pp. 71–85.

McElrea, F. (1994) 'Justice in the Community: The New Zealand Experience', in Burnside, J. and Baker, N. (eds) *Relational Justice: Repairing the Breach* (Winchester: Waterside Press), pp. 93–103.

McMahon, M. (1992) *The Persistent Prison: Rethinking Decarceration and Penal Reform* (Toronto: University of Toronto Press).

Meier, D. (1998) 'Restorative Justice – a New Paradigm in Criminal Law?', *European Journal of Crime, Criminal Law and Criminal Justice,* 6:2, pp. 125–139.

Merry, S. and Milner N. (eds) (1993) *The Possibility of Popular Justice: A Case Study of Community Mediation in the United States* (University of Michigan Press).

Miller, W. (1999) 'In Defense of Revenge', in Hanawalt, B. and Wallace, D. (eds) *Medieval Crime and Social Control* (Minneapolis: University of Minnesota Press), pp. 70–89.

Moberly, W. (1968) *The Ethics of Punishment* (London: Faber and Faber).

Moore, D. and O'Connell, T. (1994) 'Family Conferencing in Wagga Wagga: A Communitarian Model of Justice', in Alder, C. and Wundersitz, J. (eds) *Family Conferencing and Juvenile Justice: The Way Forward or Misplaced Optimism* (Canberra: Australian Institute of Criminology), pp. 45–86.

Morris, A. and Gelsthorpe, L. (2000) 'Something Old, Something Borrowed, Something Blue, but Something New? A Comment on the Prospects for Restorative Justice under the Crime and Disorder Act 1998', *Criminal Law Review,* Jan., pp. 18–30.

Morris, A. and Young, W. (2000) 'Reforming Criminal Justice: The Potential of Restorative Justice', in Strang, H. and Braithwaite, J. (eds) *Restorative Justice: Philosophy to Practice* (Aldershot: Ashgate/Dartmouth), pp. 11–31.

Morris, H. (1984) 'A Paternalistic Theory of Punishment', *American Philosophical Quarterly*, 18: pp. 263–71 [also available in Duff, R. A. and Garland, D., (eds) (1994) *A Reader on Punishment* (Oxford University Press), pp. 92–111].

Moule, C. (1998) *Forgiveness and Reconciliation: And Other New Testament Themes* (London: Society for Promoting Christian Knowledge).

Murphy, J. (2000) 'Two Cheers for Vindictiveness', *Punishment and Society*, 2:2, pp. 131–43.

Murphy, J. and Hampton, J. (1988) *Forgiveness and Mercy* (Cambridge: Cambridge University Press).

National Center for Victims of Crime (n.d.) 'Victim Impact Statements', available online at http://www.ncvc.org/vroom/impact_key.htm.

Nathanson, D. (1992) *Shame and Pride: Affect, Sex, and the Birth of the Self* (New York: W. W. Norton).

Nisbet, R. (1967) *The Sociological Tradition* (London: Heinemann).

Nokes, P. (1967) *The Professional Task in Welfare Practice* (London: Routledge and Kegan Paul).

Norrie, A. (1993) *Crime, Reason and History: A Critical Introduction to Criminal Law* (London: Weidenfeld and Nicolson).

Norrie, A. (1999) 'Albert Speer, Guilt, and "The Space Between"', in Matravers, M. (ed.) *Punishment and Political Theory* (Oxford: Hart Publishing), pp. 133–51.

Paterson, F. and McIvor, G. (1999) 'Conferencing as a Response to Youth Crime' (unpublished paper, British Criminology Conference, Liverpool, July 1999).

Pavlich, G. (1996) *Justice Fragmented: Mediating Community Disputes under Postmodern Conditions* (London: Routledge).

Pollard, C. (2000) 'Victims and the Criminal Justice System: A New Vision', *Criminal Law Review*, Jan., pp. 5–17.

Pollock, F. and Maitland, F. (1898) *The History of English Law before the Time of Edward I*, Volume 2 (2nd edn.) (Cambridge: Cambridge University Press).

Pranis, K. (1998) 'Building Community Support for Restorative Justice: Principles and Strategies' (available online at http://members.aol.com/fcadp/archives/Community.htm *or* http://www.restorativejustice.org/library/BuildingSupport_Pranis.html).

Pratt, J. (1996) 'Colonization, Power and Silence: A History of Indigenous Justice in New Zealand Society', in Galaway, B. and Hudson, J. (eds) *Restorative Justice: International Perspectives* (Monsey, NY: Criminal Justice Press), pp. 137–55.

Pratt, J. (2000) 'Emotive and Ostentatious Punishment: Its Decline and Resurgence in Modern Society', *Punishment and Society*, 2:4, pp. 417–39.

Quin, J. (1998) 'The Labour Government's New Approach to Criminal Justice', *Policy Studies*, 19:3–4, 185–9.

Real Justice (2000) *Six Conferences: A Composite View of Conferencing Programs for Troubled Youth* (videocassette) (USA: Real Justice – available at http://www.realjustice.org/).

Reitan, E. (1996) 'Punishment and Community: The Reintegrative Theory of Punishment', *Canadian Journal of Philosophy*, 26:1, pp. 57–82.

Restorative Justice Consortium (n.d.) *Manifesto* (unpublished).

Restorative Justice Consortium (2000) *Restorative Justice from Margins to Mainstream* (London: Restorative Justice Consortium).

Retzinger, S. and Scheff, T. (1996) 'Strategy for Community Conferences: Emotions and Social Bonds', in Galaway, B. and Hudson, J. (eds) *Restorative Justice: International Perspectives* (Monsey, NY: Criminal Justice Press), pp. 315–36.

Reynolds, T. (2000) 'Restorative Justice – a New Way Forward for Victims of Crime?', *Howard League Magazine*, 18:2, p. 8.

Roberts, R. (1995) 'Forgivingness', *American Philosophical Quarterly*, 32:4, pp. 289–306.

Roberts, S. (1979) *Order and Dispute: An Introduction to Legal Anthropology* (Harmondsworth: Penguin).

Roberts, Y. (1998) 'A Crying Shame', *The Guardian,* 29 Sept. 1998, G2 p.4.

Rock, P. (1990) *Helping Victims of Crime: The Home Office and the Rise of Victim Support in England and Wales* (Oxford: Clarendon Press).

Rock, P. (1994) 'Introduction', in Rock, P. (ed.) *Victimology* (Aldershot: Dartmouth Publishing), pp. xi–xix.

Rose, N. (2000) 'Government and Control' in Garland, D. and Sparks, R. (eds) *Criminology and Social Theory* (Oxford: Oxford University Press), pp. 183–208. [also available in *The British Journal of Criminology*, 40:2, Spring 2000].

Schafer, S. (1960) *Restitution to Victims of Crime* (London: Stevens & Sons).

Schluter, M. (1994) 'What is Relational Justice?', in Burnside, J. and Baker, N. (eds) *Relational Justice: Repairing the Breach* (Winchester: Waterside Press), pp. 17–27.

Schneider, C. (1977) *Shame, Exposure and Privacy* (Boston: Beacon Press, 1977).

Shafer-Landau, R. (1991) 'Can Punishment Morally Educate?', *Law and Philosophy*, 10: pp. 189–219.

Shapland, J. (1984) 'Victims, the Criminal Justice System and Compensation', *British Journal of Criminology*, 24:2, pp. 131–249.

Sharpe, J. (1990) *Judicial Punishment in England* (London: Faber & Faber).

Shearing, C. (2001) 'Punishment and the Changing Face of Governance' *Punishment and Society*, 3:2, pp. 203–20.

Sherman, L. (1993) 'Defiance, Deterrence and Irrelevance: A Theory of the Criminal Sanction', *Journal of Research in Crime and Delinquency,* 30, pp. 445–73.

Sim, J. (1990) *Medical Power in Prisons: The Prison Medical Service in England 1774–1989* (Milton Keynes: Open University Press).

Simester, A. and Sullivan, G. (2000) *Criminal Law: Theory and Doctrine* (Oxford: Hart Publishing).

Smith, D., Blagg, H. and Derricourt, N. (1988) 'Mediation in the Shadow of the Law: The South Yorkshire Experience', in Matthews, R. (ed.) *Informal Justice?* (London: Sage), pp. 123–49.

Sorrell, T. (1999) 'Punishment in a Kantian Framework', in Matravers, M. (ed) *Punishment and Political Theory* (Oxford: Hart Publishing), pp. 10–27.

Stein, J. (ed) (1979) *Random House Dictionary of the English Language*, revised edition (New York, NY: Random House).

Strang, H. and Braithwaite, J. (eds) (2000) *Restorative Justice: Philosophy to Practice* (Aldershot: Ashgate/Dartmouth).

Stuart, B. (1996) 'Circle Sentencing: Turning Swords into Ploughshares', in Galaway, B. and Hudson, J. (eds) *Restorative Justice: International Perspectives* (Monsey, NY: Criminal Justice Press), pp. 193–206.

Sullivan, D. (1998) (ed) *The Phenomenon of Restorative Justice* (special issue of *Contemporary Justice Review*, 1:1).

Sullivan, D. and Tifft, L. (1998) 'The Transformative and Economic Dimensions of Restorative Justice', *Humanity and Society*, 22:1, pp. 38–53.

Sullivan, D., Tifft, L. and Cordella, P. (1998) 'The Phenomenon of Restorative Justice: Some Introductory Remarks', *Contemporary Justice Review*, 1:1, pp. 7–20.

Sykes, G. and Matza, D. (1957) 'Techniques of Neutralization: A Theory of Delinquency', *American Sociological Review*, 22, pp. 664–70.

Taraschi, S. (1998) 'Peacemaking Criminology and Aboriginal Justice Initiatives as a Revitalization of Justice', *Contemporary Justice Review*, 1:1, pp. 103–21.

Tauri, J. (1999) 'Explaining Recent Innovations in New Zealand's Criminal Justice System: Empowering Maori or Biculturalising the State', *Australian and New Zealand Journal of Criminology*, 32:2, pp. 153–67.

Tavuchis, N. (1991) *Mea Culpa: A Sociology of Apology and Reconciliation* (California: University of Stanford Press).

Tendler, S. (1997) article in *The Times*, 18 October 1997, available online at www.penallex.org/uk/pages/pressu23.htm#49.

Thames Valley Police (1997) *Restorative Justice: Restorative Cautioning – a New Approach* (Oxford: Thames Valley Police Restorative Justice Consultancy).

Thompson, E. (1992) *Customs in Common* (London: Merlin Press).

Tönnies, F. (1887/1963) *Gemeinschaft und Gesellschaft* (translated as *Community and Society*, by Loomis, C.) (New York: Harper Torchbook).

United Nations (1998) *Guide for Policymakers on the Implementation of the United Nations Declaration of Basic Principles of Justice for Victims of Crime and Abuse of Power* (available online at http://www.victimology.nl/).

Van Dijk, J. (1985) *Compensation: by the State or by the Offender* (The Hague, Netherlands: Ministry of Justice).

Van Dijk, J. (1988) 'Ideological Trends within the Victims Movement: an International Perspective', in Maguire, M. and Pointing, J. (eds) *Victims of Crime: A New Deal?* (Milton Keynes: Open University Press).

Van Ness, D. (1993) 'New Wine and Old Wineskins: Four Challenges of Restorative Justice', *Criminal Law Forum*, 4:2, pp. 251–76.

Virgo, G. (1999) *The Principles of the Law of Restitution* (Oxford: Oxford University Press).

von Hirsch, A. (1990) 'Proportionality in the Philosophy of Punishment', *Criminal Law Forum*, 1:2, pp. 259–90.

von Hirsch, A. and Ashworth, A. (1998) *Principled Sentencing: Readings on Theory and Policy* (2nd edn.) (Oxford: Hart Publishing).

Walgrave, L. (1995) Restorative Justice for Juveniles: Just a Technique or a Fully Fledged Alternative?' *The Howard Journal of Criminal Justice*, 34:3, pp. 228–49.

Walgrave, L. (2000) 'Restorative Justice and the Republican Theory of Criminal Justice: An Exercise in Normative Theorising on Restorative Justice', in Strang, H. and Braithwaite, J. (eds) *Restorative Justice: Philosophy to Practice* (Aldershot: Ashgate/Dartmouth), pp. 165–83.

Walker, P. (1994) 'Repairing the Breach: A Personal Motivation' , in Burnside, J. and Baker, N. (eds) (1994) *Relational Justice: Repairing the Breach* (Winchester: Waterside Press), pp. 147–55.

Warner, K. (1994) Family Group Conferences and the Rights of the Offender', in Alder, J. and Wundersitz, J. (eds) *Family Conferencing and Juvenile Justice: The Way Forward or Misplaced Optimism* (Canberra: Australian Institute of Criminology), pp. 141–52.

Watts, R. (1996) 'John Braithwaite and *Crime, Shame and Reintegration*: Some reflections on Theory and Criminology', *Australian and New Zealand Journal of Criminology*, 29:2, pp. 121–41.

Webster, P. (1999) 'Restorative Justice – the Way Forward?', *Offbeat: the Newspaper for Surrey Police and the Local Community,* 304, April 1999, pp. 4.

Whitman, J. (1998) 'What is Wrong with Inflicting Shame Sanctions?', *Yale Law Journal*, 107: pp. 1055–92.

Wilson, J. (1983) *Thinking about Crime*, revised edition (New York: Vintage Books).

Wright, M. (1989) 'What the Public Wants', in Wright, M. and Galaway, B. (eds) *Mediation and Criminal Justice* (London: Sage), pp. 264–9.

Wright, M. (1996a) *Justice for Victims and Offenders: A Restorative Response to Crime* (2nd Edn.) (1st edn. published by Open University Press, 1991) (Winchester: Waterside Press).

Wright, M. (1996b) 'Can Mediation be an Alternative to Criminal Justice?' in Galaway, B. and Hudson, J. (eds) *Restorative Justice: International Perspectives* (Monsey, NY: Criminal Justice Press), pp. 227–39.

Wright, M. (1999) *Restoring Respect for Justice* (Winchester: Waterside Press).

Yazzie, R. (1998) 'Navajo Peacemaking: Implications for Adjudication-Based Systems of Justice', *Contemporary Justice Review*, 1:1, pp. 123–31.

Yazzie, R. and Zion, J. (1996) 'Navajo Restorative Justice: The Law of Equality and Justice', in Galaway, B. and Hudson, J. (eds) *Restorative Justice: International Perspectives* (Monsey, NY: Criminal Justice Press), pp. 157–73.

Young, R. and Goold, B. (1999) 'Restorative Police Cautioning in Aylesbury – From Degrading to Reintegrative Shaming Ceremonies?', *Criminal Law Review*, Feb., pp. 126–38.

Zedner, L. (1994) 'Reparation and Retribution: Are they Reconcilable?', *Modern Law Review*, 57:2, pp. 228–50.

Zehr, H. (1990) *Changing Lenses: A New Focus for Crime and Justice* (Scottdale, PA: Herald Press).

Zehr, H. (2000) 'Restorative Justice Hits the Big Time: But Will it Remain True to its Vision?', (available online at http://www.restorativejustice.org/conference/RJhitsbigtime.html).

Zehr, H. and Mika, H. (1998) 'Fundamental Concepts of Restorative Justice', *Contemporary Justice Review*, 1:1, pp. 47–55.

Zion, J. (1998) 'The Use of Custom and Legal Tradition in the Modern Justice Setting', *Contemporary Justice Review*, 1:1, pp. 133–48.

Index